The Dictionary of Health Economics

The Dictionary of Health Economics

Anthony J. Culyer

University of York, UK and Chief Scientist, Institute for Work & Health, Toronto, Canada

Edward Elgar
Cheltenham, UK • Northampton, MA, USA

© Anthony J. Culyer 2005

All rights reserved. No part of this publication may be reproduced, stored in a retrieval system or transmitted in any form or by any means, electronic, mechanical or photocopying, recording, or otherwise without the prior permission of the publisher.

Published by
Edward Elgar Publishing Limited
Glensanda House
Montpellier Parade
Cheltenham
Glos GL50 1UA
UK

Edward Elgar Publishing, Inc.
136 West Street
Suite 202
Northampton
Massachusetts 01060
USA

A catalogue record for this book
is available from the British Library

Library of Congress Cataloguing in Publication Data
Culyer, A. J. (Anthony J.)
    The dictionary of health economics / Anthony J. Culyer.
        p.   cm.
    Includes index.
    1. Medical economics—Dictionaries. I. Title.

    RA410.A3C85   2005
    362.1'03—dc22

                                                        2005041563

ISBN 1 84376 208 0 (cased)

Typeset by Manton Typesetters, Louth, Lincolnshire, UK.
Printed and bound in Great Britain by MPG Books Ltd, Bodmin, Cornwall.

Library
University of Texas
at San Antonio

CONTENTS

Preface   vii
Acknowledgments   xi
Conventions   xiii

The Dictionary of Health Economics   1

Index   377

WITHDRAWN
UTSA LIBRARIES

PREFACE

> Knowledge is of two kinds. We know a subject ourselves, or we know where we can find information on it. (Samuel Johnson, quoted in Boswell's *Life of Johnson*)

This is a book serving the second of these two kinds of knowledge, a book that I have intended that the reader should be able to dip into from time to time. I hope it may also serve that other thing with which knowledge is so often mistaken: understanding. If one's appetite is whetted, as I hope may occasionally be the case, there are loads of decent texts that provide solid main courses and desserts. The *Dictionary* is not intended to compete with them. My main hope is that it may be of use to the reader in a hurry (whether a beginning economist or someone who needs to understand what economists go on about), who wants a reminder about a topic or who wants a quick and relatively painless introduction to it. It would be great if, to borrow from Sir Topham Hat (the Fat Controller in *Thomas the Tank Engine*), the *Dictionary* were to be a 'really useful engine'.

Health economists, to a greater extent than most economists, have engaged in close collaborations with specialists in other fields (not only other social sciences) and with policy makers, especially in the area of health technology assessment. I hope, therefore, that the book may be useful to these 'others'. Multidisciplinarity and multiprofessionality also have a consequence for the inclusion criteria used: I have included many more definitions, particularly in statistics, epidemiology and medicine, than would otherwise have been the case, which I hope will be useful to health economists without causing outrage to the relevant 'others'. These are provided, however, strictly on the bikini principle: I have restricted myself to the bare essentials of definition save for cases where I have judged the other discipline to have become so intertwined with health economics that it warrants more extended treatment – even explanation. Again, this is not a textbook. I have provided definitions and occasional interpretational help on non-economic terms on the grounds that, in multidisciplinary collaborations (whether trans-disciplinary, cross-disciplinary or interdisciplinary – terms the reader will *not* find in the dictionary) between researchers/teachers who still have a primary single academic disciplinary base, it is a good thing for each side of the collaboration to have some (even if incomplete) understanding of the concepts and methods of the others. We economists certainly need such help and I have tried to provide it without, I hope, doing too much violence to the meanings of other disciplines' specialized jargon.

Nor is this a general economics dictionary, so I have not included economic terminology that is infrequently used by health economists. There is, for example, hardly any macroeconomics here. The verbal boundaries of 'health economics' are one of the four matters I have wondered more about than about any other inclusion/exclusion criterion. Should it turn out that I have been too stringent in excluding terms, or too lax in including them, I trust my users will let me know.

The second 'boundary' issue about which I have worried concerns the extent to which the *Dictionary* ought to include the names and biographies of significant health economists. I have included people's names only when they have become attached to a headword or phrase requiring an entry (for example, 'Pareto-optimality', 'Altman's nomogram') or where their name has a common adjectival form, as in 'Rawlsian' (none of these three is, of course, a health economist). Only in such cases have I provided some bibliographical information (and occasionally biographical information as well). This is a tough rule and it has produced some odd outcomes. Thus Kenneth Arrow is in (but not on account of his scientific contribution to health economics) and Alan Williams is in (but on account of his league table and 'plumbing diagram' rather than QALYs or 'fair innings', or...). Without explicit mention are Angus Deaton, Mike Drummond, Bob Evans, Martin Feldstein, Richard Frank, Victor Fuchs, Mike Grossman, Bengt Jonsson, Emmett Keeler, Herb Klarman, the two Laves, Harold Luft, Will Manning, Tom McGuire, Gavin Mooney, Joe Newhouse, Mark Pauly, Charles Phelps, Frans Rutten, Frank Sloan, Greg Stoddart, George Torrance, Burt Weisbrod and lots of (mostly younger) others who have played key roles in shaping the discipline. They are there, of course, peering through the undergrowth of the entries but anonymously, just like the 'basic science' giants, many of whom are fortunately still actively with us, on whose intellectual shoulders we all stand: Armen Alchian, Gary Becker, James Buchanan, Milton Friedman, Peter Hammond, John Harsanyi, Werner Hildenbrand, Daniel Kahneman, Ian Little, Paul Samuelson, Reinhard Selten, Amartya Sen, Vernon Smith, Joseph Stiglitz and Vivian Walsh. To venture into list-making exemplifies my problem: where does one stop, how far does one stray into psychology and other related disciplines, and how does one avoid giving offence? So I stopped barely before beginning: the case for inclusion is eponymy. The only exception I have allowed is that of Lionel Robbins, mainly on account of his famous definition of 'economics', because he was *not* a health economist and because he is dead.

A third 'boundary' issue relates to the inclusion or exclusion of organizations. I have included as many official organizations that are substantial users or commissioners of health economics as I can identify and I have also included those health economists' professional organizations of which I know.

I have not included any of the many research groups in universities and elsewhere, nor have I included the names of government departments and ministries, many of which now have teams of health economists. Where possible, I have included web addresses.

The fourth 'boundary' issue relates to references: what to include and what not. I suspect that I have been too strict here in citing only works in which the origin of a headword or phrase is to be found. Providing references on all topics of substance, whether in health economics or one of the 'others', would have been a major additional effort and one whose fruits, moreover, would be doomed to become obsolete relatively early. However this is a question that might be answered differently should the opportunity arise later.

I have not included obsolete terms, unless I have judged them to have continuing value (as, for example, with 'value in use') but I have left ones in that seem obsolescent until such time as their destiny has become clear.

I have gone well beyond a definition in many cases, especially when I have judged a topic to be a critical element of health economics, one about which there are widespread misconceptions that need putting right, or one where it seemed important to give some insight into the way an idea is used, why it is important or why it is controversial. I hope these mini-lectures will help readers to get on track. They are not, however, accompanied by further reading: again, this *Dictionary* is not a textbook and ought not to be treated as though it were. Driving a locomotive demands more than the knowledge that it is merely on the right track.

I have not hesitated to record opinions, sometimes sharp ones, some tongue-in-cheek, where it seemed appropriate. Needless to say, the opinions are mine and there is no implication that they are widely shared amongst health econo-mists. I hope both the explicit opinions and any left implicit will lighten the enquirer's search, even if it does not enlighten it. A *Dictionary* surely need not be entirely po-faced.

I have tried to ensure that the language of the *Dictionary* is inclusive. I use 'they' 'them' and 'their' instead of the tediously repetitive mantra of 'he or she', 'him or her' and 'his or hers' (or 'she or he', 'her or him' and 'hers or his').

Samuel Johnson famously defined a lexicographer as 'A writer of diction-aries; a harmless drudge that busies himself in tracing the original, and detailing the signification of words'. The really significant word in this defi-nition is 'harmless' and I am not sure of his truth in asserting it. Practical lexicographers have the power to confuse, mislead and infuriate, all of which seem to be pretty harmful things to be doing. I hope my harm is small. Moreover my risk of doing harm is further reduced by my eschewing any systematic attempts at etymology or word history.

The *Dictionary* doubtless contains mistakes. I apologize for them now. I would be grateful to hear from readers who want to put me right. My explanation for error is again Johnson's: according to Boswell, when asked how he came to give a mistaken definition of 'pastern', he replied: 'Ignorance, Madam, pure ignorance.' I hope nonetheless that I have hidden most of mine.

My particular hope is that, whatever the imperfections of this *Dictionary*, it will be judged to be of sufficient value for enquirers to want to invest their time in telling me how a recension might make it better. My e-mail addresses are: ajc17@york.ac.uk and aculyer@iwh.on.ca.

A.J.C.

ACKNOWLEDGMENTS

I am extremely grateful to Ron Akehurst, Werner Brouwer, Adriana Castelli, Li-Jen Cheng, Karl Claxton, Richard Cookson, Roman Dolinschi, Tina Eberstein, Brian Ferguson, Alastair Fischer, John Frank, William Gnam, Clyde Hertzman, Sheilah Hogg-Johnson, Paul Holyoke, Jerry Hurley, Paul Jacobson, Andrew Jones, Robin Kells, Gisela Kobelt, Andreas Maetzel, Evelyne Michaels, Charles Normand, Adam Oliver, Nirmala Ragbir-Day, Sandra Sinclair, Emile Tompa and Adrian Towse for commenting on various definitions and making suggestions for headwords and phrases to include. A particular debt of gratitude is owed to Martin Forster, Leslie Godfrey, Desre Kramer, Robin Pope and Tom Rice for their exceptionally painstaking commentaries. All these friends and their many suggested redraftings have enormously improved the *Dictionary*'s amplitude, accuracy and accessibility. I have not always followed their advice so, alas, they cannot be held accountable for the *Dictionary*'s defects. These are entirely my responsibility.

CONVENTIONS

Use of italics
Italicized terms, other than reference titles, in the text of entries are themselves entries in the *Dictionary*. Bibliographical and biographical material is included only in connection with entries that are themselves individuals or that refer to named individuals. Mention of an entry in another entry is italicized only at the first mention.

Cross-references
Cross-references are provided at the end of many entries. When there is more than one they are in alphabetical order. These are cross-references to substantive entries and not, for example, to mere synonyms or antonyms. These do not repeat cross-references indicated within the entry by italicized words.

Order of subject matter
Entries are in strict alphabetical order regardless of their nature.

References and web sites
References are as full as it has been possible to make them, though some authors' first names are not known. Web sites are current at the time of writing.

CONVENTIONS

A

Ability to Pay

This is not a technical term in economics; it is, however, frequently used as though it were – most frequently as a part of an ethical principle used in connection with the idea of fair taxation, *viz.* that a taxpayer's contribution ought to bear some relation to their 'ability to pay'. A strict definition might amount to this: ability to pay is the sum of an individual's tradable *human* and non-human *capital*, that is, their entire *wealth*, though it seems doubtful whether those who use the term actually do have this definition in mind. Some may have in mind no more than the individual's *budget constraint*. Cf. *Willingness to Pay*. See *Progressivity, Regressivity*.

Abnormal Profit

Profit in excess of the (so-called 'normal') market rate of return on assets.

Abscissa

The horizontal axis in a two-dimensional diagram. Commonly referred to as the x-axis. Sometimes a point on that axis. Cf. *Ordinate*.

Absolute Advantage

This exists when a firm or a jurisdiction can produce a good or service with fewer inputs than another. Cf. *Comparative Advantage*, with which absolute advantage is often confused.

Absolute Risk Aversion

A characteristic of *utility functions*. It is a measure of the slope of a utility function and its rate of change. See *Insurance* for an account of how a diminishing marginal utility of income generates a form of risk aversion. See *Arrow–Pratt Measure, Risk Aversion*.

Absolute Risk Difference

Same as *absolute risk reduction*. The absolute arithmetic difference in occurrences of adverse *outcomes* between experimental and control participants in a *clinical trial*. The reciprocal of number needed to treat (NNT). Often referred to as ARR. See *Number Needed to Treat, Relative Risk Reduction, Odds Ratio*.

Absolute Risk Reduction

The absolute arithmetic difference in occurrences of adverse *outcomes* between experimental and control participants in a *clinical trial*. The reciprocal of *Number Needed to Treat* (NNT). Often referred to as ARR. See *Relative Risk Reduction, Odds Ratio*.

Absorbing State

This is a condition or 'state' in a *Markov chain* in which the *transition probability* is zero. 'Death' is such a state. Once in such a state, there is no escape from it. See also *Markov Model, Transition Matrix*.

Academic Detailing

A method of continuing professional education in which physicians are visited by an expert health professional to discuss prescribing and other aspects of clinical practice. Cf. *Detailing*.

Acceptability Curve

A graphical way of showing more information about uncertainty in a *cost–effectiveness analysis* than can be done by using only *confidence intervals*. See *Cost–effectiveness Acceptability Curve*.

Access

Access to health care, or its 'accessibility', is often regarded as an important determinant of the *equity* of a health care system, but the meaning and significance of 'access' or 'accessibility' are nonetheless often left unclear. Insofar as it is important in *equity* it seems that it is cheapness of access that really matters, usually because the writer will have some notion underlying their concern for equity about the importance of meeting *need*, and access seems to be a precondition for having needs assessed in order that they might be met. Economists typically treat accessibility as a comprehensive term for 'price'; that is, any user monetary fee that is to be paid plus time and transport costs, waiting, and any other element that constitutes a 'barrier' whether or not that barrier takes a monetary form or can be converted into a monetary form. This emphasizes financial barriers to access. Other barriers may be physical, institutional or social. Some may be direct, others indirect. For example, access to insurance may be the only route to accessing health care itself. The following have all been found to be important practical barriers: the service was not there; it was too costly; transport was too difficult; the appointment time was not convenient; the language available was not suitable; the service was not known about; the social distance between clients and caregivers was too great. Absence of a service that is 'needed' or demanded is plainly a very real barrier.

Accessibility unimpeded to any significant extent by financial or other barriers is a characteristic of a health care system that is commonly desired or sometimes (as in Canada) required by statute.

Account

Either (a) a record of financial transactions covering a period which is usually a year or (b) an agreement between buyer and seller that the seller will not expect to be paid until an agreed date. See *Balance of Payments*, *Balance Sheet*.

Accreditation

A process of certification that an organization or individual meets particular quality standards. See, for an example of an organization that provides such certification, *Joint Commission on Accreditation of Healthcare Organizations*.

Act Utilitarianism

Under act utilitarianism, it is the value of the consequences of an action that matters in determining whether the action is right. See *Utilitarianism*.

Activities of Daily Living

A frequently used set of basic activities of daily life, such as eating, bathing, dressing, toileting and transferring, each of which can be rated on a simple scale. The activities and their measurements vary according to the groups for whom they are being developed. The scores are sometimes combined in the construction of indices of healthy functioning or to measure changes in response to treatments. The acronym ADL is in common use. See *Barthel index*, *Quality-adjusted Life-year*.

Activity-based Financing

A method of financing public hospitals used in Norway. It uses *Diagnostic Related Groups* and *block contracts*.

Actuarially Fair

An insurance premium is actuarially fair when it is equal to the monetary value of the expected loss insured multiplied by its probability of occurring.

Acute

Adjective used to describe a sudden, possibly brief, ill-health occurrence, in contrast to *chronic*. Sometimes used to indicate severity.

Adaptive Conjoint Analysis

A form of *conjoint analysis* in which a computer program adapts the range of choices amongst many *attributes* of services to suit the subject doing the ranking. Cf. *Full Profile Conjoint*.

Addiction

Economists have not always modelled addictive substance use in terms of the four common *attributes* of addictiveness: persistence of use, tolerance, withdrawal and reinforcement. In health economics they have modelled addiction in broadly three ways. The first is in imperfectly *rational* models in which individuals effectively have two mutually incompatible but each internally consistent *utility functions* (for example, a farsighted one and a shortsighted one). Second, there are myopic irrational models, in which future consequences are not well understood or, if understood, are heavily discounted or ignored. Finally, there is 'rational addiction', in which the addictive habit enhances both current and future *utility* sufficiently to overcome the (rationally perceived) negative consequences for the user.

Addition Rule

A property (also called 'additivity') according to which the probability of either of two mutually exclusive events occurring is the sum of the probabilities of each occurring.

Additive Separability

A quality of *utility* measurement required in some measures of *health*. It amounts essentially to the idea that the weights or *utilities* attached to entities amongst which one is choosing, or which are components of an index of health, can be combined at any point in time and over time by adding without adjusting for any interaction between them that might make the whole more (or less) than the sum of its parts (apart from *discounting*). See *Quality-adjusted Life-year*.

Additivity

Same as *addition rule*.

Adjusted Odds Ratio

An *odds ratio* that has been corrected for the effects of other variables in the equation.

ADL

An acronym for *activities of daily living*.

Administered Prices

Prices set by regulatory agencies (for example, *Medicare's prospective reimbursements* in the USA) or by sellers as distinct from the prices that emerge in the marketplace.

Administrative Costs

Expenditures by an organization on management and administration and associated internal functions like accounting, finance, human resource management and (sometimes) research.

Advance Directive

An advance directive instructs doctors and other health care professionals about the kind of care one wishes to receive in the event of being unable to specify it in person (as when one is in a coma). It can specify both what treatments are wanted and those that are not.

Adverse Event

Usually refers to the consequences of using a pharmaceutical product, medical device or surgical procedure. Serious adverse events might be listed as death, a life-threatening drug experience, inpatient hospitalization, prolongation of existing hospitalization, a persistent or significant disability/incapacity, a congenital anomaly/birth defect, and other important medical events that may jeopardize the patient or subject and may require subsequent corrective medical or surgical intervention to prevent one of the other outcomes listed above.

Adverse Selection

Insurers tend to set their premiums in relation to the average experience of a population. If, in fact, members of subsets of the population have different probabilities of illness (or at any rate they believe they have different probabilities) then those with low probabilities (or low perceived ones) may not buy insurance and those with high probabilities (or perceptions) may eagerly seize their opportunity. If this happens, insurers end up with clients who are likely to prove costlier than expected. High-risk individuals tend to 'drive out' low-risk individuals. See *Asymmetry of Information, Market Failure*.

Aetiological Fraction

The proportion of an outcome that can be attributed to a particular *risk factor*. Also known as the etiological fraction and the attributable fraction.

Aetiology

The study of the causes of disease. Also 'etiology'.

AETMIS

See *Agence d'Evaluation des Technologies et des Modes d'Intervention en Santé*.

Affine Function

A function with constant slope and non-zero intercept.

Affordability

A term that has no clear meaning in economics, though its one unambiguous possible meaning, *viz.* referring to entities whose purchase price is lower than the value of the purchaser's realizable wealth, seems not to be the one people usually have in mind when using this term. It is sometimes taken as a synonym for *budget impact*. Some may have in mind any combination of entities that lies beneath a *budget constraint*.

A Fortiori

A Latin tag meaning 'more strongly' or 'even more conclusively'.

Agence d'Evaluation des Technologies et des Modes d'Intervention en Santé

Quebec's provincial agency for health technology assessments. Its website is at www.aetmis.gouv.qc.ca/en/mod.php?mod=userpage&menu=17&page_id=2.

l'Agence Nationale d'Accréditation et d'Evaluation en Santé

The French national agency that conducts health technology *appraisals*. Its website is at www.anaes.fr/ANAES/anaesparametrage.nsf/HomePage? ReadForm.

Agency

See *Agency Relationship*.

Agency for Health Care Research and Quality

A US agency responsible for, amongst other things, health technology assessments for the US Medicaid and Medicare Programs. Its website is at www.ahrq.gov/.

Agency Relationship

Classically, the role of a physician or other health professional in determining the patient's (or other client's) best interest and acting in a fashion consistent with it. The patient or client is the *principal* and the professional the *agent*. More generally, the agent is anyone acting on behalf of a principal, usually because of *asymmetry of information*. In health care, the situation can become rather complicated by virtue of the fact that doctors are expected (in many systems) to act, not only for the 'patient', but also for 'society' in the form, say, of other patients or of an organization with wider societal responsibilities (like a *managed care* organization), or taxpayers, or all potential patients. See also *Market Failure, Multi-task Agency, Supplier-induced Demand*.

Agent

A professional or similar person who acts on behalf of another (the *principal*). See *Agency Relationship*.

Aggregation

A process of adding up smaller parts to make a greater whole. For example, aggregate demand is the sum of expenditures by consumers, investors, government and net exports and is usually modelled as a function of (aggregate) income and/or the (aggregate) price level.

Aggregation Problem

A faulty interpretation that arises by using associations that seem to hold at an aggregate level (say, the level of a community) as evidence that they hold also at the individual level. It is also known as the *ecological fallacy*. For example, while the (aggregate) observation may be made that US states with a high proportion of foreign-born residents are also states with high literacy in American English, it does not follow that foreign-born people are more literate in English than the rest. In fact studies at the individual level have shown that the 'ecological correlation' of foreign-born and literacy rates arises because foreign-born people tend to settle in states that already have high literacy in English. At the individual level, the correlation between being foreign-born and ability in English is (as one may expect) in fact negative. A subtler example arises in the analysis of the causes of differences in the average health of *populations* and the idea that income inequality may be correlated with (or might even cause) lower average health. If everyone has the same *demand for health* at a variety of incomes and *health* (however measured) rises with income but at a declining rate, then more income inequality implies lower average health (*ceteris paribus*). As income disparities widen, an increase in income for the rich will generate an increase in health that is less than sufficient to compensate for the fall in health generated by an equivalent reduction in income for the poor. Should this be the case, caution is the order of the day in evaluating claims that it is inequality per se that is deleterious to health. Such claims may be right but they are not the only possible explanation: the phenomenon may arise simply because of the underlying *income-elasticity* of the demand for health.

AHRQ

Acronym for *Agency for Healthcare Research and Quality.*

AIES

Acronym for *Associazione Italiana di Economia Sanitaria.*

Algorithm

A mathematical procedure or formula for solving a problem in a sequential fashion, with each step depending on the outcome of the previous one. Named after Mohammed ibn-Musa al-Khwarizmi (780–850) who lived in what is now called Iraq.

Allais Paradox

This is a famous paradox of *expected utility theory* that has caused some to question the validity of the theory. Suppose a subject has the following choices under uncertainty:

Gamble A: a 100% chance of receiving $1 million.
Gamble B: a 10% chance of receiving $5 million, an 89% chance of receiving $1 million and a 1% chance of receiving nothing.

Most people choose A over B, even though the expected pecuniary value of B is $1.39 million. Presumably, certainty is preferred. In terms of expected utility they are revealing that

$$U(\$1m) > 0.1U(\$5m) + 0.89U(\$1m) + 0.01U(\$0)$$

and, subtracting $0.89U(\$1m)$ from each side of the inequality, we get

$$0.11U(\$1m) > 0.1U(\$5m) + 0.01U(\$0).$$

Now present the same subject with a further two gambles:

Gamble C: an 11% chance of receiving $1 million, and an 89% chance of receiving nothing.

Gamble D: a 10% chance of receiving $5 million, and a 90% chance of receiving nothing. Most people choose D over C.

In terms of expected utility, they are revealing that

$$0.1U(\$5m) + 0.9U(\$0) > 0.11U(\$1m) + 0.89U(\$0).$$

Now, as expected utility theory permits, subtract $0.89U(\$0)$ from each side to get

$$0.1U(\$5m) + 0.01U(\$0) > 0.11U(\$1m),$$

which is the opposite from what was chosen in the first choice situation. Expected utility theory excludes this possibility because preferring A to B implies preferring C to D. See Maurice Allais (1953), 'Le comportement de l'homme rationnel devant le risque: Critique des postulats et axiomes de l'école américaine', *Econometrica*, **21**, 503–46.

Alliance

A term used in the pharmaceutical industry to describe the relationship between a pharmaceutical company and its partners in research and development (usually biotechnology companies).

Allocation Bias

A statistical term for *bias* arising from the manner in which subjects are assigned to treatment groups in *clinical trials*.

Alternative Hypothesis

A term used in statistical hypothesis testing: a hypothesis about the effect of interest that is false if the *null hypothesis* is true (but not necessarily true if the null hypothesis is false).

Alternatives

A feature of all *option appraisals* is that various (alternative) courses of action are identified and evaluated.

Altman's Nomogram

Mathematically it is quite a complicated exercise to calculate the size of a *sample* necessary to achieve a given *statistical power* in *clinical trials*. Altman's *nomogram* is a graphical method of assessing the power and *statistical significance* of a test at a variety of sample sizes. The right-hand vertical axis of the nomogram shows various power values, from 0.05 to 0.995. The left-hand vertical axis represents the 'standardized difference': a ratio which relates the difference of interest to the *standard deviation* of the observations. There are two axes within the nomogram, one for a significance level of 0.05, the other for 0.01, with total sample sizes indicated on each. The nomogram can be used to evaluate the optimal sample size once the power is specified, the significance level 5 per cent or 1 per cent is chosen and the standardized difference is calculated. This nomogram can be found at p. 456 of Douglas G. Altman (1991), *Practical Statistics for Medical Research*, London: Chapman and Hall.

Altruism

In economics this is usually seen as a form of *utility* interdependence in that one person gains utility from the knowledge that another's lot in life is improved. In some versions the utility may come from the act of improving the other's lot or at least from contributing (or maybe only to be seen to be contributing) to the improvement. See *Utility Function*.

Ambiguity

A term used by decision and game theorists in the context of certain kinds of decisions being made under uncertainty which from the perspective of subjective *utility* theory is a kind of *bias* in the human psyche. Suppose there are two urns, each containing a hundred balls, which are either red or black. One urn has fifty red and fifty black balls. The proportion of red and black in the other urn is unknown. You can draw one ball from one of the urns, without looking, and if you draw a red ball you win a hundred dollars. Most people choose the 50–50 urn, even though, if we take the view that there are insufficient reasons for discriminating between the two urns, there is no higher probability of getting a red. When offered a hundred dollars for a black ball, they also choose the 50–50 urn. They seem to be averse to the 'ambiguity' represented by the other urn and strongly prefer the apparently clear-cut. This is also known as the Ellsberg Paradox (Daniel Ellsberg, 1961, 'Risk, ambiguity, and the Savage axioms', *Quarterly Journal of Economics*, **75**, 643–69).

Ambulatory Care

Health care provided on an outpatient (non-hospitalized) basis. It includes preventive, diagnostic, treatment and rehabilitation services.

ANAES

Acronym for *l'Agence Nationale d'Accréditation et d'Evaluation en Santé*.

Anaesthesia

The medical specialty concerned with desensitization to pain, usually through injection or gas. It includes pain management for people with chronic painful conditions. (An alternative usage is 'anaesthesiology'.)

Analysis of Covariance

A statistical procedure used to control for the effect of a *covariate* on the relationship between an *independent* and a *dependent variable*. Also ANCOVA.

Analysis of Variance

ANOVA uses the *F-test* to test the *null hypothesis* that the *means* of two or more groups are equal. It involves comparison of within and between group *sample* sums of squares (which is where the '*variance*' bit comes in).

Analytic Epidemiology

That branch of *epidemiology* concerned with the testing of hypotheses about the relationships between exposures and disease outcomes.

ANCOVA

Acronym for *analysis of covariance*.

Andrology

The science of diseases of the male sex.

Annual Equivalent Charge

A constant sum paid annually whose *present value* is the same as (equivalent to) a *capital* cost.

Annuitized Value

See *Equivalent Annual Cost*.

Annuity

A constant amount of money per year received in perpetuity or for a specified period of time. The *coupon* on a bond is a specific type of annuity.

ANOVA

Acronym for *analysis of variance*.

Antenatal

The period between conception and birth. Same as *prenatal*.

A Posteriori

A Latin tag meaning 'proceeding inductively', 'inferring cause from effect'. Literally 'from what comes after'. Cf. *A Priori*.

Appraisal

The process of assessing costs and benefits in relation to a set of objectives and a set of alternative means (options) of realizing them. See *Cost–benefit Analysis*, *Cost–effectiveness Analysis*, *Cost–utility Analysis*, *Option Appraisal*.

Appreciation

An increase in the value of an *asset*. It may occur as the result of *inflation* or real factors such as increased *productivity* or greater *demand*. Cf. *Depreciation*.

A Priori

A Latin tag meaning 'proceeding logically from assumption to implication' or, sometimes, 'presumptively'. Literally 'from what is before'. Cf. *A Posteriori*.

AQOL

Acronym for *assessment quality of life*.

Arbitrage

The practice of exploiting price differences between two (or possibly more) markets: matching deals are struck that leave a profit: the difference between the market prices. One who engages in arbitrage is called an arbitrageur.

Area Probability Sample

A form of *stratified sampling* in which the unit of analysis is a geographical area.

Area Wage Index

An index of labour costs used to reimburse hospitals in the US *Medicare* system.

Arithmetic Mean

A measure of the central tendency of a set of numbers. The average of a set of numbers. The sum of the observations divided by their number. Arithmetic mean = $\Sigma X_i/N$, where the X_i are the values of X and N is the total number of observations. The qualifier 'arithmetic' is usually dropped.

ARR

Acronym for *absolute risk reduction*.

Array

Data sorted in order from the lowest to the highest values.

Arrow Award

A prize for health economists awarded annually by the International Health Economics Association for the best published paper in health economics. Its title honours Kenneth Arrow.

Arrow–Debreu Equilibrium

This forms the basis for modern *general equilibrium* theory in economics. The model is static but assumes multiple individuals, multiple goods and services and multiple possible states of the world. It specifies the economic environment, a resource allocation mechanism and a system of property rights. See Kenneth J. Arrow and Gerard Debreu (1954), 'Existence of an equilibrium for a competitive economy', *Econometrica*, **22**, 265–90.

Arrow Impossibility Theorem

One of the astonishing findings of modern economics (and from a student's PhD thesis at that) is that a set of quite reasonable sounding requirements about social choice orderings necessarily implies that there is no method for constructing social preferences from *ordinal* individual preferences. In other words, there is no rule, such as majority voting (nor any other), for deriving social preferences from arbitrary individual preferences of the kind commonly assumed by economists. The reasonable requirements are completeness: in a choice between alternatives A and B either A is socially preferred to B, or B is preferred to A, or there is a social indifference between A and B; transitivity: if A is socially preferred to B and B is preferred to C then A is also preferred to C; if every individual prefers A to B then socially A should be preferred to B; non-dictatorship: social preferences should not depend upon the preferences of only one individual; social preferences should be independent of irrelevant alternatives: that is, the social preference of A compared to B should be independent of preferences for C. Health economists seem to be less reluctant to use cardinal and interpersonally comparable '*utilities*' than economists working in many other areas of application. See Kenneth J. Arrow (1951), *Social Choice and Individual Values*, New York: Wiley.

Arrow–Pratt Measure

A measure of *absolute risk aversion*. Loosely, it is a measure of the curvature of a *utility function*. See Kenneth J. Arrow (1970), *Essays in the Theory of Risk Bearing*, North Holland: Amsterdam; John W. Pratt (1964), 'Risk aversion in the small and in the large', *Econometrica*, **32**, 122–36.

Arrow Social Welfare Function

A form of *social welfare function*, specifying how one arrives at social welfare from individual utilities by having reasonable requirements. These are completeness: in a choice between alternatives A and B either A is socially preferred to B, or B is preferred to A, or there is a social indifference between A and B; transitivity: if A is socially preferred to B and B is preferred to C then A is also preferred to C; if every individual prefers A to B then socially A should be preferred to B; non-dictatorship: social preferences should not depend upon the preferences of only one individual; social preferences should be independent of irrelevant alternatives: that is, the social preference of A compared to B should be independent of preferences for C. See *Arrow Impossibility Theorem*, *Bergson–Samuelson Social Welfare Function*, *Pareto Optimality*.

Ascertainment Bias

Same as *detection bias*.

Asociación de Economía de la Salud

The Spanish Association for Health Economics. Its website is at www.aes.es/entrada.asp?acceso=1.

Aspiration Adaptation

An alternative way of doing *decision analysis* to the use of *expected utility theory*. See *Bounded Rationality*.

Assessment Quality of Life

An Australian measure of health-related quality of life having five dimensions (Illness, Independent living, Social Relationships, Physical senses and Psychological well-being). A website for this instrument is www.chpe.buseco.monash.edu.au/pubs/wp66.pdf. See *Disability-adjusted Life-year*, *EQ-5D*, *EuroQol*, *Health Gain*, *Health Status*, *Health Utilities Index*, *Healthy Year Equivalents*, *Quality-adjusted Life-year*, *SF-6D*, *SF-8*, *SF-12*, *SF-36*.

Asset

Any property or entities with marketable worth owned by a person or business. Assets include real property, *human capital* and enforceable claims against others (including bank accounts, stocks and debts).

Associazione Italiana di Economia Sanitaria

The Italian Association for Health Economists. Its website is at www.aiesweb.it.

Assortive Matching

The non-random selection of trading partners with respect to one or more traits (for example, productivity, potential health gain); it is positive when like matches like more frequently than would be expected by chance (for example, people with high potential health gain are matched with effective health technologies) and is negative when the reverse occurs (for example, when infectious people match susceptible people).

Asymmetry of Information

The usual asymmetry relates to the difference in the information known to a patient, or member of the public, and that known to a professional such as a doctor or nurse. While it is sometimes thought that the informational advantage is all on one side (the professional's), this is to take too narrow a view of what the information may be about. For example, while it may be realistic to imagine that a doctor will have more knowledge about the probable consequences of a particular clinical intervention on a person's health, the doctor will usually have less competence in assessing the consequences for that person's home and working life; here the advantage lies with the patient, who will also usually be more competent in judging the value (*utility*) of alternative clinical possibilities that the professional may propose (including 'doing nothing'). It would seem to follow that decisions intended to be of real benefit to a patient ought to be taken in a mutual fashion, with professional and patient in effect pooling their respective sets of information and the patient then either reaching the final decision or delegating it to the professional. See *Agency Relationship*.

Another important form of asymmetry that is important in health economics is the difference in information available to an insurer and an insured person. The insurer will typically set premia according to broad averages of probability and expense to cover the expected liability while the insured person may possess information, for example about private lifestyle and the risks to health that it entails, which is not available to the former and that indicates that the probability is higher or lower than the one embodied in the premium calculation. If higher, the incentive to buy *insurance* is, *ceteris paribus*, greater and the risk of financial loss to the insurer is also greater. If lower, it becomes less likely that insurance will be purchased. The use of *experience rating* and no-claims 'bonuses' are two ways used by insurers to overcome this difficulty. See *Adverse Selection*.

Asymptote

A straight line that is the limiting value of a curve. The asymptote of a curve can be thought of as a line that is continuously approached but never touched by the curve.

Asymptotic Property

In statistics, this usually refers to a property of a statistic that applies as the *sample* size approaches infinity. See *Asymptote*.

Attention Bias

Same as *Hawthorne effect*.

Attributable Fraction

Same as *aetiological fraction*.

Attribute

A generic characteristic of something or someone. In health economics, it is often an element of human function such as *activities of daily living* which may form components of a measure of *health status*. Sometimes called 'dimension of health' or 'domain of health'. In *conjoint analysis*, an attribute may be part of a vignette describing the character of, say, a service that is being valued. In clinical research, the term is used to indicate an independent variable that cannot be manipulated by the researcher. Note also the verbal usage: 'to attribute' is to assign a consequence to a cause or an idea to its author.

Attrition Bias

Bias caused by non-response in *panel data*. The bias arises if the characteristics of non-responders differ from those of responders.

Audiology

The study of hearing and hearing impairment. In some countries the specialty includes the study of the nature, causes and treatment of diseases of the ear. See *Rehabilitation Medicine*.

Audit Trail

A systematic method of documenting and interpreting *qualitative* data.

Autarky

The state of a non-trading economy or individual. Self-sufficiency. A Latinate derivative not to be confused with the Greek derivative 'autarchy', which means 'despotism'.

Autocorrelation

Autocorrelation occurs when a *variable* is *correlated* with earlier values of itself.

Average Cost

As used in economic theory, the average cost is the *total cost* of producing a specified rate of output (in the technically most efficient way) divided by that rate of *output*. See *Opportunity Cost*.

Average Fixed Cost

Total *fixed cost* divided by the rate of *output*. See *Opportunity Cost*.

Average Product

Total product (*output* rate) divided by the amount of *variable factor* used.

Average Revenue

Total revenue divided by the rate of *output*.

Average Total Cost

Total cost divided by the rate of *output*. See *Opportunity Cost*.

Average Variable Cost

Total *variable cost* divided by the rate of *output*. See *Opportunity Cost*.

Aziende Sanitarie Locali

Italian local health organizations that commission hospital services on behalf of their local communities. See *Purchaser–provider Split*.

B

Balance Billing

The practice whereby health care providers collect from patients the difference between the fees they have charged and the reimbursement they receive from insurers. In some jurisdictions (for example, Canada) it is prohibited by statute. See *Extra Billing*.

Balance of Care

The determination of the efficient allocation of clients to types of medical and social care. See *Efficiency*.

Balance of Payments

The balance of payments is the record of one country's trade dealings with the rest of the world. It has two main parts. The current account shows the flows of trade in visible and invisible goods (like services) plus the net effect of interest, profits, dividends and transfers. The capital account shows flows of investment and other (financial) capital (payment and repayment of debts). 'Official financing', in the form of changes in the central bank's holdings of gold and foreign currency and debt, meets any overall deficit when the current and capital accounts are added together (ignoring statistical errors). By definition the balance of payments must balance. 'Balance of payments surplus' or 'balance of payments deficit' are therefore slightly misleading terms. A current account balance of payments deficit that is judged to be unsustainable will need remedial action. Although it is often seen as a symbol of a country's economic virility, a balance of payments surplus is not necessarily beneficial since it involves the central bank holding more assets in the form of short-term foreign government debt, and this typically earns a lower *rate of return* compared to other ways of investing taxpayers' contributions to public investment.

Balance of Trade

A component of the *balance of payments*.

Balance Sheet

A statement at the end of a period (usually a year) of the wealth of a person or organization. The balance sheet consists of various *stocks*: assets (cash, bank deposits, stocks of goods and other easily realizable assets, debts owed to the person/organization, investments, for example other organizations that are owned by the person/organization and fixed assets like buildings less *depreciation*); and liabilities (debts owed to lenders, such as bank loans and overdrafts; debts to other creditors, and the shares owned by shareholders). Cf. profit and loss account, which records flows: changes in an organization's net worth or *wealth* over the period.

The basic equation in accounting is assets = liabilities + *equity*, so equity is assets less liabilities.

Balanced Panel

Opposite of *unbalanced panel*. A *panel* in which only respondents with complete data for all sampling waves are included.

Bar Chart

A diagram showing the distribution of a non-continuous *variable* (e.g. social

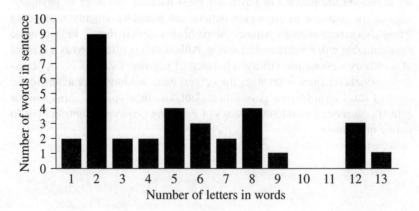

class) in which the height of the column (bar) above each value is proportional to the relative frequency of observations in that category of the variable. For example, the figure shows the frequency with which words of various lengths appear in the first sentence of this entry (with 'e.g.' counting as a two-letter word). Cf. *Piechart*.

Barrier to Entry

An impediment to the flow of resources (such as the entry of a new firm) into an industry or segment of a market. It usually refers to man-made impediments, though many also occur naturally, for example from *economies of scale*, which might make it very costly for a potential new entrant to achieve a scale large enough to enable *competition* on similar terms with extant organizations. Barriers include such arrangements as *patents* and *licences*. Many barriers arise through the operation of regulatory agencies. The existence of barriers ought not to lead automatically to the inference that they are invariably undesirable and ought to be removed. Such an inference is best reached (or rejected) after a careful analysis of the costs and benefits of reducing or removing them. Similar considerations apply to the setting up of new barriers or increasing the height of existing ones. Enormous resources are sometimes devoted to the surmounting of barriers, particularly the barriers deliberately created by society to illegal activities like the production and distribution of narcotics. See *Contestable Market*.

Barrier to Exit

Limitations, usually imposed by government or regulatory agencies, or arising from a locally politically hot situation, on an organization's ability to cease activity. It is notoriously difficult to close hospitals for political reasons (central or local). On the other hand, it is much less difficult to replace (senior) management teams, which is a common recourse in health care when the institution must survive.

Barthel Index

An index of the *activities of daily living* on a scale of 0–20. Its website is at http://www.strokecenter.org/trials/scales/barthel.html. See Florence I. Mahoney and Dorothea W. Barthel (1965), 'Functional evaluation: the Barthel Index', *Maryland State Medical Journal*, **14**, 56–61.

Baumol Effect

An argument initially promulgated by William Baumol that accounts for the increasing share of service industries (like health care) in *Gross Domestic Product*. The phenomenon is explained in terms of steadily increasing productivity in *capital*-intensive industries, leading to steadily declining relative prices in those industries. The value (or the productivity) of health care is in general extremely imperfectly revealed in any known markets, even in situations where there are markets for care, so the story is a bit like Hamlet without the prince: the increasing share is visible but not the slow productivity growth. Despite this, and despite the high capital intensity of some modern medicine, and despite the fact that the *efficiency* of much health care remains untested, many regard Baumol's conjecture as having broad plausibility in health care. See William Baumol (1967), 'Macroeconomics of unbalanced growth: the anatomy of the urban crisis', *American Economic Review*, **57**, 415–26.

Bayes' Rule

See *Bayes' Theorem*.

Bayes' Theorem

The general form of Bayes' theorem (sometimes called Bayes' rule) is:

$$p(A|X) = \frac{p(X) \times p(A)}{p(X|A) \times p(A) + p(X|{\sim}A) \times p({\sim}A)},$$

where

$p(A)$ is the prior (our prior knowledge, for example, of the prevalence of cancer in the population as a whole);

$p(A|X)$ is the posterior probability (a revised estimate of the probability of A, given X, in our example, of there being cancer, given that the test result was positive);

$p(X|A)$ is the conditional probability of X, given A (in our example, of a positive test when a patient has cancer);

$p(X|{\sim}A)$ is the conditional probability of X, given not-A (in our example, of a positive test when a patient does not have cancer).

Same as *Bayes' rule*. See *Bayesian Method*.

Bayesian Method

The Bayesian method is a way of revising beliefs about *probabilities* or the value of a *parameter* as new information is obtained. The old information might, for example, be based on a *systematic review* or a *consensus panel* of experts or a straightforwardly subjective judgment. It is termed the prior probability (or the prior *distribution* within which the true value of a parameter is believed to lie). The new information might be obtained from a recently completed *clinical* trial. The revised probability (or distribution) is called the posterior.

Suppose there is a *population* in which a characteristic (like having cancer) is true for a given fraction and untrue for the rest. It is uncontroversial to calculate the *conditional probability* that a particular observation comes from a person truly having the characteristic. The following example is due to Eliezer Yudkowsky, on http://yudkowsky.net/bayes/bayes.html. It is generally known that 1 per cent of women at age 40 who participate in routine screening have breast cancer (this is the prior); 80 per cent of women with breast cancer will get positive mammographies (*true positives*); 9.6 per cent of women without breast cancer will also get positive mammographies (*false positives*) (these are data obtained from a *clinical trial*). Now suppose a woman in this age group has a positive mammography in a routine screening. What is the probability that she actually has breast cancer? The correct answer is 7.8 per cent. To see why, these are the steps: out of 10 000 women, 100 have breast cancer; 80 of those 100 have positive mammographies. From the same 10 000 women, 9900 will not have breast cancer and of those 9900 women, 950 will also get positive tests – but falsely. This makes the total number of women with positive (true and false) tests 950+80 or 1030. Of those 1030 women with positive tests, 80 will have cancer. Expressed as a proportion, this is 80/1030 or 0.07767 or 7.8 per cent.

This example of *diagnosis* illustrates how Bayesian methods allow a prior belief (the probability of cancer) to be revised in the light of new information from the test results (probability of a test result conditional on having cancer) to form a posterior belief (the probability of cancer conditional on the test results). The example also enables one to intuit better the general form of Bayes' theorem (sometimes called Bayes' rule):

$$p(A|X) = \frac{p(X) \times p(A)}{p(X|A) \times p(A) + p(X|{\sim}A) \times p({\sim}A)},$$

where

p(A) is the prior (our prior knowledge, in the example, of the prevalence of cancer in the population as a whole);

p(A|X) is the posterior probability (a revised estimate of the probability of *A*, given *X*, in our example, of there being cancer, given that the test result was positive);

p(X|A) is the conditional probability of *X*, given *A* (in our example, of a positive test when a patient has cancer);

p(X|~A) is the conditional probability of *X*, given not-*A* (in our example, of a positive test when a patient does not have cancer).

The issues raised in considering the relative merits of Bayesian or *frequentist* approaches to probability arise acutely because of the all-pervading nature of uncertainty in medicine, where evidence may accumulate over time from a variety of sources. For purposes of *cost–effectiveness analysis* there is often uncertainty about the detailed natural history of a disease (for example, the probability that a breast cancer detected *in situ* by mammography will progress to invasive cancer is not known and, if it does progress, the time between preclinical detectability and symptomatic disease is also unknown), the character of outcomes beyond a period of a clinical trial is often unknown, along with the distribution across types of patients of beneficial and harmful outcomes and whether the way measured outcomes have been defined is appropriate or correlated with outcomes that are appropriate (*construct validity*). In addition, the use of Bayesian methods enables probability statements to be made in the form of the probability of a hypothesis being true, given the evidence, which are of direct relevance to decision making. For example, in the context of *economic appraisal*, it allows statements about the probability of an intervention being cost-effective given the accumulated evidence. However the often subjective nature of forming Bayesian priors, which may require judgment or a particular interpretation of existing evidence, means that it is important to consider the *sensitivity* of the posterior results to alternative specification of the priors.

The approach is named after Thomas Bayes (1702–1761). He was an English Presbyterian minister. An amateur mathematician, he was elected a Fellow of the *Royal Society* in 1742 even though he had no published works on mathematics – and published none in his lifetime under his own name.

Before and After Study

A study in which outcomes are measured before an intervention is implemented and compared to outcomes measured afterwards. Sometimes called a 'pre-post study'. This form of experimental design is particularly prone to *bias* mainly because of failure to control for potential *confounding variables*.

Benefit

The gains, before *costs* are deducted, of any particular course of action, therapy, treatment, preventive programme and so on. In principle, these gains are valued by the total amount that individuals are *willing to pay* to acquire them (including any externally affected individuals who may not be the direct beneficiaries). In principle, again, since willingness and *ability to pay* are often correlated (and these are, in turn, correlated with *health status*), many economists are reluctant to attach any significance to individuals' willingness to pay, though, in principle, weighting systems might be adopted to compensate for unequal abilities to pay. Similarly, in principle, weights might be applied to different individuals when adding benefits accruing to different persons. In practice, owing to the difficulties inherent in undertaking these tasks, health benefits are left in non-monetized form, especially in *extra-welfarism*, under which health maximization is commonly taken as the social *maximand*. Partly because of these difficulties and partly because of the stated objectives of health policy in many jurisdictions, many health economists have directed their energies to the development of direct measures of *health* without seeking also to assess its monetary value. These factors also doubtless account for the popularity of *cost–effectiveness* and *cost–utility analyses*. See *Assessment Quality of Life, Disability-adjusted Life-year, EQ-5D, Health Gain, Health Status, Health Utilities Index, Healthy Years Equivalent, Quality-adjusted Life-year, SF-6D, SF-8, SF-12, SF-36*.

Benefit–cost Ratio

A statistic commonly used to describe the conclusion of a *cost–benefit* study. It is the ratio of the *present value* of *benefits* to the present value of *costs*. Given that the classification of some entities as costs or negative benefits, and benefits or negative costs, is ambiguous, the ratio can be a misleading indicator of *efficiency* and, as a ratio, it gives no indication of the size of the benefits or costs in question. It is often better to use the difference between the present values rather than their ratio.

Benefits Transfer

This term applies to a variety of techniques for transferring the values ascribed to a good, service or *attribute* in one survey or experimental context in relevant ways to another decision or policy context, thereby avoiding the necessity of repeating the experiment or survey.

Bequest Value

Same as *existence value.*

Bergson–Samuelson Social Welfare Function

The original idea for a *social welfare function* is due to Abram Bergson (1914–2003) and definitively and rigorously developed by Paul Samuelson (b.1915) in his PhD thesis with astonishing virtuosity. Bergson's original idea was extremely general, for the value of social welfare was understood to depend on all the variables that might be considered as affecting it. It is usually interpreted as being defined over a particular profile of individual *utilities*. This is what is usually meant by the term 'welfarist': social welfare is deemed to depend on utilities (and not, for example, quantities of goods or anything else). See Abram Bergson (1938), 'A reformulation of certain aspects of welfare economics', *Quarterly Journal of Economics*, **52**, 310–34; Paul A. Samuelson (1947), *Foundations of Economic Analysis*, Cambridge: Harvard University Press. See *Arrow Impossibility Theorem, Arrow Social Welfare Function, Pareto Optimality, Social Welfare.*

Best–worst Conjoint Analysis

A procedure for estimating utilities in *conjoint analysis* in which subjects are shown varieties of levels of *attributes* of a service in combinations and are asked to select the combinations that they like best and least. The process is repeated several times, each time with a different combination.

Beta Distribution

A frequency distribution having two parameters, usually labelled α and β, mean = $\alpha/(\alpha + \beta)$, variance = $\alpha\beta/[(\alpha + \beta)^2(\alpha + \beta + 1)]$ and which is bounded on the interval 0–1. It is flexible, and can be symmetrical about the *mean* or positively or negatively *skewed*. Cf. *Normal Distribution.*

Bias

In empirical work, any systematic difference between the empirical results of an analysis and the true facts of the case (for example, the difference between the distribution of values in a sample and the actual values of the population from which the sample is drawn). In non-statistical areas it is any distorting influence which might lead to wrong or misleading results, for example, a search of the (English language) literature on a subject might lead one to ignore all Chinese contributions (unfortunately, no reviewer knew Chinese) and to conclude something wrong about the results (apart from the apparent fact that the Chinese were not in the field). Research sponsorship (whether by commercial or non-commercial sponsors) can lead to pressure on researchers to produce particular results or suppress 'unwanted' results. Common types of bias in *clinical trials* and surveys include *allocation bias*, *ascertainment bias*, *design bias*, *detection bias*, *exclusion bias*, *information bias*, *interviewer bias*, *lead-time bias*, *measurement bias*, *observer bias*, *performance bias*, *publication bias*, *recall bias*, *referral bias*, *sample selection bias*, *selection bias*, *surveillance bias*, *therapeutic personality bias*, *volunteer bias*, *withdrawal bias* and *work-up bias*. See also *End of Scale Bias, Omitted Variable Bias, Spacing out Bias, Starting Point Bias.*

Bidding Games

An alternative to the traditional open-ended questionnaire approach which is often used in *willingness to pay* studies. Depending on how a subject responds to a prompted value, a search *algorithm* bids them up or down until a final value is settled upon.

Bimodal Distribution

A *distribution* of a *variable* that has two peaks (*modes*).

Binary Variable

A *variable* that can take one of only two values: usually 1 and 0, such as 'yes' or 'no', 'well' or 'ill', 'inpatient' or 'outpatient', 'home delivery' or 'hospital delivery'. Same as *dummy variable, dichotomous variable.*

Binomial Distribution

A distribution used with discrete random variables. When a fair coin is flipped, the outcome is one of two mutually exclusive possibilities: heads or tails. If a coin is flipped n times, then the binomial distribution can be used to determine the probability of obtaining exactly r heads in the n outcomes. The formula that is used assumes that the observations are dichotomous, mutually exclusive, independent and randomly selected.

Bioassay

The quantitative assessment of a substance's potency through experimental measurement of its effects on tissue or living creatures.

Bio-equivalence Study

Same as *equivalence study*.

Birth Rate

See *Crude Birth Rate*.

Birth Weight

An infant's weight as recorded at birth. Low birth weight is conventionally <2500g, Very low birth weight is <1500g. Ultra low birth weight is <1000g.

Bivariate

Data on two (possibly linked) *variables*.

Bivariate Probit Model

A non-linear statistical model that has two binary *dependent variables*.

Black Report

A report commissioned by the Department of Health and Social Security from Sir Douglas Black on the inequality of health in the UK. Notorious for being published in only duplicated form for several years in an apparent government attempt to hide bad news. Eventually published as a Penguin. Originally: Sir Douglas Black *et al.* (1980), *Inequalities in Health: a Report of a Research Working Group*, London: Department of Health and Social Security. Later: Sir Douglas Black, Peter Townsend and Nick Davidson (1992), *Inequalities in Health: the Black Report*, 2nd edn, London: Penguin.

Blinding

Blinding (sometimes called 'masking') refers to a set of techniques designed to reduce *bias* in *clinical trials*. A double-blind trial is where neither the patient nor the observer/clinician is aware of whether the patient is in the *control* or *experimental* arm of a trial. A single-blind trial is where the patient (or observer/clinician) is aware of which arm they are in but the observer/clinician (or patient) is not. A triple-blind trial is one in which subjects, observers/clinicians and analysts are unaware of patient assignment to the arms of the trial. In trials of different styles of patient management or many surgical procedures, full blinding is often, alas, impossible. The seriousness of the potential bias will then depend on the circumstances. For example, blinding patients to the treatment they receive in a controlled trial matters less when the outcome measures are objectively observable events, like death, rather than subjective, like the relief of pain. However, even in surgery, patient blinding is possible. For example, in a trial of surgery for osteoarthritis of the knee the controls underwent a sham procedure, having a small slit cut in the side of the knee that was then sewn up again.

Block Contract

A form of contract between health care *purchasers* (*commissioners*) and health care providers, in which a wide range of services is agreed to be provided in exchange for a *global budget*. Cf. *Cost and Volume Contract*. See *Purchaser–provider Split*.

Boolean Logic

The use of the terms 'and', 'or' and 'not' for refining database searches of literature, as in *systematic reviewing*. Named after the English mathematician George Boole (1815–1864).

Bootstrap Method

The bootstrap is a statistical method of estimating the distribution of an estimator or test statistic by 'resampling' the data. The term comes from the old idea that you might be able to lift yourself off the ground by pulling on the straps on the backs of your boots. Suppose you have a *sample* of 20. You 'bootstrap', or approximate, the *population* from which the sample came by duplicating the sample many times over in a computer simulation of the population. You then draw lots of samples (each size 20) from this artificial bootstrap population. Bootstrapping is particularly useful when data are *skewed* and sample sizes are modest. It is frequently used in estimating probability distributions of *cost–effectiveness ratios*, their *confidence intervals* and *variances*.

Bootstrapping

A *non-parametric method* of estimating the *distribution* of an estimator or test statistic by 'resampling' the data. See *Bootstrap Method.*

Bottom-up Studies

A term used in costing methods for *cost–effectiveness* and similar analyses, according to which data sources for costs are directly obtained from a specific population or sample. Cf. *Top-down Studies.*

Bounded Rationality

One usage of this term assumes that individuals behave in a manner that is as optimal with respect to their goals as their resources will allow. Loosely, it means they are content with outcomes that are merely satisfactory rather than ideal, operate by rules of thumb, take short cuts and so on. In essence, this version of the theory recognizes that making decisions is itself a costly exercise and the resources used in weighing up the pros and cons of any choice need themselves to be economized. Another usage avoids entirely the idea that individuals have precisely defined goals that they seek to maximize even if only approximately or by rule of thumb and so on. Instead, people have aspirations which they can adapt up or down according to the ease of realizing them. Both types of bounded rationality relax one or more assumptions of standard *expected utility theory.*

Box Plot

Sometimes a 'box and whisker' plot. This is a figure in which the ends of the 'box' indicate the upper and lower values of the *interquartile range* of a *variable*, the vertical line through the box indicates the *median value*; the 'whiskers', which are the lines extending from either side of the box, indicate the 95 per cent central range of the variable; points beyond the extremities of the whisker identify the maximum and minimum values (in some box plots, the ends of the whiskers are the two extreme values). In *descriptive statistics* the two extreme values, the two limits of the interquartile range and the median are sometimes referred to as the '5 number summary' of the data. In some versions, the box plot is presented vertically.

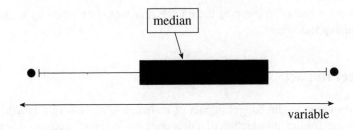

median

variable

Brand Name

The particular name given to a patented drug. Cf. its *generic* name.

Budget Balance

The difference between the government's current revenue and current expenditure. When they are equal the budget is said to be 'balanced'. When revenue exceeds expenditure there is a 'budget surplus' and when expenditure exceeds revenue there is a 'budget deficit'.

Budget Constraint

The limit to expenditure imposed by a cash-limited budget. Often represented as a straight line in geometrical representations of a consumer's choice possibilities between two goods or services, where it shows the limiting boundary of combinations of purchases that are possible with that budget. Sometimes termed 'budget line'. Often used in conjunction with

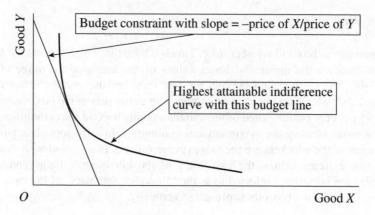

indifference curves to indicate the choice that would be made by a *utility-maximizing* individual.

Budget Impact

The estimation of the budget impact of a change in the use of a health care technology (or the introduction of a new one) is a frequent accompaniment to a *cost–effectiveness* analysis. Budget impact is a forecast of rates of use (or changes in rates of use) with their consequent short- and medium-term effects on budgets and other resources to help health service managers plan such changes.

Budget Sets

The sets of bundles of goods and services an individual can purchase. The bundles available on or under the *budget constraint*.

Bulk-billing

Bulk-billing is an Australian term to describe the system under *Medicare* whereby a doctor bills Medicare directly, accepting the Medicare benefits as full payment for a service. The practitioner cannot make any additional charge for a service, nor can any other person or company.

Burden of Disease

A measure of the total *morbidity* from a particular disease or disease in general, or its impact in terms of unfavourable consequences, or the cost of treating the victims. While such measures have their uses, one common use, which is not recommended, is as an indicator of the pay-off to research (since it takes no account of the probable success of the possible research) or as an indicator of priorities for treatment (as it takes no account of the *productivity* of treatments). Moreover the burden of disease does not measure the 'burden' (that is, the *opportunity cost*) of any measures that might be taken to reduce it. And a final caution: measures of 'burden' often fail to calibrate *quality of life*.

Burden of Taxation

There are two kinds: the direct cost to taxpayers (though this is not a cost to society as a whole since what taxpayers lose others gain) and the 'excess burden' or 'deadweight loss'. The excess burden is a subtler idea and is best seen in a demand and supply figure. Suppose a market is initially in *equilibrium* at price P and rate of output/consumption Q. An indirect tax is then imposed in the form, say, of a constant excise tax which has the effect of vertically displacing the supply curve by the amount of the tax per unit. The new equilibrium price is P_1 and the new output rate is Q_1. The burden is shared (depending on the *elasticities* of demand and supply) between buyers and sellers. The direct cost to demanders is the rectangle labelled a, the direct cost to suppliers is b. The excess burden for demanders is c and that for

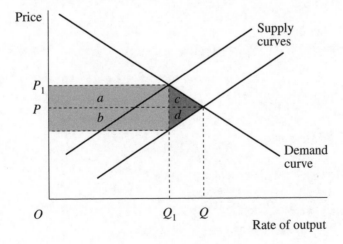

suppliers is *d*. The excess burdens represent the value over and above their cost of production of goods and services no longer bought and sold. Since nearly all health care systems involve a degree (sometimes very large) of government expenditure, it is plain that a part of the price paid for this is the excess burden (which, incidentally, exists also in connection with direct taxes) and not just the proportion of the tax revenue accounted for by public expenditure on health care.

C

CAHTA

Acronym for *Catalan Agency for Health Technology Assessment and Research*.

Canadian Coordinating Office for Health Technology Assessment

A Canadian federal organization with a mandate to encourage the appropriate use of health technology by influencing decision makers through the collection, analysis, creation and dissemination of information concerning the *effectiveness* and cost of technology and its impact on health. Its web address is www.ccohta.ca.

Capacity

A measure sometimes of the *throughput* or *output* of which a plant or organization is capable and sometimes of the *stock* of an input such as hospital beds which may determine a limit to throughput or output.

Capacity to Benefit

In health economics, this term usually refers to the potential *health gain* an individual or group might achieve through the use of health services.

Capacity Utilization

The extent to which the *capacity* of an organization like a hospital is actually being used. For hospitals, a common measure is the fraction of beds filled.

Capital

Viewed variously as a physical *stock* of assets (buildings, land plant, equipment and so on) which can earn income or generate *utility*, as a stock of financial *assets* (government bills, *equities*, bank balances and so on), or as the *present value* of the net value of a *flow* of services over time that a particular asset or programme may yield. Capital (a stock) is measured at a point in time in contrast to *investment* (a flow), which takes place through time. *Human capital* is the stock of valuable resources embodied in a human being, not all of which are (or ought to be) marketable. Health can be seen as an element in human capital which can depreciate and be invested in. Selling one's stock of human capital (in contrast to selling its flow) is one way of defining (voluntary) slavery, though this is more commonly called 'indenture'.

Capital Account

A component of the *balance of payments*.

Capital Consumption

A national income accounting term: the amount by which *gross investment* exceeds *net investment*. Synonymous with replacement investment.

Capital Cost

The *cost* of acquiring, owning or using an item of capital equipment net of depreciation. See *Capital*.

Capital Market

The market for long-term loans.

Capitalized Value

The sum of a discounted *flow* of future *costs* or *benefits*. See *Present Value*.

Capitation

A method of paying doctors a fixed fee per period per patient registered (sometimes differentiated according to age or sex of patient) regardless of the amount of service provided. Cf. *Fee-for-service*.

Card Sorts

An instrument used in *conjoint analysis*. Combinations of the *attributes* of services are written on cards which subjects are asked to sort into piles indicating their rank order of preference.

Cardinal Scale

Ratio scales and *interval scales* are both cardinal scales, in contrast to any scale that indicates no more than the order of entities (for example, by their size). Cardinality is sometimes vulgarly confused, especially when associated with *utility*, with interpersonal comparability, with which, however, it has nothing intrinsic to do at all. Interpersonal comparisons may be made ordinally or cardinally. Cf. *Ordinal Scale*. See *Utility*.

Cardinal Utility

A characteristic of *utility* measurement.

Cardiology

The medical specialty concerned with diseases and abnormalities of the heart.

Carides Two-stage Method

A method of estimating *cost functions* when the data are *censored*, typically because of staggered start dates in *clinical trials*. The method involves weighting a cost function by a survival function. See George W. Carides (2003), 'Methods for analysing censored cost data', in Andrew H. Briggs (ed.), *Statistical Methods for Cost-Effectiveness Research: A Guide to Current Issues and Future Developments*, London: Office of Health Economics, ch. 6.

Caring Externality

A type of externality in which one person derives utility from the consumption, perceived well-being, and so on of another. See *External Effects*.

Carryover Effect

A temporary or permanent change (for example, in health) that is the result of past treatment.

Cartel

A grouping of producers which acts as a *monopoly*. Suppliers of similar products may coordinate their behaviour implicitly or explicitly by setting common prices and agreed market quotas, and acting as a single organization might act to increase profit (and prices). Professional organizations often act as though they were cartels, through such devices as negotiating a standard fee schedule (per item of service), banning advertising, making particular acts (such as performing injections) legal only for members (and illegal for members of closely related professions). See *Competition*.

Case-control Study

A study comparing a series of patients with a particular condition (the cases) with a comparison group of patients (*controls*) who do not have the condition in order to determine previous exposure to a *risk factor*.

Caseload

The number of cases handled in a given period of time by a health care professional or a health care institution.

Case Management

A method of cost control and quality assurance used in many systems of health care that directs individual patients to the most appropriate amount, duration and type of health service and social care, and monitors outcomes.

Case-mix

The proportions in the total stock or flow of patients of the various types into which they may be classified (surgical, medical, for example, or more refined categories). It is often used as a variable in hospital cost analysis. See also *Diagnosis Related Group.*

Case-series Study

A study using patients' accumulated case notes over a period of time. There is no *control* group.

Cash Terms

Expenditure measured in terms of current (nominal) prices. See *Constant Prices.*

Catalan Agency for Health Technology Assessment and Research

An agency of the Catalan Health Service in Spain that encourages the introduction, adoption, diffusion and utilization of efficient health technologies, while promoting the needs assessment and *equity* analysis in the delivery and financing of health care services. Its website is at www.aatrm. net/ang/ang.html.

Categorical Variable

A variable (sometimes called a 'nominal' variable) that has two or more categories, but where there is no intrinsic ordering to the categories. For example, gender is a categorical variable having two categories (male and female) and it is not acceptable to order them intrinsically.

Category Rating Scale

A scale measure of health, or health-related quality of life, in which numerals (1, 2, 3, ...) correspond to states of health (categories) usually having verbal descriptions (such as 'can perform limited activities of daily living'). The numerical categories are sometimes assumed to have equal intervals between them (but sometimes not).

CBA

Acronym for *cost–benefit analysis.*

CCOHTA

Acronym for *Canadian Coordinating Office for Health Technology Assessment.*

CCR

Acronym for *cost-to-charge ratio.*

CEA

Acronym for *cost–effectiveness analysis.*

CEAC

Acronym for *cost–effectiveness acceptability curve.*

CEDIT

Acronym for *Comité d'Evaluation et de Diffusion des Innovations Technologiques.*

Ceiling Effect

A phenomenon whereby a drug reaches a maximum effect, so that increasing its dosage does not increase outcome. It may also be the product of a measurement instrument, as when, for example, a measure of cognitive performance has an insufficient number of the more difficult tasks or nearly everyone can score 100 per cent because the tasks in general are too easy.

Ceiling Ratio

The maximum acceptable (to a decision maker) *incremental cost–effectiveness ratio*.

Censored Data

Runs of data, for example, in a *clinical trial*, can be cut off at various points for various reasons. This is called 'censoring'. In some cases, the data are censored because the trial observation period was shorter than *time to event*. Other reasons include *loss to follow-up* and death from some unrelated cause.

Census Tract

A geographical area defined within a population census with well-defined boundaries.

Centers for Medicare & Medicaid Services

The Centers for Medicare & Medicaid Services (CMS) is a Federal agency within the US Department of Health and Human Services. Programmes for which CMS is responsible include Medicare, Medicaid and the State Children's Health Insurance Program. It was formerly known as the *Health Care Financing Administration*. Its web address is http://www.cms.hhs.gov/default.asp?

Centile

Also termed percentile. When a continuous *variable* is split for convenience into 100 equal-sized chunks of data the cut-off points between them are called centiles. See *Quantile*.

Centripetal Bias

Same as *referral bias*.

CER

Acronym for *control event rate*.

Certainty Equivalent

The certain and sure money or utility ('sure thing') that a subject would have to receive to be indifferent between it and a given gamble ('uncertain prospect') is called the gamble's 'certainty equivalent'. The certainty equivalent is less than the expected value of the gamble if an individual has a diminishing marginal utility of money income and obeys the axioms of *expected utility theory*. This indicates a kind of *risk aversion*. In health economics, the usual experiment contains a certain outcome, such as five years of healthy life, and an uncertain prospect consisting of the combination of two or more uncertain outcomes such as probability p of having two years of healthy life and probability $(1 - p)$ of having 15 years of healthy life. P is then experimentally adjusted until there is *indifference*.

Certificate of Need

A method of regulating hospital *capital* developments that requires state (USA) agencies to review and approve changes in hospital bed *capacity* and major purchases of equipment above certain threshold levels. Abbreviated to CON.

CES Production Function

See *Constant Elasticity of Substitution Production Function*.

Ceteris Paribus

A Latin tag meaning 'other things equal' or (better) 'other things remaining unchanged'. Cf. *Mutatis Mutandis*.

Chemotherapy

The use of a chemical to treat a disease.

Cherry Picking

Same as *cream skimming*.

Chiropody

Treatment of the feet.

Chiropractor

A person licensed to practise chiropractic care using manipulation mechanically to restore displaced bones, especially the vertebrae, to their proper alignment.

Chi-squared Test

χ^2 (chi-squared or 'chi-square' – statisticians are not agreed) is a statistical test based on a comparison between a test statistic and a critical value from a chi-squared distribution. A chi-squared variable can be regarded as the sum of a number of squared independent normal variables, each with zero mean and unit variance. The number of such squared terms is the number of degrees of freedom of the χ^2 distribution. A chi-squared test can be used to test the null hypothesis that two or more population distributions do not differ. When comparing observed values with those expected under the null hypothesis, it is the sum of the ratio of the squared differences between observed (O) and expected (E) values to the expected value:

$$\chi^2 = \sum \frac{[O_i - E_i]^2}{E_i}.$$

There are two well-known versions, the Pearson χ^2 test and the Mantel–Haenszel test. See *Statistical Significance*.

Choice Modelling

A *conjoint analysis* procedure for estimating *willingness to pay* for services using a weighted set of *attributes* of the services in question.

Choice Theory

Any theory that purports to explain or account for or to recommend human choices. *Utility maximizing* and *expected utility theory* are two examples.

Chronic

Long-lasting. The US National Center for Health Statistics defines it as of three or more months' duration.

Churning

Refers variously to such practices as the transfer of patients between long-term care hospitals and colocated acute care hospitals simply for financial gain. It is also used as a synonym for staff turnover. The term originates in financial markets (where it is also referred to as 'twisting'): an unethical practice by brokers to increase their commissions by trading excessively on a client's behalf.

Citizens Council

This council (note the cowardly absence of an apostrophe in 'Citizens') advises the *National Institute for Health and Clinical Excellence* in England and Wales on critical value judgments associated with *health technology appraisals* and *clinical guideline* development. It is essentially a *consensus panel* or *focus group* and the membership is designed to represent the broad characteristics of the population of England and Wales.

Citizens' Jury

Similar to *consensus panel*.

Clinical Budgets

A procedure whereby physicians or teams of physicians in a given specialty in hospitals are assigned a fixed sum of money for their activity to cover the expenses of, for example, pharmaceutical prescriptions, use of pathology laboratories or staff salaries.

Clinical Epidemiology

The methods of *epidemiology* applied to clinical matters, especially in determining the *effectiveness* or *efficacy* of clinical interventions in the treatment of medical conditions.

Clinical Governance

The most widely used definition of clinical governance, as used in the UK National Health Service, is a framework through which NHS organizations are accountable for continually improving the quality of their services and safeguarding high standards of care by creating an environment in which excellence in clinical care will flourish. Introduced in 1998, it was a programme to implement extensive culture change: at the professional level, with individual health care professionals adopting 'reflective practice' and patients being placed at the centre of professional thinking; at team level, with teams becoming multidisciplinary groups, where understanding about roles, about sharing information and knowledge and about support for each other becomes part of everyday practice; and at the organizational level, with organizations putting in place systems and local arrangements to support teams and assure the quality of care provided with commitment and leadership from the board level down.

Clinical Guidelines

Clinical guidelines are recommendations on the appropriate treatment and care of patients with specific diseases and conditions. They are usually drawn up by multidisciplinary groups of experts and ought to be based on systematic reviews of the literature. Some, such as those developed by the *National Institute for Health and Clinical Excellence*, take account of *cost-effectiveness*.

Clinical Significance

A difference between the effects of different treatments judged by expert clinicians to be important for clinical or policy decisions. It is independent of statistical significance or cost-effectiveness.

Clinical Trial

Clinical trials are generally tests of the *effectiveness* of medical and surgical interventions. With pharmaceuticals, trials go through various *phases*, identifying safety and *efficacy* beyond the *preclinical trial* stage. Trials use samples of patients drawn from a relevant population of patients or people at risk and many are multi-centred and international in nature. They vary greatly in their use of controls (for example, some compare the procedure being studied with a *placebo*, others with a common practical alternative) and in other aspects of their design, their size, duration, choice of *outcome*, *endpoint*. See *Phases in Clinical Trials*.

Clinimetrics

The science of measuring clinical phenomena such as signs and symptoms.

Closed-ended Questionnaire

An interview schedule or questionnaire in which the respondent has to choose one of a specific set of predetermined mutually exclusive and exhaustive answers. Cf. *Open-ended Questionnaire*.

Cluster

Groupings of health-related events that are thought not to be the product of mere chance.

Cluster Analysis

Statistical methods used to group entities that are interrelated.

Cluster Sample

A *sample* obtained through a two-stage procedure in which the population is divided into mutually exclusive and exhaustive *clusters* from which a random sample of clusters is then taken. If all the observations in the selected clusters are used, the procedure is termed 'one-stage' cluster sampling; if a sample from the selected clusters is taken, the procedure is 'two-stage' cluster sampling. Cf. *Stratified Sample, Subgroup Analysis*.

CMA

Acronym for *cost-minimization analysis*.

CMS

Acronym for *Centers for Medicare & Medicaid Services*.

Cobb–Douglas Production Function

The Cobb–Douglas *production function* has the form:

$$Y = AK^{\alpha}L^{\beta},$$

where A, α and β are constants; A is commonly interpreted as 'technology' and K and L are *capital* and *labour* services, respectively. If there are *constant returns to scale*, then $\alpha + \beta = 1$. With increasing/decreasing returns to scale the sum is >1 and <1, respectively. Named after the US mathematician Charles W. Cobb (dates untraceable) and the US economist Paul H. Douglas (1892–1976).

Cobb–Douglas Utility Function

A utility function taking the form:

$$U = AX_1^{\alpha}X_2^{\beta},$$

where the X_i are goods or services. See *Cobb–Douglas Production Function*.

Cochrane Collaboration

This is an international network of clinicians, researchers and consumers which develops and maintains a collection of *systematic reviews* and *meta-analyses* of the effectiveness and efficacy of technologies for treating medical conditions. Its website is at www.cochrane.org/docs/siteindex.htm.

Coding

Assigning numerical values to *categorical variables*, especially in data processing.

Coefficient of Concordance

See *Kendall's Coefficient of Concordance*.

Coefficient of Determination

Same as R^2.

Coefficient of Variation

A measure of dispersion: the *standard deviation* divided by the *arithmetic mean* and multiplied by 100. Usually referred to as CV.

Cohort

A well-defined group of subjects having a common experience or exposure, which is then followed up over time.

Cohort Case-control Study

A *case-control* study conducted within a *cohort study*. Also known as a nested case-control study.

Cohort Study

A study of a group of patients initially with the characteristic of interest (for example, they have been exposed to a *risk factor*) who are then compared with another group, identical as far as possible in all other respects, without the characteristic of interest (that is, they have not been exposed to the risk factor) in order to estimate the impact of the characteristic (the risk factor in this case) on health. Also called 'follow-up' study or 'longitudinal' study.

Coinsurance

Coinsurance is the practice whereby the insured person shares a fraction of an insured loss with the insurer. For example, the insurance policy may require the insured person to pay 10 per cent of the expenses of medical care, with the insurer paying 90 per cent. The sum paid by the insured person is known as a *copayment*, so if the expenses are $1000 and the coinsurance rate is 10 per cent, the copayment is $100. Some policies require *deductibles*, sometimes known as 'excess', to be paid. Under this arrangement the insured person pays a fixed sum if the event insured against occurs and the insurer pays all other expenses. Thus, if the deductible is $100 and the coinsurance rate 10 per cent, should the event involve an expense of $1000, the insured person pays $190 ($100 plus $90 copayment).

The effects of deductibles and coinsurance can be shown using the figure, which assumes that individuals are *expected utility* maximizers. The vertical axis shows the price of health care P (assumed – implausibly – to be set equal to *marginal cost*) and the *marginal value* placed upon health care consumption by an individual. The horizontal axis indicates the rate of consumption of health care (so much per day, week, month and so on). The bold curve, equivalent to the *demand curve*, is the marginal value curve and the horizontal line is the (constant) marginal cost curve. In a world of no insurance, the individual faces a price OP, at which OC_1 care will be consumed when ill. Let the individual (while healthy) consider buying insurance. Suppose neither the individual nor the insurer is in any doubt about the probability, p, of illness striking in any period (another tall order). Given that the insured, when uninsured, would consume $OPaC_1$ the actuarially *fair premium* is p of this amount. We assume also that there is zero *loading*: that is, the insurer adds nothing to the premium to cover the administrative costs of operating the insurance service. Now let an individual consider insurance. They are comparing consumption (if sick) C_1 at a user price P and no premium, with consumption C_3 at a zero price and the payment of a premium. The difference between C_3 and C_1 is due to *moral hazard*. The fair premium payable will be *p* (the probability of the event occurring) times the cost of care ($OPdC_3$). Given such a premium, whether the individual buys insurance cover will partly depend on whether $Pea > adC_3$. (Note that the individual will definitely buy insurance if the insurer foolishly sets the premium at *p* times $OPaC_1$, the expense that will be incurred under self-insurance.)

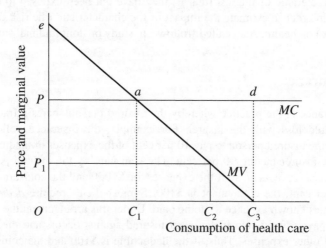

Suppose that cover is purchased, the individual judging that it is worth buying insurance to avoid the financial risk. A policy containing a deductible may still be to the individual's advantage. A deductible does not affect the marginal cost of consumption so, once an individual is insured, they will consume C_3. Suppose there is a deductible of $100. If insurance is taken out, the individual will thus pay $100 and consume C_3 care. If the value of the additional consumption over self-insurance (C_3–C_1) exceeds $100, this will seem a good deal and the care will be purchased. Whether insurance will be purchased, however, depends on the premium combined with the effects of the deductible. The deductible reduces the net benefit of the additional consumption (C_1aC_3) by $100. So long as the advantage of avoiding the risk of the financial consequences of ill-health remains high enough, the individual will purchase this policy. Plainly, there will be some deductible high enough to overwhelm this advantage and the individual will then self-insure. Deductibles, by reducing the number of small claims (that is, claims at or below the value of the deductible), may reduce insurance companies' administrative costs and hence enable the *loading* element of the premium to fall.

With coinsurance, the individual pays a percentage of the cost, say OP_1, which causes a fall in the amount demanded when insured (from C_3 to C_2) leading to a reduction in the actuarially fair premium as the cost of the care chosen falls. Coinsurance thus can reduce the effect of moral hazard and reduce premiums. Taken to the extreme, let the coinsurance rate approach P. Plainly, at P, there is self-insurance, the premium is zero (and so is moral hazard). The consumer is fully exposed to the financial risk of ill-health. One might expect an optimal coinsurance rate to exist between O and P, though it needs to take account of external effects. The 'excess' consumption that the coinsurance reduces is in excess only of the optimum seen from the particular individual's viewpoint and, from a wider social viewpoint, may not be excessive at all (a *second best* solution is preferable to attempting a first best one). See *Copayment, Insurance*.

Cointervention

In a *randomized clinical trial*, the application of additional procedures to subjects in either arm (experimental or control) of the study.

Collège des Economistes de la Santé

The French health economists' association. Its website is at www.cesasso.org/PagesGB/defaut_gb.htm.

Collinearity

This occurs when pairs of *explanatory variables* in a *regression analysis* are correlated. See also *Multicollinearity*.

Comfort Care

Same as *palliative care*.

Comité d'Evaluation et de Diffusion des Innovations Technologiques

CEDIT is a French hospital-based agency for the assessment of medical technologies. Its website is at www.cedit.aphp.fr/english/index_present.html.

Commissioner

This has a specific meaning in the context of the UK *National Health Service*, where it refers to authorities like *Primary Care Trusts* that are responsible for commissioning health care on behalf of local communities. See *Commissioning, Purchaser–provider Split*.

Commissioning

A term used in the UK *National Health Service* to describe the process through which collective purchasers of health care such as *Primary Care Trusts* reach agreements with providers in an *internal market*.

The Common Drug Review

A Canadian organization that provides participating federal, provincial and territorial drug benefit plans with systematic reviews of the best available clinical evidence, critiques of manufacturer-submitted pharmacoeconomic studies and formulary listing recommendations made by the Canadian Expert Drug Advisory Committee. Its website is at www.ccohta.ca/entry_e.html.

Communicable Disease

An *infectious disease* due to an infectious agent (such as bacterium, virus, parasitic worm) or any toxic products that arise through its transmission from an infected person, animal or reservoir (such as swamps, contaminated needles) to a susceptible host, either directly or indirectly through an intermediate plant or animal host, *vector*, or the inanimate environment. See *External Effects*.

Community Medicine

The study of health and disease in communities. The underlying discipline to support *public health medicine*.

Community Rating

Setting health care insurance premia according to the utilization of a broad population (for example, one defined by employer type or geography). Cf. *Experience Rating*.

Comorbidity

The coexistence in a patient of a disease or diseases in addition to the condition that is the object of study or treatment.

Comparative Advantage

This exists when a firm or a jurisdiction can produce a good or service with less forgone output (*opportunity cost*) than another can. Cf. *Absolute Advantage*, with which comparative advantage is often confused. Call centres are increasingly located in India, not because their location there involves fewer inputs for any given number of calls dealt with (absolute advantage), but because the output lost from using (mainly, in this case) people in this way rather than another is smaller than it would be in, say, most European countries or North America. Some countries have an absolute advantage in producing nearly everything, but it is impossible for them to have a comparative advantage in everything. Conversely some countries have an absolute advantage in virtually nothing but they necessarily have a comparative advantage in something. Total world production increases, and therefore consumption possibilities increase, if countries specialize according to their comparative, not absolute, advantages. Of course, how these gains from specialization are shared is another matter.

Comparative Health Systems

The general term used to describe studies that compare the various health care systems (though the word 'care' is dropped) that exist internationally.

Comparative Price Level

See *Purchasing Power Parity*.

Comparative Statics

A procedure in economics whereby two *equilibrium* states are compared, usually in a context where one state is the consequence of altering a *parameter*, *ceteris paribus*. Cf. *General Equilibrium*.

Compensating Variation

The compensating variation in income is the minimum (maximum) amount of money that has to be given to (taken away from) an individual to make them as well off in their own judgment as before a price rise (fall). Cf. *Equivalent Variation, Willingness to Accept, Willingness to Pay*.

Compensation Test

This is a way of measuring the desirability of a proposal for change. If the people who are expected to gain from the change are willing to compensate those who lose (that is, fully compensate them such that they are at the least indifferent between accepting and not accepting the change), then the change is judged to be *welfare* enhancing. An alternative test is to discover whether the expected losers can compensate (just) the potential gainers for going without the proposed change; if so, then the change is not welfare enhancing. Or one might apply both tests. These are ways of trying to identify *Pareto-improvements* and *potential Pareto-improvements* in *social welfare*. See also *Kaldor–Hicks Criterion* and *Scitovsky Criterion*.

Competition

In economics, there is a variety of descriptors of types of market competition, most of which relate to competition amongst producers or sellers of goods and services: 'perfect', 'imperfect', 'monopolistic', 'duopolistic' 'oligopolistic' are the five most likely to be encountered. Perfect competition is the modelling of a situation in which there are sufficiently large numbers of producers for the activity of any one not to affect the market price. It is sometimes called '*price-taking*'. Imperfect competition refers to a situation in which the activity of any one of several producers will affect the price. Monopoly stands at the end of the spectrum farthest from perfect competition and refers to a situation in which there is a single seller. A duopoly exists when there are but two producers. An oligopoly exists when there are just a few sellers. The idea that there is a direct link between the number of sellers and the 'amount' of competition is not a very good one. It is usually more insightful to consider the nature of the influence that one producer may have on another, or on consumers or employees, and the ease of access to information about competitors' activities and plans, than simply to consider numbers. Nonetheless, within broad bands, numbers of producers in similar fields do form the basis for measuring the *concentration ratio* of an industry. See also *Cartel*.

There can also be degrees of competition between buyers. For example, one of the arguments for concentrating purchasing power for health care in the hands of a *managed care* organization, or the state at regional or national level, is that this creates substantial influence over the prices that can be obtained from producers and the wages and salaries that must be paid to health service professionals. When buyers are sufficiently large in relation to the market, the condition is termed 'monopsony'.

Economists tend to regard competition with favour, though there are some markets in which competition can be extremely damaging, of which the most important is probably the *insurance* market. See *Risk Selection*.

Complement

A good or service whose demand rises or falls as the price of another good falls or rises is said to be a complement. The *cross-elasticity of demand* is negative. Infliximab and methodextrate, two drugs used in combination in the treatment of rheumatoid arthritis, are an example. So are golf clubs and balls. They tend to be goods that are used together.

Complete Case Analysis

A method of dealing with *incomplete data*. It involves using only complete cases, with no values imputed to missing data, with the risk of *bias* if the sample with omissions is not representative.

Complete Market

A market is said to be theoretically 'complete' when individuals can obtain insurance against any future time and state of the world.

Completeness

One of the standard axioms of choice theory. It requires that an individual either prefers entity *A* to entity *B*, or *B* to *A*, or that they are indifferent between the two. See *Utility*.

Compliance

The extent to which patients follow the health advice they receive.

Comprehensiveness

A characteristic of a health care system that is commonly desired or sometimes (as in Canada) required by statute. It relates to the range of services that are or ought to be provided, typically including all those deemed 'medically necessary' (which is not equivalent to 'cost-effective') and covering *inpatient* and *outpatient* care, and community-based services including pharmacy, dentistry and *ophthalmic* services. Cf. *Universality*.

CON

Acronym for *certificate of need*.

Concentration Curve

See *Concentration Index*.

Concentration Index

In health economics, a *concentration index* is a means of quantifying the degree of income-related inequality in health. Where there is no income-related inequality, the concentration index is zero. The *concentration curve* in the figure shows the cumulative percentage of the population or sample on the horizontal axis sample, ranked by income, beginning with the poorest and the cumulative percentage of ill-health (say, fractions of deaths in a period) on the vertical axis. The concentration index is defined as twice the area between the concentration curve and the line of equality (the 45° line running

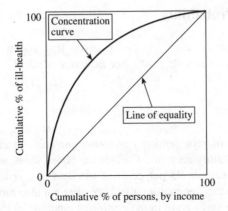

from the south west corner to the north east). The convention is that the index takes a negative value when the curve lies above the line of equality, indicating disproportionate concentration of ill-health among the poor, and a positive value when it lies below the line of equality. Cf. *Lorenz Curve*.

Concentration Ratio

The share of the market (usually by sales or employment) occupied by the largest firms (typically, four firms). See also *Herfindahl Index*.

Concept Mapping

A concept map is a diagram for identifying and linking ideas and for gathering and sharing information. It will have 'nodes' that contain a concept, activity or question and links to other nodes. The links have descriptive labels and will have an arrow if there is an obvious direction of flow. It is increasingly used as a means of brainstorming or creating coherence in a managerial team.

Concurrent Review

A review of a patient's records to determine their *need* for continuing care.

Conditional Probability

The probability of an event occurring given that another event has also occurred or a particular state exists. See *Bayesian Method*.

Confidence Box

A graphical way of representing *confidence intervals* in cost–*effectiveness analysis* or *cost–utility analysis*. Confidence boxes show where a specified percentage (for example 95 per cent) of the data in a *scatter plot* will lie. Consider a health care technology that is costlier but also more effective than its comparator, so that we are in the north east quadrant of the *cost–effectiveness plane* shown in the figure. The slope of rays such as *a* and *b* shows the *incremental cost–effectiveness ratio* ($\Delta C/\Delta E$) of the technology under investigation relative to an alternative (*control*). The steeper the ray, the greater the *marginal cost* per marginal gain in output compared with the comparator. The upper and lower confidence limits of incremental cost are plotted against the upper and lower confidence limits of the *effectiveness* measure in the form of a box. Rays *a* and *b* are the outer limits of the confidence interval (usually 95 per cent). Cf. *Confidence Ellipse*.

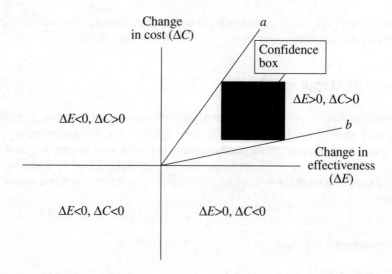

Confidence Ellipse

A graphical way of representing *confidence intervals* in *cost–effectiveness analysis* or *cost–utility analysis*. Confidence ellipses show where a specified percentage (such as 95 per cent) of the data in a *scatter plot* will lie. Consider a health care technology that is costlier but also more effective than its comparator, so that we are in the north east quadrant of the *cost–effectiveness plane* shown in the figure. The slope of rays such as a' and b' shows the *incremental cost–effectiveness ratio* ($\Delta C/\Delta E$) of the technology under investigation relative to an alternative (*control*). The steeper the ray, the greater the *marginal cost* per marginal gain in output compared with the comparator. The upper and lower confidence limits of incremental cost are plotted against the upper and lower confidence limits of the *effectiveness* measure in the form of an ellipse (inside the confidence box). Rays a' and b' are the outer limits of the confidence interval (usually 95 per cent) and will lie within the rays defined by the corners of the *confidence box*. Confidence ellipses are visual indicators of correlation: they are stretched out from south west to north east if there is a positive *covariance* between ΔC and ΔE. The confidence ellipse is more circular when two variables are uncorrelated. Cf. *Confidence Box.*

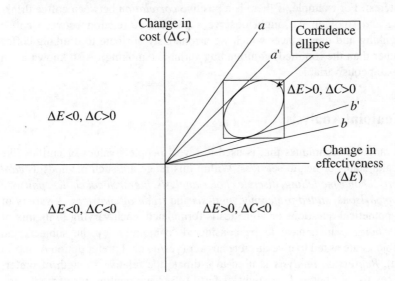

Confidence Ellipsoid

Same (roughly speaking) as *confidence ellipse.*

Confidence Interval

The range of values within which a population *parameter* such as the population *mean* or *variance* is expected to lie with a given degree of confidence. The convention is to set the 'confidence' level at 95 per cent, in the (*frequentist*) sense that, with repeated sampling, there is a 95 per cent chance that the true parameter value lies within that range.

Confidence Limits

The upper and lower bounds of a *confidence interval*.

Confounding

Confounding occurs when an effect is attributed to an *independent variable X* when in fact it is due to an omitted variable (a confounding variable) *B*, which is correlated with both *X* and the outcome (*dependent variable*) of interest. For example, if there is a positive *correlation* between coffee drinking and smoking we might observe a positive correlation between coffee drinking and lung cancer which we erroneously attribute to drinking coffee rather than the (omitted) confounding variable (smoking). Also known as an 'extraneous variable'.

Conjoint Analysis

A range of techniques that is used to reveal people's values of entities like health states or health services. Within this range are such methods as *card sorts, choice modelling, discrete choice analysis, hierarchical choice, pairwise comparisons, stated preference analysis* and *trade-off matrices*. A variety of hypothetical questions or vignettes is formulated, each varying in its mix of *attributes* (which have to be considered 'conjointly' by the subject) and subjects are asked to give discrete answer (yes/no or 'I prefer option A' and so on). *Regression analysis* is used to estimate the relative strength of preferences for attributes. In a study of fertility service quality, for example, the attributes to do with quality might include attitudes of staff to the patient (uncaring/unsympathetic; caring/sympathetic), continuity of contact with staff (see same staff; see many different staff), time on waiting list for first IVF attempts (1, 3, 6, 18, 36 months), cost to patient per attempt ($0, $750, $1500, $2500, $3000), chances of taking home a baby (5, 10, 15, 25, 35 per cent), follow-up support (yes; no). The resultant scores are usually treated as utilities. *Willingness to pay* estimates are also sometimes made. See also *Adaptive Conjoint Analysis*, *Quality-adjusted Life-year*, *Utility Measurement*.

Consecutive Sampling

Recruiting subjects as they become available. The potential *bias* inherent in this method is plain. Cf. *Convenience Sample*.

Consensus Conference

Similar to *consensus panel*.

Consensus Panel

A panel (sometimes called a consensus conference, focus group or citizens' jury) of people selected for their expertise and other *attributes* deemed to be relevant, which is invited to answer one or more questions about which there may be considerable doubt or disagreement on the part of a parent body. Panellists will usually have available to them the consensus questions, one or more *systematic reviews*, summaries of the available evidence and the ability to interview invited experts and other stakeholders. There may be a facilitator. The conferences usually take place over two or three days. The *Citizens Council* is a form of consensus panel. Topics addressed have included factors to take account of in assessing 'need', whether age of patients should be taken into account in deciding what treatments are available in the *National Health Service* and whether orphan drugs ought to be given special consideration.

Consequences

A term used in *cost–effectiveness analysis* to describe the necessary (or predicted) future effects of a decision. It embraces all the effects that may be deemed relevant, usually classified into costs and benefits, some being in monetary and others often in non-monetary forms.

Consequentialism

The idea that the ethical merit or otherwise of any proposed course of action (for example, changing the financial terms of access to health care, or the exclusion of a drug from the list of approved benefits in an insurance plan) is to be evaluated in terms of its consequences (as distinct, say, from the motives of those advocating it, or because one is conceived to have a duty to adopt it, or because God commands it). Cf. *Deontological, Utilitarianism.*

Consistent Estimate

An estimate that converges on the true *parameter* value as the sample size approaches infinity.

Constant Elasticity of Substitution (CES) Production Function

A type of *production function* having, in the case of two inputs, the form:

$$Y = A[\alpha K^{\rho} + \beta L^{\rho}]^{(1/\rho)},$$

where α and β are constants; A is a *variable* broadly representing 'technology' and K and L are *capital* and labour services, respectively; ρ is constant and is a measure of the substitutability of labour for capital services or vice versa. The *elasticity* of substitution (σ) is $1 / (1 + \rho)$. Since ρ is constant, then so is σ; hence the name for this type of *production function*. If $\rho = 0$ then the function becomes a *Cobb–Douglas production function* and $\sigma = 1$.

Constant Prices

The use of the prices of a given year in calculating costs and benefits in other years so as to eliminate the effect of inflation. This is usually done by means of a *price index* or price deflator. An example of such an index (deflator) is $P_1 Q_1 / P_0 Q_1$, where P_1 is a set of prices at date 1, Q_1 is a set of commodities at that date and P_0 is the set of prices for those same commodities at an earlier date.

Constant Proportional Time Trade-off

An assumption made in the construction of *quality-adjusted life-years* (QALYs). Subjects must be willing to sacrifice a constant proportion of future years of life for a given QALY gain.

Constant Returns to Scale

A feature of *production functions*. A production function exhibits constant returns to scale if increasing all *factors of production (inputs)* in the same proportion increases *outputs* by the same proportion. Note that the way that output responds to changes in a single input is not the same as a response to a change of scale, where all inputs may vary. See *Law of Variable Proportions*.

Constraint

The limits (real and imaginary; budgetary, resource, political and so on) on what it is possible to accomplish. Careful examination of imagined constraints often results in their being seen to be movable, though usually at some cost. Releasing decision makers from the curse of unimaginative thinking about constraints is one of the potentially great benefits of well-conducted *economic appraisals*.

Construct

A notional measure of something that is not directly measurable, such as 'quality of life' or 'severity of illness'.

Construct Validity

A *construct* that correlates well with other conventionally trusted measures of the underlying concept and that discriminates as one would expect (that is, in ways predicted by theory) between cases having and not having particular characteristics. Cf. *Convergent Validity, Criterion Validity, Discriminant Validity, External Validity, Face Validity, Predictive Validity, Test–retest Validity*.

Constructed Preferences

Preferences that are revealed by experimental subjects but that are not their 'true' preferences, being expressed under circumstances when they feel they have to express something but are unsure about what it is (or ought to be). In health economics, this is perhaps most likely to occur when people are weighing up small changes in low probabilities.

Consultation Fee

A money charge made for consulting a doctor. See *Fee-for-service*.

Consumer Good

An *economic good* used by households for final consumption (that is, not for selling on or for investment purposes).

Consumer Price Index

A measure of the weighted price change over a period of time of a bundle of goods typically purchased by 'consumers'. See *Price Index*.

Consumer Sovereignty

This is not a technical term in economics. It refers to the idea that consumers ultimately determine (sometimes that they ought to determine) the goods and services that are produced, their quantities, qualities and availability in time and space. The nearest idea to it that is used in (welfare) economics is the idea of individual welfare, in which the welfare of all individuals (and not just consumers) is taken as comprising the welfare of society, but it is a vulgar error to muddle the two. It is also sometimes used to mean that consumers are the only (or possibly ought to be the only) judges of their own welfare. See *Pareto Optimality*.

Consumer's Surplus

The difference between what a consumer pays for a good or service and the maximum they would pay rather than go without it. In the first figure below, showing a *demand curve* (here *linear*), it is the patterned area bounded by the demand (*marginal valuation*) curve, the vertical axis and the horizontal line at *P*. Under particular assumptions it is the maximum that someone will pay for the right to purchase the good at price *P* or the minimum they must receive to forgo that privilege. In the second figure below, imagine the consumer being constrained to purchase under circumstances where they must reveal the maximum they would pay for a small amount of a good rather than none. This is indicated by the first tall rectangle in the second figure. Then they are asked the maximum they would pay for a second small increment, indicated by the second rectangle, and so on. Now imagine that the increments become increasingly tiny and we consider all such increments up to

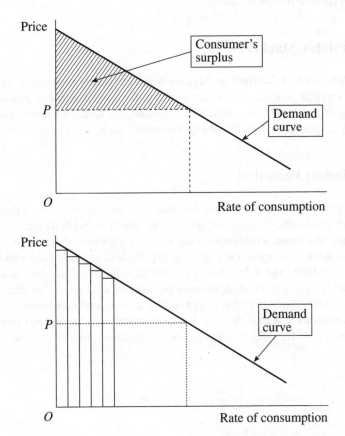

the marginal valuation that equates to the going price. In the first figure the whole of the area below the demand curve up to that rate of consumption is thus the maximum the individual is willing to pay, the rectangle below the price line is the amount that would actually be paid in a market (price times quantity) and the difference between them is consumer's surplus. Practical estimation of consumer's surplus usually makes the assumption that the relevant section of a demand curve, when one has but two observations, is *continuous* and *linear*. See *Compensation Test, Producer's Surplus*.

Contagious Disease

A *communicable disease* that is transmitted through physical contact (touching) and infected water droplets. Often used much more loosely as a virtual synonym for 'infectious disease' and hence inclusive of airborne, insect and other *vectors* of transmission.

Contestable Market

A market in which *barriers to entry* are low. A perfectly contestable market has a complete absence of barriers to entry: no special *licences*, *patents* or copyrights, no high *fixed costs*, and where no marketing barriers (whether legal or illegal) have been created by incumbent firms. See *Competition*.

Contingent Valuation

Contingent valuation is so called because it is an experimental method for eliciting valuations of goods or services by which individuals are asked to state their maximum willingness to pay or the minimum willingness to accept going without, contingent on a specific hypothetical scenario (like making a market purchase) and a description of options available. It is also known as the *stated preferenc*e method, because the method asks people to state their values directly (and hypothetically), rather than inferring *revealed preferences* values from actual choices. A related procedure that depends more on inferring values from the characteristics of services is *conjoint analysis*.

Continuity

One of the standard axioms of *utility* theory. It requires that there is an *indifference curve* such that all points to its north east are preferred to all point to its south west.

Continuous Variable

A numerical *variable* that can in principle take the value of any real number within an interval. Of course, practical measurement constraints may in practice mean that not all possible values are actually observed. Examples include temperature, blood pressure, cholesterol concentration, labour costs, waiting time. *Demand curves* are generally drawn as continuous or empirically modelled as though they were continuous. Cf. *Discrete Variable*.

Contract Curve

A locus in an *Edgeworth Box* showing a series of *Pareto-optimal* distributions of a fixed quantity of two goods between two people, each distribution being an allocation of the two goods between the two people that can be reached by (assumed costless) contracting (trading). The contract curve is found by connecting the tangencies of the two individuals' *indifference curves*.

Control

An individual without the disease being investigated in a *case-control* study or one not receiving the treatment whose effects are being investigated in a *clinical trial*, or someone without the baseline characteristic of interest being studied in a cohort study.

Control Event Rate

The percentage or proportion of events that occur in a *control* group.

Control Group

A group of people acting as *controls* in a *clinical trial* or economic experiment.

Controlled Trial

In *clinical trials*, one group of subjects receives an experimental drug, while another group (the *control* group) receives the usual treatment for the disease or another treatment of interest or a *placebo*. The control group provides a standard against which the experimental observations may be evaluated.

Convenience Sample

A *sample* that uses the most readily available subjects and is an easy method to obtain subjects (for example, the first 20 patients to enter the clinic on a particular day). Not much recommended, as the potential *bias* is plain. Cf. *Consecutive Sampling*.

Convergent Validity

This is an aspect of *construct validity*, whereby a measure is correlated with other measures that are deemed to be acceptable empirical measures of the underlying concept.

Convexity

One of the axioms of *utility* theory. It stipulates that *indifference curves* are convex (to the origin in a two-good diagram). See *Utility*.

Cooperative Game

A type of game in *game theory* in which the players may cooperate before choosing what each will do. Cf. *Non-cooperative Game*.

Copayment

An arrangement whereby an insured person pays a particular percentage of any bills for health services received, the insurer paying the remainder (cf. *Deductible*). See *Coinsurance*.

Core

The core of an economy (if one exists) is a state in which (a) no subset of members of the community can improve upon their position (as they see it) through trade or production and (b) which is also a *Pareto optimum*.

Corner Solution

A corner solution is a choice outcome that entails the individual being on a constraint such as a *budget constraint* at the points at which the constraint touches one of the axes. It arises from one's being unable to purchase negative quantities of a good or service or from the absence of negative prices. It is a limiting case in which the usual maximizing conditions, say of *marginal value* being set equal to price, cannot apply. Cf. *Interior Solution*.

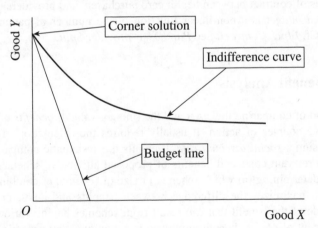

Correlation Coefficient

A measure of how closely two *variables* are linearly related. Generally denoted by 'r', its absolute value provides an indication of the strength of the relationship. The value of *r* varies between +1 and –1, with –1 or 1 indicating a perfect linear relationship, and $r = 0$ indicating no linear relationship. The sign of the correlation coefficient indicates whether the slope of the line is positive or negative when the two variables are plotted in a scatter diagram. Also known as 'Pearson's correlation coefficient' after the British statistician Karl Pearson (1857–1936). Cf. *Spearman's Rank-order Correlation Coefficient.*

Correlation does not imply causation. There is evidence that the density of the stork population is correlated with the human birth rate. The reason for the relationship is probably that both variables are related to the number of chimney stacks, which are favourite nesting sites for the birds and an indicator of the size of the human population.

Cost

For the main entry, see *Opportunity Cost.* See also *Average Cost, Capital Cost, Direct Cost, Fixed Cost, Indirect Costs, Marginal Cost, Overhead Costs, Productivity Cost, Sunk Cost, Total Cost.*

Cost and Volume Contract

A species of contract between health care purchasers and providers in which the *global budget* is a non-linear function of the number of patients to be treated. Cf. *Block Contract.* See *Purchaser–provider Split.*

Cost–benefit Analysis

A method of comparing the *costs* and the (money-valued) *benefits* of various alternative courses of action. It usually requires the calculation of *present values* using a *social discount rate.* It entails the systematic comparisons of all those relevant costs and benefits of proposed alternative schemes with a view to determining (a) which scheme, or size of scheme, or combination of schemes, maximizes the difference between benefits and costs, or (b) the magnitude of the benefit that can result from schemes having various costs. The concept of cost or benefit employed is sometimes that of *social cost* or *social benefit.*

However in other cases the scope of the cost and benefit concepts is defined by the interests of the clients for whom the analysis is conducted after discussion between clients and analysts about the options to be considered and the objectives to be sought. This is known as the *perspective* of the study.

The virtues of explicitness (in the objectives postulated, the assumptions and methods adopted) and consistency (the principle that decisions between alternatives should be consistent with objectives) are common to all forms of cost–benefit analysis. Beyond these, however, there are two broad perspectives that analysts may follow: one is often termed the 'social decision makers'' perspective and the other the 'societal' perspective. Under the social decision makers' approach, the analyst addresses the question of concern to the decision maker (which may in practice take considerable eliciting) and adopts the decision maker's values. This way of approaching the cost–benefit analyst's task is somewhat akin to a consultant's role. The social decision maker is the client.

The other approach involves the analyst in stipulating the social objectives and making the necessary value judgments (or making a value judgment about where they might be obtained other than from decision makers). In this role the analyst is somewhat distanced from those who make decisions, which may, on the one hand, have the useful consequence of exposing some choices that a decision maker may prefer to leave unexposed but, on the other, may result in the fruits of the analysis gathering dust on someone's shelves. The former approach is sometimes characterized as being consistent with *extra-welfarism*, perhaps because the client may reject *welfarism*, though there is no particular reason why the analyst adopting the second approach should not also take an extra-welfarist view.

Making value judgments is inherent in the practice of cost–benefit analysis. In addition to choosing the perspective, other critical choices, all of which involve making value judgments on behalf of society, usually include choice of outcome measure (and, if complex, like 'health gain', its constituents, their reasonable measures, their scaling and their combining); choice of cost measure; and matters concerning the distribution and weighting (geographical, between patient or disease groups, ages and sexes, and so on) of consequences, whether costs or benefits. To treat these weights as 'equal' is, of course, not to escape making a value judgment: it is to value them equally.

Explicitness in cost–benefit analysis also extends to the treatment of *uncertainty*. It is convenient to identify uncertainty in relation to the parameters of parts of the analysis and uncertainty in relation to the data themselves.

The usual *decision rule* in cost–benefit analysis is for the benefit–cost ratio (B/C) to exceed unity or for $(B - C) > 0$. See also *Benefit–cost Ratio*, *Cost–effectiveness Analysis*, *Cost–utility Analysis*, *Equity*, *Shadow Price*.

Cost–consequence Analysis

A method of assembling the components of the *marginal costs* of a project or investment *option*, perhaps in non-comparable units, without any attempt to combine them into a single monetary cost figure.

Cost Containment

Controlling medical care expenditures within a predetermined limit or range by limiting budgets (cash limits), imposing or increasing *cost sharing*, using *clinical budgets*, and so on.

Cost Curve

A graph of *cost* (*average*, *marginal* or *total*) against *output* rate.

Cost–effectiveness Acceptability Curve

A cost–effectiveness acceptability curve (CEAC) is a graphical way of showing more information about uncertainty in a *cost–effectiveness analysis* than can be done by using only *confidence intervals*. For each of a variety of possible incremental cost–effectiveness *ceiling ratios* or thresholds, the curve shows the proportion of estimates of the *incremental cost–effectiveness ratios* (ICERs) that are lower. It thus provides a visual image to aid judgments as to whether a technology actually is cost-effective.

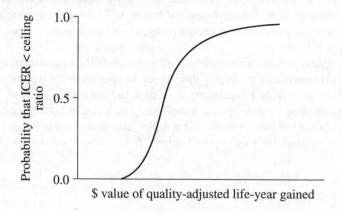

Cost–effectiveness Analysis

A method of comparing the *opportunity costs* of various alternative courses of action having the same *benefit* or in terms of a common unit of output, outcome or other measure of accomplishment. This procedure is used when benefits are difficult to value monetarily, when those that are measurable are not commensurable, or when the objectives are set in terms of health itself. It is similar to *cost–benefit analysis* except that benefit, instead of being expressed in monetary terms or in terms of several non-commensurable benefits, is expressed in terms of a homogeneous index of results achieved. These may be natural units such as the number of lives saved or number of days free from disease, they may be units that are specific to the procedures being compared (like the speed of healing of a wound), or they may be generic (like *quality-adjusted life-years*) thus enabling comparisons of cost-effectiveness to be made across many different technologies and patient groups. Some gurus advocate the use of the term *cost–utility analysis* for this latter type of analysis, though there seems to be little practical advantage in so doing. Many of the issues that arise in cost–benefit analysis, such as those of *perspective*, scope of consequences, *discount rate*, *sensitivity analysis* and *modelling*, also arise in cost–effectiveness analysis.

Cost–effectiveness Plane

A diagrammatic way of comparing technologies. A four-quadrant figure of cost difference plotted against effect difference yields quadrant I, intervention more effective and more costly than comparator; quadrant II, intervention more effective and less costly than comparator; quadrant III, intervention less

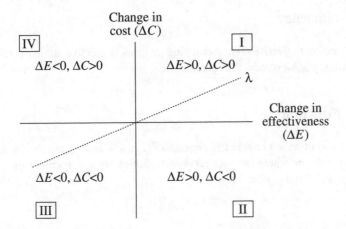

effective and less costly than comparator; and quadrant IV, intervention less effective and more costly than comparator. In quadrant II, the intervention dominates the comparator and, in quadrant IV, the comparator dominates the intervention. Quadrants I and III are the more interesting cases. Here the cost-effectiveness of the alternatives depends upon the size of the *incremental cost–effectiveness ratio* ($\Delta C/\Delta E$) and on whether the ΔE is positive or negative. Let there be a maximum amount a decision maker will pay for an increment of outcome (ΔE) indicated by the dotted line λ. Any point to the left of λ indicates that comparator treatment is more cost-effective, while points to the right of λ indicate that intervention is more cost-effective. All points below λ are in the 'region of acceptability' (note that $\Delta C/\Delta E$ is lower – actually negative – than λ in quadrant IV, but that this quadrant cannot be in the region of acceptability since ΔE is actually negative here). See also *Confidence Box, Confidence Ellipse*.

Cost–effectiveness Ratio

The ratio of *cost* to the output or outcome in a *cost–effectiveness analysis* or *cost–utility analysis*. See also *Incremental Cost–effectiveness Ratio*.

Cost–effectiveness Threshold

The maximum acceptable *incremental cost–effectiveness ratio* acceptable to a decision maker. Beyond this threshold, health care technologies will not be adopted on *efficiency* grounds alone. See *Cost–effectiveness Plane*.

Cost-efficiency

Same as *cost-effectiveness*. Achieving a given objective at least *cost*, or maximizing achievement at a given cost.

Cost Function

A function in which *cost* is the *dependent variable* and output the *independent variable*, or where the independent variables are the prices of the inputs of a *production function*.

Cost-minimization Analysis

A primitive form of *cost–effectiveness analysis*, in which cost is the dominant determining factor in a choice between alternatives (perhaps because the outcome or the value of the outcome is the same for each). The valid application of the method plainly depends on establishing the (empirical) truth of the proposition that cost is indeed the dominant determinant.

Cost of Capital

Loosely, the real borrowing rate of interest, that is, the *nominal* rate of interest less the rate of inflation.

Cost of Illness

A narrow interpretation of the cost imposed by illness focuses merely on the financial consequences of poor health (often misleadingly – and, to economists, offensively – described as 'economic') such as lost earnings from work, expenditure on health services, drugs and so on. A wider interpretation seeks to identify the true social *opportunity costs* of being ill with perhaps *shadow prices* being attached to lost working time, carers' time spent nursing, health services received and so on.

Cost-per-QALY Analysis

Analysis, otherwise usefully called *cost–utility analysis* (CUA) or *cost–effectiveness analysis* (CEA) where the decision criterion is cost per *quality-adjusted life-year* (QALY). The term appears to have been invented by taxonomizers who are unsure whether CUA is a subdivision of CEA or of *cost–benefit analysis* and who apparently believe that, if they rename it, the problem is solved. Actually the problem becomes worse, for we now have to ask whether cost-per-QALY analysis is a subset of CEA, CUA or CBA. It is not compulsory, fortunately, to answer this question.

Cost Sharing

Usually used to refer to a method of *financing health care* that involves some portion of the expenditure falling directly on the user. The cost is then shared between user and employer, government, taxpayer, insurance agency and so on. This is sometimes referred to as 'demand-side cost sharing'. It is viewed both as a means of deterring relatively 'trivial' consumption (and of course assumes a non-zero price-*elasticity* of demand) and as a means of enlarging the financial bases from which health services are financed. What is meant by 'trivial' is anyone's guess. The term 'supply-side cost sharing' is occasionally used to describe a situation where the provider receives from a third party payer less than the full costs of providing a given service.

Cost Shifting

A loose term used to describe any activity through which costs are shifted from one decision maker to another. As examples, the activity of both health care insurers in increasing *copayments* for insured workers and hospital physicians in prescribing drugs whose cost will fall on community-based practice budgets is a way of shifting costs, in the one case from employers to workers and in the other from *secondary* to *primary care* institutions.

Cost Subgroup

Individuals in an experimental group (as in a *cost–effectiveness analysis*) who are likely to cause similar costs to be incurred or avoided.

Cost-to-charge Ratio

A term used in the USA, meaning the ratio of the cost to a hospital of an item of service relative to the charge made for it. Abbreviated to CCR.

Cost–utility Analysis

A close relative of *cost–benefit* and *cost–effectiveness analysis*, but where benefit is measured in neither monetary terms nor natural units like 'deaths prevented'. It takes its name from the use of *utility*-type measures of outcome (like *quality-adjusted life-year*), though whether these really are utilities is a matter of controversy. The attempt to stress a major difference between CEA and CUA seems a somewhat overdone and fruitless bit of taxonomizing as in practice it is often hard to distinguish between the two, CEAs often having some elements of the distinguishing feature of CUA: its more subtle treatment of outcome, which is much closer to the way that many real-world decision makers consider outcome (*viz.* in terms of 'health').

Cost–value Analysis

A method for conducting *cost–effectiveness analysis* that embodies societal concerns about fairness. It is an example of the confusing proliferation of names for what is probably best simply called 'cost–effectiveness analysis'.

Count Data

This term refers to the number of occurrences of an event that have been counted.

Coupon

Coupon is the annual rate of interest on a bond's face value that the issuer promises to pay the bondholder. The term originates from the fact that coupons were once actually attached to bonds and had to be cut off or 'clipped' for the holder to receive the due interest.

Covariance

A measure of the extent to which the values taken by two *variables* are associated. It is measured as the expected value of the product of the deviations of the variables from their *arithmetic mean*. The unbiased estimator of the covariance of a population sample is formally defined as:

$$s_{xy} = \frac{\sum_i (x_i - \bar{x})(y_i - \bar{y})}{n-1},$$

where the (x_i, y_i) are independent, $i = 1 \ldots n$, and the bars over the variables x and y denote sample means. See *Analysis of Covariance*.

Covariate

A *variable* that covaries with a *dependent variable* and which one usually wants to control in order to explore the relationship between independent variables and the dependent variable(s). See *Analysis of Covariance*.

Cox Proportional Hazards Model

A semiparametric model for duration analysis. A form of *multiple regression* used in exploring the simultaneous effects of multiple variables on survival. Not a technique for non-econometricians. The model is named after Sir David Cox (b.1924). See David F. Cox (1972), 'Cox regression models and life tables', *Journal of the Royal Statistical Society*, **B** (34), 187–220. See *Hazard Function*.

Cream Skimming

A practice in private health *insurance* markets by which the insurer obtains a higher proportion of good risks (people with a low probability of needing care or who are likely to need only low-cost care, or both) in their portfolio of clients than the insurance premium is calculated on.

Creaming

Same as *cream skimming*.

Criterion Function

Same as *loss function*.

Criterion Validity

The ability of an instrument (like a measure of health-related quality of life) to replicate a gold standard. Similar to *construct validity*.

Cronbach's Alpha

A measure of how well a set of variables measures a single unidimensional underlying construct (such as 'health'). See Lee J. Cronbach (1951), 'Coefficient alpha and the internal structure of tests', *Psychometrika*, **16**, 297–333.

Cross-elasticity of Demand

The responsiveness of the consumption of a good or service to a change in another good's price. See *Elasticity*.

Crossover Design

A type of *clinical trial* in which each subject receives more than one of the interventions under investigation and in random order. Contrast this with a *parallel groups* design, where some subjects receive one treatment and different subjects receive another. The crossover design represents a special situation where there is no separate comparison group, each subject in effect serving as their own *control*.

Cross-product Ratio

Same as *odds ratio*.

Cross-sectional Data

Data in which each respondent is observed and each observation recorded only once, giving a snapshot picture of the population at a point in time.

Cross-sectional Study

A study in which the observations of dependent and independent variables, or exposure and outcome, are taken at a single point in time (cf. *longitudinal* study). Such studies are incapable of examining the temporal causes/effects of disease agents or interventions.

Crowding Out

In general, a reduction in private expenditure (especially *investment*) that occurs when a government's expansionary fiscal policy (which may be to the advantage of the health care sector) causes *interest rates* to rise. In health economics, the term has been used to describe the effect that public health insurance programmes may have on the demand for private health care insurance.

Crude Birth Rate

The number of live births in a year divided by the population.

Crude Death Rate

The number of deaths in a year divided by the population. Cf. *Standardized Mortality Ratio*.

CUA

Acronym for *cost–utility analysis*.

Culyer–Wagstaff Diagram

A four-quadrant figure showing the construction of a *health frontier* in a two-person world from a *budget constraint*, two *production functions* and an assumed initial distribution of health. Used to analyse alternative constructs of *equity* and how they relate to *efficiency*. See Anthony J. Culyer and Adam Wagstaff (1993), 'Equity and equality in health and health care', *Journal of Health Economics*, **12**, 431–57.

Cumulative Frequency

The number of individuals with values below and including some designated value.

Cumulative Incidence Rate

The proportion of an initially disease-free population which develops the disease in an interval of time. Also called simply 'cumulative incidence'.

Current Account

A part of the *balance of payments*.

CV

Acronym for *coefficient of variation*.

D

DALE

Acronym for *disability-adjusted life expectancy*.

DALY

Acronym for *disability-adjusted life-year.*

Danish Centre for Evaluation and Health Technology Assessment

The Danish national centre for *health technology assessment.* Its website is at www.sst.dk/Planlaegning_og_behandling/Medicinsk_teknologivurdering. aspx?lang=en.

DASH

Acronym for *disabilities of the arm, shoulder and hand*, a 30-item self-reporting system for assessing upper extremity function.

Data Envelope Analysis

A *linear programming* technique that uses empirical evidence of the most efficient producers of *outputs* to locate an envelope that predicts the maximum outputs achievable with a variety of different *inputs* or *factors of production*. It is particularly vulnerable to *omitted variable bias*.

Data Mining

This has two (altogether different) meanings. The first usage is overusing data (especially without any theoretical expectation as to what the data might reveal) to draw invalid inferences. The second, more recent, usage is an efficient process of discovering non-obvious regularities in large data bases, often using *algorithms* based on decisions trees or networks.

DBC

A form of *diagnostic related group* used in the Netherlands. See *Diagnosis Treatment Combination*.

DCEHTA

Acronym for *Danish Centre for Evaluation and Health Technology Assessment*.

DCF

Acronym for *discounted cash-flow*.

DDD

Acronym for *defined daily dose*.

DDMAC

Acronym for *Division of Drug Marketing, Advertising and Communications*.

DEA

Acronym for *data envelope analysis*.

Deadweight Loss

A measure of the loss of *welfare* resulting from misallocations of resources (that is, inefficient allocations; ones that are not *Pareto-optimal*). For some examples see *Excess Burden, Insurance*.

DEALE

Acronym for *declining exponential approximation to life expectancy.*

Decile

When a continuous *variable* is split for convenience into ten equal-sized chunks of data, the cut-off points between them are called deciles. See *Quantile.*

Decision Analysis

This typically refers to a formal, essentially *utilitarian*, method for quantifying decision problems under conditions of uncertainty, in which the probability of each event in a chain of events, along with the consequences of such events, is explicitly stated. Some approaches, like *bounded rationality*, do not, however, use quantified probabilities. See *Decision Rule*, *Decision Tree*, *Expected Utility Theory*, *Markov Chain*, *Quality-adjusted Life-year.*

Decision Rule

A criterion (or set of criteria) to aid a decision maker in selecting between alternative options. In the context of a *cost–benefit analysis* it may be 'rank all projects in terms of their *benefit–cost ratios* and work down the list until the budget is exhausted'. In *cost-effectiveness* contexts, the rule might be 'adopt all projects for which the *incremental cost–effectiveness ratio* exceeds a given threshold'.

Decision Tree

A diagrammatic representation of a *decision analysis* in which chains of choices are identified, each conditional on a prior choice and with outcomes and probabilities built in. In the figure, ■ indicates a decision node, ● indicates a chance node and ◄ indicates an end node. In this decision tree, the issue is whether to give therapy. If it is given (the *Rx* group), there is a probability p of life and of $1-p$ of death. In the untreated (control) group there is a probability r of life and $1-r$ of death. Of the surviving patients in either arm, they may become inpatients or treatment may no longer be needed

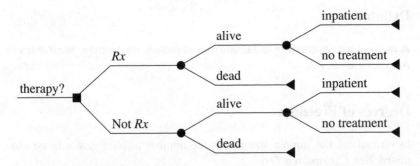

beyond a certain point. If the costs of the therapy, and the probabilities of life or death, and the probabilities that living patients will become hospitalized or no longer need treatment, together with the costs of these options (for both arms), are known then the (probable) *cost-effectiveness* of the two courses of action may be computed.

Declining Exponential Approximation to Life Expectancy

An algorithm for calculating life expectancy when death rates are constant. Commonly abbreviated to DEALE. See *Gompertz Function*.

Decreasing Returns to Scale

Same as *diminishing returns to scale*.

Deductible

An arrangement under which the insured person pays a fixed sum if the event insured against occurs and the insurer pays all other expenses. It is known as 'excess' in the UK. See *Coinsurance*.

Defined Daily Dose

The estimated average maintenance dose of a drug when used to treat its main clinical indication.

Deflator

A method for eliminating inflation from monetary time series. See *Constant Prices*, *Price Index*.

Degrees of Freedom

In estimation, the sample size minus the number of *parameters* to be estimated. See *Chi-squared Test*.

Delphi Method

A systematic method for obtaining a collective opinion, usually of a group of experts, in the absence of more reliable assessments (of, say, *cost-effectiveness* or some other quantitative measure or indicator). The basic method involves a facilitator soliciting opinions which are then fed back anonymously to the group, whose members may then revise their opinions and feed them back again. After a few rounds, the facilitator averages the opinions.

Demand Curve

A bivariate geometrical representation of a *demand function* where the *dependent variable* is rate of consumption or use and the *independent variable* is price. In general, a demand curve shows the maximum rate of demand for a good or service per unit of time at a variety of prices, and also the maximum price that will be paid for a small amount more, *ceteris paribus*. Conventionally the price variable is measured on the *y* axis and quantity on the *x* axis, even when quantity is the dependent variable. When price is the dependent variable, the demand curve is commonly referred to as a *marginal valuation curve*. This shows the maximum amount someone is willing to pay for a small increment in the rate of consumption. Under particular conditions (for example, when the *income elasticity* of demand is zero) the two curves coincide.

Care needs to be taken in distinguishing between using the word 'demand' in the sense of a particular rate at a particular price and using it in the sense of the whole range of rates at a range of prices (a point on the demand curve versus the entire curve itself). It evidently makes (logical) sense to say 'price rose and so demand fell' and also 'demand fell, so price fell', and a little thought reveals that the apparent paradox is resolved once it is seen that 'demand' is being used in two different senses.

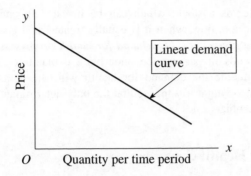

Let the amount of something demanded be a function of its relative price and buyers' incomes. The demand curve is a two-dimensional representation of this function in which responses to changes in price are seen as movements along the demand curve and responses to changes in income are seen as shifts of the entire demand curve.

In most situations in the health field 'demand' is not the demand by traders or dealers, who demand only in order to be able to supply; it is the demand by users either because it is a *final good* (as in the case of the *demand for health*) or an *intermediate good* or service (as is the case with the *demand for health services*).

Some of the demand-side characteristics that ought always to be borne in mind when using demand curves in the context of health care, especially when making *normative* statements about *welfare*, are the following: uncertainty about the probable *incidence* of disease, its consequences, the *effectiveness* and likely *cost* of treatments; the (strong?) possibility that the 'rationality' assumptions underlying utility theory do not apply when someone is worried, sick, incapacitated or in pain; the fact that there may well be *external* demands for the care of the person(s) whose demand is under consideration in addition to their own demand; and the fact that the price to which a demander is imagined to be responding may not be at all an accurate reflection of the *marginal cost* of providing the care in question. See *Law of Demand*.

Demand for Health

The maximum amount of *health* chosen as a function of various *independent variables*, such as the *rate of return* to investment in health, expected wages from work, the price of health care (not to mention many other variable not often considered by economists, such as early parenting, developmental cultural influences, social norms and family circumstances). 'Health' itself can be treated either as a stock, which can be invested in and is subject to depreciation, or as a flow, when it is usually treated as a *construct* such as *quality-adjusted life-years*. The *demand for health services* is a *derived demand* that depends in part on the underlying demand for health. It is a vulgarism to muddle the demand for health with the demand for health services. It is also vulgar to suppose that the only determinants of health are economic or pecuniary ones.

Demand for Health Care

Same as *demand for health services*.

Demand for Health Services

The maximum rate of use of health service facilities as a function of various *independent variables* like health status, price, distance from facility, time spent obtaining the service, income, wealth, educational attainment and so on. The demand for health services is usually treated as a *derived demand* (that is, derived from the demand for health). The *income elasticity* has commonly been found to be around unity, so an increase in income normally leads to a roughly similar increase in the demand for service. The price elasticity is usually low. See *Demand Curve, Demand for Health, Elasticity.*

Demand Function

The demand function is a mathematical representation of the maximum rate of demand as the *dependent variable* and its various determinants. A simple example would make the amount of something demanded a function of its relative price and buyers' incomes. The *demand curve* is a two-dimensional representation of this function in which responses to changes in price are seen as movements along the demand curve and responses to changes in income are seen as shifts of the entire demand curve. See *Law of Demand.*

Demand-side Cost Sharing

See *Cost Sharing.*

Demography

The study of the characteristics of human populations, such as their size, growth, density, distribution and vital statistics.

Deontological

Deotological theories are ethical theories broadly based on the idea that what matters (or ought to matter) in moral discourse is categorical: it's either right or wrong. A typical form is any moral theory based on the idea of 'doing one's duty'. This approach is especially associated with Immanuel Kant. 'Lying is always wrong, even if it has good consequences' has characteristic deontological tones. It is very remote from most economic theorizing about what is 'good' for societies, which is generally calculating and *consequentialist*. (Note that the root of the word is the Greek for 'it is binding on' not 'deus', the Latin word for 'god'.) Cf. *Utilitarianism*.

Dependency Ratio

A measure of the portion of a population which is composed of people who are too young or too old to work. The dependency ratio is equal to the proportion of individuals aged below 15 or above 64, divided by the proportion of individuals aged 15 to 64, expressed as a percentage. Thus:

$$\text{Dependency ratio} = \frac{(\% \text{ under } 15) + (\% \text{ over } 65)}{\% \text{ between } 15 \text{ and } 64} \times 100$$

Dependent Variable

A variable (often denoted by y) that is postulated to be determined by an *independent variable* (usually x). For example, the rate of consumption of a good (dependent variable) may be regarded as behaviourally determined by (amongst other things) its price (independent variable), or the *marginal value* placed on a good (dependent variable) may be regarded as being determined by (amongst other things) its rate of consumption (independent variable). See *Demand Curve*.

Depreciation

The change in the value of a *capital* good over time, usually expressed annually. The value will typically fall as a result of wear and tear, supersession by other capital items, or through changes in fashion. When the value rises, the term is *appreciation*. The values in question are in *constant prices*: allowance for inflation is a separate matter.

Derived Demand

The maximum the buyer is willing to pay for a good or service as a result of a demand for something else, usually more fundamental. For example, the *demand for health care* is said to be derived from the *demand for health*.

Dermatology

The medical specialty concerned with diseases and abnormalities of the skin.

Descriptive Statistics

The type of statistics in which the emphasis is on describing the principal, or most interesting, features of a set of data. For example, *variables* may be characterized as *qualitative* or *quantitative*, or data may be distributed in a particular way around a *mode*, or two sets of data may be related, one rising (or falling) as the other falls (or rises).

Descriptive Study

A study that intends to record (or at any rate only actually records) a situation or a distribution of data without any analysis of cause and effect or hypothesis testing.

Design Bias

Bias in *clinical trials* arising from bad design, such as lack of controls or poorly chosen controls.

Desmoteric Medicine

Medical practice in a prison. From the Greek for 'prison'.

Detailing

The process by which pharmaceutical companies send agents to doctors in order to promote their products via information dissemination and the emphasis of positive product *attributes*. The idea is to encourage *prescriptions* rather than directly to encourage purchase. Cf. *Academic Detailing*.

Detection Bias

A form of *bias* in *clinical trials* arising from systematic differences in the ways in which outcomes are defined and/or measured. For example, women taking an oral contraceptive will have more frequent cervical smears than women who are not on the pill and so are more likely to have cervical cancer diagnosed (if they actually have it). Thus, in a *case-control* study that compared women with cervical cancer and a control group, at least part of any higher pill consumption rates amongst the former group may be due to this effect. Also called 'ascertainment bias'.

Determinant

A factor, characteristic, causal agent that affects the character, size or some other feature of interest in another. It has nothing to do with 'determinism' as a philosophical point of view.

Deterministic Model

A model in which the *parameters* and *variables* are not subject to random fluctuations. Cf. *Stochastic Model*.

Deutsches Institut für Medizinische Dokumentation und Information

The German federal agency for conducting *cost–utility analyses* and *health technology assessments*. Its website is at: www.dimdi.de/dynamic/de/index.html.

Diagnosis

The attaching of a disease label to a patient's (or family's or larger group's) condition after examining symptoms and performing various tests.

Diagnosis Related Group

Same as *Diagnostic Related Group*.

Diagnosis Treatment Combination

The Dutch version of *Diagnostic Related Group* covering *episodes of care*.

Diagnostic Related Group

DRGs are groupings of diagnoses according to their clinical similarity and the cost of treatment. Under US *Medicare*, patients are classified according to their DRG, of which there are about 500, and the provider is reimbursed by a fixed price for the 'standard' treatment under that DRG.

Dichotomous Variable

Same as *binary variable*.

Difference Principle

This states that social and economic inequalities are justifiable only if they are to the advantage of the least advantaged person. See *Fairness*.

DIMDI

Acronym for *Deutsches Institut für Medizinische Dokumentation und Information*.

Dimension of Health

A characteristic, like *attribute*, but particular to measuring *health*.

Diminishing Marginal Utility

A property of a *utility function*, to the effect that increments of a good or service are assumed to add positive but diminishing additions to total *utility*. It is not to be conceived of as a successive phenomenon, in which the additions take place over time, but as an instantaneous characteristic of human preferences. Now largely superseded, save in *expected utility* theory, by the more general 'ordinalist' idea of a diminishing *marginal rate of substitution* in consumption or a negatively sloped *indifference curve*. See *Marginal Utility, Ordinal Utility, Utility*.

Diminishing Returns to Scale

A feature of production functions. A production function exhibits diminishing returns to scale if increasing all inputs in the same proportion increases outputs by a smaller proportion. Cf. V*ariable Proportions*. See *Production Function*.

Direct Cost

The *internal cost* of an activity or decision in terms of the resources used to the agency creating the cost. It includes the cost of labour, other goods and services, *capital* (usually considered as a rental value) and *consumables*. It excludes *external costs*, *productivity costs*, uncompensated forgone earnings and elements of cost that may be undervalued by market prices. See *External Effects, Opportunity Cost*.

Direct Health Care Corporation

A form of US corporation providing direct health care services to its members and subscribers through contracts with licensed health service personnel and health service institutions but one that does not pay cash indemnity benefits.

Direct Tax

A tax on income (a *flow*) or wealth (a *stock*).

Disabilities of the Arm, Shoulder and Hand

DASH is a self-administered outcome instrument developed as a measure of self-rated upper-extremity disability and symptoms for use mainly in studies of occupational health and safety. The DASH consists of a 30-item disability/ symptom scale, scored 0 (no disability) to 100. A short form is *QuickDASH*. Its website is http://www.dash.iwh.on.ca/.

Disability

The International Classification of Functioning, Disability and Health (ICF) developed by the *World Health Organization*, currently (2004) defines disability in the following way: 'ICF is a classification of health and health related domains that describe body functions and structures, activities and participation. The domains are classified from body, individual and societal perspectives. Since an individual's functioning and disability occurs in a context, [it] also includes a list of environmental factors. ICF is useful to understand and measure health outcomes. It can be used in clinical settings, health services or surveys at the individual or population level.' The definition can be found on the WHO site at www3.who.int/icf/icftemplate. cfm?myurl=introduction.html%20&mytitle=Introduction. Cf. *Handicap*, *Impairment*.

Disability-adjusted Life Expectancy

DALE is a measure of healthy *life expectancy* developed by the *World Health Organization*. Years of expected ill-health are weighted according to severity and subtracted from the expected overall life expectancy to give the equivalent years of healthy life. The measure was developed to facilitate international comparisons of *health* and health outcomes.

Disability-adjusted Life-year

A measure of the burden of disability-causing disease and injury. Age-specific expected life-years are adjusted for expected loss of healthy life during those years, yielding states of health measures or, when two streams of DALYs are compared, potential health gain or loss in different scenarios or as a consequence of different decisions. Cf. *Assessment Quality of Life, EQ-5D, EuroQol, Health Gain, Health Status, Health Utilities Index, Healthy Year Equivalents, Quality-adjusted Life-year, SF-6D, SF-8, SF-12, SF-36.*

Disability Days

Days of restricted activity due to disease or injury.

Discount Factor

The discount factor for year t is given by $1/(1 + r)^t$ where r is the annual discount rate. Thus, if $r = 0.1$, the discount factor for $t = 1$ is 0.909 and for $t = 5$ it is 0.620. See *Discounting* for a general description.

Discount Rate

The *rate of interest* used to calculate a *present value* or to discount future values. See *Discounting*.

Discounted Cash Flow

A *flow* of money over a time period in which each period's cash is adjusted by an appropriate *discount factor* to represent its (reduced) future value (fundamentally due to *time preference*). The *present value* of the flow is the sum of these discounted values over the period in question. See *Discounting*.

Discounting

A procedure for reducing costs or benefits occurring at different dates to a common measure by use of an appropriate discount rate. Thus, with an annual discount rate r (expressed as a decimal fraction) the *present value* (*PV*) of a cost (*C*) in one year's time is $PV = C/(1 + r)$. In two years' time, it is $PV = C/(1 = r)^2$. The *PV* of a stream of future costs is the sum of every year's *PV*. For a stream, C, that is constant, the discrete time formula is *PV* $= C\left[\dfrac{(1+i)^n - 1}{i(1+i)^n}\right]$. Of course, the same procedure applies to benefits as to costs. There is controversy as to whether benefits (for example, future *quality-adjusted life-years* gained) ought to be discounted.

Discrete Choice Analysis

A procedure in *conjoint analysis* in which subjects select discrete combinations of *attributes* of services, often written down on cards, and rank them.

Discrete Time Model

A model in which the decision points, outcomes or other events are conceived as occurring at specific points in time, for example, the start or end of a calendar year, rather than continuously. The points are often equidistant from one another.

Discrete Variable

A variable that is not *continuous* and can take on values only at isolated points, such as the non-negative integers, 0, 1, 2, ... Examples include life, death, discharge from hospital, onset of disease, purchase of health insurance.

Discriminant Function Analysis

An alternative to *logistic regression analysis* that is used with *discrete dependent variables* that enables one to allocate entities from two or more populations to the correct one with minimal error.

Discriminant Validity

A measure has discriminant validity when it distinguishes between groups in ways prescribed by the analyst.

Disease Costing

A procedure for assigning the expenditures of a health system or part thereof to the particular disease for which care is provided.

Disease Management

A systematic approach to a health condition or health care intervention that involves organizing preventive, interventional and care approaches across the entire spectrum of the relevant professional groups and which measures outcomes in terms of effects on the population rather than on an individual.

Diseconomies of Scale

Opposite of *economies of scale*.

Disposable Income

The income left to an individual after payment of taxes and receipt of *transfer payments*.

Disposable Personal Income

The share of *national income* accruing to households net of taxes and other contractual deductions but including *transfer payments*.

Distribuendum

The good or service that is to be distributed (or redistributed), for example, income, wealth, health or health care.

Distribution

A distribution is usually described mathematically or graphically (or both). The distribution shows how probability is allocated over the range of possible values. If the variable is *discrete*, probability is assigned to isolated values. If the variable is continuous, probability is assigned to intervals, with the probability of a single variable being treated as zero. The best-known example of a distribution is the bell-shaped curve (the *normal distribution*) shown in the figure for the variable *y*, where µ is the mean (and also the median). See *Frequency Distribution, Mean, Median*.

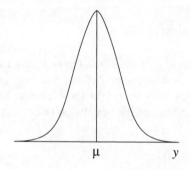

Distribution Function

A mathematical function that gives the *probability* with which a random variable falls at or below particular values. Examples include those for the *binomial, normal, log-normal, chi-squared, t* and *F*.

Distributional Value Judgments

Distributional *value judgments* are value judgments about the desirability or otherwise of various distributions of entities to which moral significance is attached, like health or health care, or the accessibility of health care. They may relate to, or derive from, more fundamental value judgments, for example about the relevance of a person's desert or need. See *Equity*.

Distributive Justice

The fairness with which some entity is distributed between people or groups of people. See *Equity*.

Divisibility

The idea that *goods* (including *inputs*) do not come in chunks but are usable in infinitely small increments (or decrements). In economics this characteristic (which is often useful in mathematical models) is often achieved, even when the good in question is manifestly lumpy in physical expression, by investigating rates of use or consumption (since *time* is infinitely divisible). In *cost–effectiveness analysis* the use of combinations of options (such as programmes of health care) in identifying those that have *dominance* usually requires programmes to be divisible.

Division of Drug Marketing, Advertising and Communications

The branch of the US Food and Drug Administration that deals with the economic *appraisal* of pharmaceuticals and medical devices. It licenses drugs, offers guidance to industry, professionals and consumers, and acts as a regulator.

DMF

Acronym for 'decayed missing filled' (teeth).

Domain of Health

Same as *attribute*.

Dominance

Dominance exists when one option, technology or intervention is more effective and has costs no higher than another or when it is at least as effective and has costs lower. See *Cost–effectiveness Plane, Extended Dominance*.

Donut Hole

Same as *doughnut hole*.

Dose–Response Curve

This is a figure in which the X axis plots concentration of a drug (or some other exposure variable, harmful or beneficial) and the Y axis plots responses such as secretion of a hormone, heart beat or health outcome. It is similar to the diagrammatic representation of a *production function* where there is a single variable input and a single output. The standard dose–response curve has four parameters: the baseline response, the maximum response, the slope and the exposure concentration that provokes a response halfway between baseline and maximum.

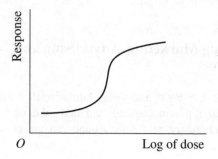

Double Blind Trial

A trial in which neither the patient nor the observing/measuring clinician is aware of whether a patient is in the *control* or the *experimental* arm. See *Blinding*.

Doughnut Hole

This term, coined in the USA (where it is 'donut hole'), refers to an insurance plan in which there is a gap within the range of expenditures over which no cover is provided. The *Medicare* prescription drug benefit scheduled to go into effect in 2006 provides a clear example. Enrollees will pay the first $250 (US) as a *deductible*, 25 per cent of the next $2000 in annual covered *prescription drug* expenditures, 100 per cent of the next $2850 in drug expenses and only 5 per cent after their expenditure exceeds $5100 in a year. The 'hole' is the $2251–$5100 range. Although doughnut hole benefits do not seem to have any economic logic, there is political appeal: if the deductible is kept low enough, most people will enjoy at least some covered benefits, and costs are lower than if there were no doughnut hole.

DRG

Acronym for *Diagnostic (Diagnosis) Related Group*.

DRG Creep

Changes in diagnostic coding by hospitals and other providers in order to take advantage of better remunerated *Diagnostic Related Groups*.

Drug Lag

A term used to describe the slow approval of drugs by the US *Food and Drug Administration* before drugs are permitted to reach the market.

Dummy Variable

An alternative name for a *binary variable*, which takes the value 1 or 0.

Dumping

A refusal by a health care provider to treat patients whose costs are expected to exceed the compensation payable to the provider. It arises particularly in systems that are dependent on private health insurance arrangements. In the USA, federal patient-dumping law entitles people in emergency situations to be screened, receive emergency care and to be appropriately transferred to another provider. A hospital must provide 'stabilizing care' for a patient with an emergency medical condition. The hospital must screen for the emergency and provide the care without inquiring about *ability to pay*. Although emergency cover is thus assured (in the USA), there is less assurance about non-emergency care for people who lose their jobs or change jobs (and who lose cover that was previously provided through a workplace arrangement).

Note that this is quite different from the usual notion of 'dumping' in international trade: selling goods abroad below their normal market value or below the price charged for them in the domestic market of the exporting country. This form of dumping can be a predatory trade practice whereby the international market, or a certain national market, is flooded with dumped goods in order to force competitors out of the market and establish a monopoly position.

Duopoly

A market in which there are but two sellers. See *Competition.*

Duration Analysis

The analysis of the time spent by an individual in a particular state (say, of health). Cf. *Survival Analysis* in medical statistics.

E

Earmarking

Associating particular forms of tax with particular forms of expenditure. It is usually seen as a bad thing by politicians, since it reduces their discretion, and a good thing by libertarians, for the same reason.

EBM

Acronym for *evidence-based medicine.*

Ecological Fallacy

The ecological fallacy consists in thinking that relationships observed for groups necessarily hold for individuals. Thus, while the (aggregate) observation is made that US states with a high proportion of foreign-born residents are also states with high literacy in American English, it does not follow that foreign-born people are more literate than the rest. For one thing, there may be a large *variance* to which the use of an average gives no clue; for another, there may be many other determinants (*confounders*); for yet another, to observe a *correlation* is not to observe cause and effect or the direction of cause and effect. For that one needs a hypothesis. In fact studies at the individual level have shown that the 'ecological correlation' of foreign-born and literacy rates arises because foreign-born people tend to settle in states that already have high literacy. At the individual level, the correlation between being foreign-born and ability in American English is (as one may expect) in fact negative. See *Aggregation Problem.*

Econometrics

The application of statistical and mathematical methods in the field of economics to test economic theories, quantify relationships and other entities of interest, and the methodological development of the techniques for doing these things.

Economic Appraisal

A general term for the economic evaluation of options. This can be done from a variety of *perspectives*. See *Cost–benefit Analysis*, *Cost–effectiveness Analysis*, *Cost–utility Analysis* and *Financial Appraisal*.

Economic Evaluation

Same as *economic appraisal*.

Economic Good

A good or service of which more is wanted. It corresponds to the *non-satiation* axiom of economic choice theory. It is not necessarily a good or service that commands a market price. Health care commonly meets the definition.

Economics

Economics is the science which studies human behaviour as a relationship between given ends and scarce means which have alternative uses. This is the classic definition given by Lord Robbins in *An Essay on the Nature and Significance of Economic Science* (London: Macmillan, 1932).

Economics of Health

Same as *health economics*.

Economics of Hospitals

See *Hospital Behaviour*, *Hospital Costs*, *Hospital Economics*.

Economies of Scale

This is a result of *increasing returns to scale*: the amount of *resource* used per unit of *output* falls at higher output rates. It implies a falling unit *cost* as output rates increase, so long as *input* prices do not increase so as to offset the scale effect, as they might if the organization in question is a principal user of a resource and there is a degree of *monopsony*. Diseconomies of scale are the contrary phenomenon. See *Production Function*.

Economies of Scope

Economies of scope enable a firm to produce several goods or services jointly more cheaply than producing them separately. The simultaneous production of hospital care and medical teaching is an example. Cf. *Economies of Scale*.

Ecuity Project

An international research project funded by the European Union whose full title is 'Equity in the finance and delivery of health care in Europe'. Their website is at www2.eur.nl/bmg/ecuity//.

Edgeworth Box

Named after the Oxford economist Francis Ysidro Edgeworth (1845–1926), this is a diagram showing the possible allocations of given quantities of two goods between two people and how, given conventional assumptions about their preferences, they can achieve a *Pareto-optimal* distribution of the goods between them from any initial starting distribution.

EER

Acronym for *experimental event rate*.

Effect Modification

A change in the size of an effect in a trial due to some *variable* that is not an immediate *determinant*; that is, an interaction between the independent variable of interest (such as treatment with a drug) and another, unrelated, variable (such as gender). For example, age is a modifier of the effect of measles infection on the risk of death.

Effect Size

The average change in an outcome *variable* divided by its standard deviation in *before and after studies*. In epidemiological studies with dichotomous (binary) outcomes and exposures it is often expressed as a *relative risk*.

Effectiveness

A measure similar to *efficacy* except that it refers to the effect of a particular medical technology or procedure on outcomes when used in 'actual' practice. It thus differs from efficacy in that efficacy concerns only the technical relationship between the procedure and its effects under 'ideal' conditions (in practice, typically the conditions that obtain in a research-oriented teaching hospital or primary care practice). 'Actual' practice is thus conceived to be practice as conducted by average professionals working with average resources. In economic jargon, the idea of effectiveness is encompassed within the notion of a *production function.*

Effectiveness Subgroups

Groups of individuals in a larger experimental group for whom the *effectiveness* is expected to be the same.

Efficacy

The maximum benefit or utility to the individual of the service, treatment regimen, drug, preventive or control measure advocated or applied under 'ideal' conditions. The probability of benefit to individuals in a defined population from a medical technology under 'ideal' conditions of use. More generally, the maximum potential effect of a particular medical action in altering the natural history of a particular disease for the better. 'Ideal' might refer to the excellence of the team running the experiment or trial, or to the quality of the establishment in which they are working. Cf. *Effectiveness.*

Efficiency

In a restrictive sense defined either as minimizing the *opportunity cost* of attaining a given output or as maximizing the output for a given opportunity cost. The general term used by economists is known as *Pareto-efficiency*. This is an allocation of resources such that it is not possible to reallocate them without imposing uncompensated losses of *utility* on some individual. A variant is *potential Pareto-efficiency*, where it is not possible to reallocate resources without imposing uncompensatable losses on someone (that is, the losses may not actually be compensated). It is common to see the notion of efficiency expressed at three different levels: technical efficiency, where more inputs are not used than are technically necessary to attain a given *output*; cost-efficiency or *cost-effectiveness*, where a given output is produced using the least-cost technically efficient combination of inputs (or, conversely, output is maximized for a given level of cost); Pareto-efficiency, where output is not only technically efficient and cost-efficient but is also set at an efficient rate such that any diminution or increase would impose uncompensated losses on some individual. Pareto-efficiency is also termed 'allocative efficiency' (a somewhat unhelpful term since all three ideas of efficiency are about resource allocation). The first two ideas concern the allocation of inputs to outputs; the third concerns the allocation of outputs to consumers, clients or users.

A variant idea of efficiency is known as *extra-welfarism*. With this (rather than general utility or welfare) as the framework, the maximand may be whatever the analyst or policy maker selects as appropriate. In health policy, health or health gain are common objectives. In such cases, health may be set as the maximand and efficiency implies either achieving a given overall level of health in the population at the least opportunity cost or, for a given set of resources, maximizing their impact on overall health. The idea of 'overall' health implies, of course, some means of 'adding up' the health of individual people, which will entail some distributional value judgments concerning the weight each is to have. In extra-welfarism, it is common not to extend the idea of efficiency to achieve an efficient distribution of outputs to clients, leaving this as a matter of *equity*, to be determined in other ways and by other criteria. Needless to say, equity objectives can themselves also be achieved with varying degrees of efficiency.

It should be plain that 'efficiency' is an inherently *normative* term. It tends to commend itself to economists, who do not always stop to think that whether it is good to be efficient may depend on what it is one is being efficient at doing. An efficiently run torture chamber scarcely commends itself, indeed it were better for such places to be inefficient than efficient. See also *Interpersonal Comparisons of Utility*, *Kaldor–Hicks Criterion*, *Utility*, *X-inefficiency*.

Elasticity

The responsiveness of a *dependent variable* (for example, output or demand) to changes in one of the variables determining it (for example, an input, price or income), *ceteris paribus*. It may be positive or negative. Numerically it is given by

$$\text{elasticity} = \frac{\%\ \text{change in dependent variable}}{\%\ \text{change in determining variable}}.$$

Commonly encountered elasticities are income elasticity (the responsiveness of consumption to changes in income); demand elasticity or own-price elasticity (the responsiveness of the consumption of a good or service to a change in its price), cross (price) elasticity (the responsiveness of the consumption of a good or service to a change in the price of another good or service) and elasticity of substitution (the responsiveness of the ratio of two *inputs* to a change in the *marginal rate of substitution*).

Elasticity of Substitution

A measure of the curvature of an *isoquant*. See *Elasticity*.

Ellsberg Paradox

An awkwardness for *expected utility theory*. In experiments, subjects have displayed an aversion to ambiguity contrary to the assumptions of expected utility theory. See *Ambiguity*.

Empirical

Of experience, evidence, observation or experiment as distinct from *a priori* or being based on reason only.

Employee Benefit Plan

A US plan created or maintained by an employer or employee organization that provides benefits for employees. The term may cover retirement pension plans, other plans for life insurance, health and dental insurance and disability income insurance. A plan's cost may be completely paid for by the employer or be shared with employees. A plan may also cover such benefits as sick leave, disability, profit sharing or stock purchasing.

Emporiatics

The medical specialty concerned with diseases and treatments of travellers.

End of Scale Bias

A form of bias found in some instruments for measuring *health status*. It involves a reluctance on the part of experimental subjects to use the extremes of the scale they are offered.

Endemic

Disease *prevalences* in a particular location that do not vary much over time.

Endocrinology

The medical specialty concerned with the structure and *physiology* of endocrine glands (glands that secrete directly into the bloodstream).

Endogenous

Usually descriptive of a characteristic of a *variable* in an economic model. A variable is endogenous if it is a function of parameters or variables in the model. Cf. *Exogenous*.

Endowment

In economics this usually refers to the bundle of goods and money that each individual is assumed to hold at the beginning of an analysis.

End-point

Defines the ultimate outcome in a *clinical trial*. Common end-points are severe toxicity, disease progression or death. These end-points (other than death) are rarely end-points of the sort to satisfy economists because they are not easily interpretable in welfare terms and/or because they mark an end-point in time beyond which further measurement and observation is not done (which may require modelling if there are significant post-end-point events for cost-effectiveness purposes). From such a perspective, such end-points plainly are not 'ultimate'.

ENT

Acronym for ear, nose and throat, the surgical specialty of *otorhinolaryngology*.

Entitlement Theory

This is a libertarian theory that holds that a distribution of goods, or income and wealth, is just if it arises in a non-coercive way (for example via voluntary trading between individuals). Cf. *Fairness*, *Utilitarianism*.

Epidemic

A rapid increase in the *prevalence* of a disease. Levels of an infection. Cf. *Endemic*, *Pandemic*.

Epidemiology

The study of the relationship between *risk factors* and disease in human populations, including factors that can change the relationship, and the application of such analysis to the design and management of health care systems. Clinical epidemiology is studied in clinical settings, usually by clinician epidemiologists, and usually with patients as subjects. Experimental epidemiology involves controlled experiments as in laboratory experiments or *randomized controlled trials* (RCTs). An epidemiological experiment seems to be a synonym for an RCT. Epidemiology may be descriptive (which merely records the facts as they appear to be) or analytic (usually involving the development and/or the testing of hypotheses). See *Clinical Epidemiology*.

Episode of Care

The course of treatment from a patient's first encounter with a health care provider through to the completion of the last encounter.

EQ-5D

EQ-5D is a standardized instrument for use in developing a measure of health outcome. It is particularly associated with the QALY (*quality-adjusted life-year*). It is designed for self-completion by respondents and is suited for use in postal surveys, clinics and face-to-face interviews. It is cognitively simple, taking only a few minutes to complete. Instructions to respondents are included in the questionnaire. The current 3-level, 5-dimensional format of the EQ-5D has the following dimensions: Mobility, Self-care, Usual activity, Pain/discomfort and Anxiety/depression, each scored on a three-point scale (1– no problem, 2 – some problem, 3 – extreme problem). This generates 245 separate states of health (3^5 + 'perfect health' and 'dead'). See *Assessment Quality of Life, Disability-adjusted Life-year, EuroQol, Health Gain, Health Status, Health Utilities Index, Healthy Year Equivalents, Quality-adjusted Life-year, SF-6D, SF-8, SF-12, SF-36*.

Equilibrium

In economics, equilibrium is the term used usually to describe the (not necessarily unique) solution to a set of simultaneous equations that represent the key relationships in an economy. Thus the equilibrium price and quantity in a simple three-equation model of the economy are those at which demand equals supply, there being an equation for demand, for supply and the equilibrium condition that the price at which transactions take place is the same for demanders and suppliers and that the quantity supplied be equal to that demanded. Unless something changes (that is, the *ceteris paribus* qualifier is violated), these equilibrium values will, granted some side conditions, be stable, so the system as a whole is in a kind of balance which no one has any particular reason to want to change. See *General Equilibrium, Nash Equilibrium, Partial Equilibrium*.

Equity

This has two quite distinct meanings in economics. One is from accounting. (See *Balance Sheet*.) The other is from political philosophy. While *efficiency* is one ethical imperative in the design and operation of health services and other determinants of health, equity is the second major consideration. It is not necessarily to be identified with equality, but relates in general to ethical judgments about the fairness of income and wealth *distributions*, *cost* and *benefit* distributions, accessibility of health services, exposure to health-threatening hazards and so on. Although not the same as 'equality', equity nearly always involves the equality of something (such as opportunity, health, accessibility). Horizontal equity refers to the fairness in the treatment of apparent equals (such as persons with the same income). Vertical equity refers to fairness in the treatment of apparent unequals (such as persons with different incomes). A *distribution* of something (such as health, income or health insurance costs) is said to be horizontally equitable when people are treated the same in some relevant respect. Thus, if the relevant respect (a value judgment) is 'need', then an equitable distribution is one that treats people with the same need in the same way. A distribution is said to be vertically equitable when people who are different in some relevant way are treated appropriately differently. Thus, if the relevant respect is again 'need', an equitable distribution will accord more (of some relevant entity) to those in greater need. How much more will normally entail further value judgments.

Equivalence of Numbers

A preference measurement technique in which subjects are asked how many patients in a designated state of health should have their lives extended by one year for that to be equivalent to extending the lives of 100 healthy people by one year. See *Person Trade-off Method*.

Equivalence Scale

A scale used in equivalizing incomes or expenditures in order to make fair comparisons between households of different sizes and composition. See *Equivalization*.

Equivalence Study

A type of *clinical trial* where the aim is to establish whether one treatment is as effective (or equivalent to) another. It is most commonly used when the new treatment is expected to be as effective as an existing one but also to have fewer side-effects, a faster recovery rate, lower cost, or other relevant difference. Same as *equivalence trial*.

Equivalence Trial

Same as *equivalence study*.

Equivalent Annual Cost

The constant annual sum of money having the same *present value* as a stream of actual annual costs. Also known as annuitized value.

Equivalent Variation

The equivalent variation in income is the minimum (maximum) amount of money which would have to be given to (taken away from) an individual to make them as well off as they would have been after a price fall (rise). Cf. *Compensating Variation*. See *Kaldor–Hicks Criterion, Willingness to Accept, Willingness to Pay*.

Equivalization

An adjustment made to incomes or expenditures to enable fair comparisons to be made between households of different sizes and composition.

Ergonomics

The study of the interaction between people, their workplace and working environment, including assessing the physiological effects on workers of the design of tools, equipment and working methods.

Error Components Model

A regression model for *panel data*. See *Multiple (Linear) Regression*.

Error Term

Consider the following simple regression model:

$$Y_i = a + bX_i + \varepsilon_i,$$

where the subscript i refers to the ith observation. The random error term ε_i (epsilon) captures all the variation in the *dependent variable* Y_i that is not explained by the X_i (independent) variables.

Ethics Committee

Ethics committees are agencies (some statutory) that are designed to protect people who are directly or indirectly the subjects of, or might be affected by, research. Their approval is normally required for research involving patients, relatives or carers of patients; access to data, organs or other bodily material of past and present patients; foetal material and IVF involving patients; the recently dead in hospitals; the use of, or potential access to, health care premises or facilities; health care staff, recruited as research participants by virtue of their professional role.

Ethnography

The *qualitative study* of human races and cultures.

Etiology

The study of the causes of disease. Also 'aetiology'.

EuroQol

Same as *EQ-5D*.

EuroQol Group

An international group of economists and decision theorists (mainly but not exclusively European) who developed the *EQ-5D* measure of health-related quality of life (*quality-adjusted life-year*). Their website is at www.euroqol. org/.

Event Rate

The proportion of patients in a group in whom the event is observed. Thus, if the event is observed in 33 out of 100 patients, the event rate is 0.33.

Evidence-based Medicine

The practice of medicine informed by the best available evidence of *effectiveness* and other empirically amenable aspects of the clinical management of a patient. There is a lot of argument as to what constitutes 'evidence' and the weight to put upon different kinds of evidence (for example, evidence got from randomized control trials or from observational studies). There is remarkably little evidence that evidence-based medicine (often abbreviated to EBM) leads to better health outcomes for patients, though it must be said that this is absence of (good) evidence rather than (good) evidence of absence.

Ex Ante

A Latin tag meaning a *variable* as it was before a decision or event, sometimes used to mean the planned value of a choice variable as in 'ex ante saving'. Cf. *Ex Post*.

Excess

A term used in insurance to mean the sum payable by the insured person, or deducted from the insurer's compensation, in the event of a claim. See *Coinsurance*, *Copayment*.

Excess Burden

A loss of *consumer's* and/or *producer's surplus*. See *Burden of Taxation, Deadweight Loss, Moral Hazard*.

Excess Demand

A condition that exists when the *demand* for a good exceeds its *supply* at the prevailing price.

Excess Supply

A condition that exists when the *supply* for a good exceeds its *demand* at the prevailing price.

Exchangeability

Sometimes used in a similar way to *generalizability*. In statistics it has a technical meaning. The random vectors $\{x_1, \ldots \ldots x_n\}$ are *exchangeable* if their joint *distribution* is invariant under permutations.

Exchequer Cost

A cost that falls ultimately on taxpayers.

Exchequer Revenue

Revenue that ultimately acts to reduce claims on taxpayers.

Exclusion Bias

A form of *bias* in a *clinical trial* arising from non-random withdrawals from the trial.

Existence Value

The value placed upon the continued existence of an asset. In the context of benefits accruing to future generations, it is sometimes termed *bequest value.*

Exogenous

Usually descriptive of a characteristic of a *variable* in an economic model. A variable is exogenous if it is not a function of parameters or variables in the model. Cf. *Endogenous.*

Expansion Path

A locus in a two-input diagram which is the set of tangencies between *isoquants* and *isocost* lines as output expands.

Expected Utility

A *utility* number weighted by the probability of its occurrence. See *Expected Utility Theory.*

Expected Utility Theory

Expected utility theory postulates that a decision maker chooses (sometimes, ought to choose) between risky or uncertain prospects by comparing their *expected utility* values. Essentially the approach entails assuming that people maximize a weighted sum of utilities under uncertainty, where the weights are probabilities and choices are between gambles or lotteries containing goods and services of various kinds. The theory was developed in eighteenth-century Switzerland and became popular after it was axiomatized in the mid-twentieth century. There are many alternative axiomatizations but all share the key features of *transitivity* and *continuity* (common to all utility theories), *completeness* and von Neumann–Morgenstern (VNM) independence. Completeness implies that, if lottery x is preferred to lottery y and lottery y is preferred to lottery z, then there is some combination of x and z that will be preferred to y. The VNM axiom means, roughly speaking, that adding a third lottery to two lotteries, whose ranking has already been determined, will not affect that ranking. The

VNM tag honours those who axiomatized the theory in the last century, John von Neumann (1903–1957) and Oscar Morgenstern (1902–1976), whose book *Theory of Games and Economic Behaviour* (Princeton: Princeton University Press, 1944) laid many of the foundations of expected utility theory (though not, oddly, that of the axiom bearing their names). This was also the beginning of *game theory* since expected utility theory's axioms were offered (and accepted by many influential scientists) as a justification for the use of expectations in game theory. Cf. *Prospect Theory*, *Regret Theory*. See *Utility*.

Expected Value

The weighted average of all possible values of a *variable*, where the weights are probabilities.

Expected-value-of-information

The use of *Bayesian* and *frequentist* probabilistic approaches to uncertainty in decision-analytic situations like *cost–effectiveness analysis* usually builds on data that are at best only partially relevant. One therefore needs to adjust empirical *distributions*, use explicit judgmental distributions, or collect new data. In determining whether or not to collect additional data, the expected-value-of-information (EVPI) approach, as its name implies, invites the analyst to consider the expected value (in the form of a reduction in *opportunity loss*) of additional (perfect) information (and the costs of getting it). EVPI comes in two forms: global, in which the reduction in opportunity loss from making a decision is estimated across all uncertain parameters; and partial, in which the reduction in loss relates to getting perfect information about a specific parameter.

Expenditures on Health Care

The total expenditures (public and private) on health care services in a country (or on/by a client group) over a period of time. There have been innumerable international comparisons of health care expenditures, often motivated by the false idea that there is a magic benchmark somewhere 'out there' that other decision makers (can they be politicians?) have got right and that you can use to buttress your case for more (less) spending in your own neck of the woods. The variation in per capita spending (public or private or both combined) and in fractions of *GDP* taken up by health care is substantial, as may be seen in the table.

Health expenditures as a percentage of GDP

	1960	1970	1980	1990	1995	1996	2001
Australia	4.9	5.7	7.3	8.3	8.6	8.5	8.9
Austria	4.3	5.3	7.7	7.2	8.0	8.0	7.7
Belgium	3.4	4.1	6.5	7.5	7.9	7.8	9.0
Canada	5.5	7.1	7.2	9.1	9.6	9.5	9.7
Czech Republic	—	—	—	5.4	7.5	7.2	7.3
Denmark	3.6	6.1	6.8	6.5	6.4	6.3	8.6
Finland	3.9	5.7	6.5	8.0	7.6	7.4	7.0
France	4.2	5.8	7.6	8.9	9.9	9.7	9.5
Germany	4.8	6.3	8.8	8.7	10.4	10.5	10.7
Greece	2.9	4.0	4.3	5.2	7.2	4.7	9.4
Hungary	—	—	6.1	7.1	6.7	6.8	—
Iceland	3.3	5.0	6.2	7.9	8.2	8.2	9.2
Ireland	3.8	5.3	8.7	6.7	7.0	5.9	6.5
Italy	3.6	5.2	7.0	8.1	7.8	7.7	8.4
Japan	—	4.4	6.4	6.0	7.2	7.2	7.6
Korea	—	2.1	2.9	3.9	3.9	4.0	5.9
Luxembourg	—	3.7	6.2	6.6	7.0	7.3	5.6
Mexico	—	—	—	—	4.9	4.6	6.6
Netherlands	3.8	5.9	7.9	8.3	8.7	8.5	8.9
New Zealand	4.3	5.2	6.0	7.0	7.1	7.1	8.2
Norway	2.9	4.5	7.0	7.8	8.0	7.9	8.3
Poland	—	—	—	—	4.4	5.0	6.3
Portugal	—	2.8	5.8	6.5	8.2	8.3	9.2
Spain	1.5	3.7	5.6	6.9	7.3	7.4	7.5
Sweden	4.7	7.1	9.4	8.8	7.2	7.3	8.7
Switzerland	3.1	4.9	6.9	8.3	9.6	9.7	10.9
Turkey	—	—	—	2.4	3.3	2.9	—
United Kingdom	3.9	4.5	5.6	6.0	6.9	6.9	7.6
United States	5.2	7.3	9.1	12.6	14.1	14.0	13.9

Notes:
1. Notwithstanding considerable efforts at homogeneity, part of the inter-country differences is caused by statistical artefacts.
2. 1996 ratios are preliminary estimates.
3. Some 2002 data are for 2001.

Source: Adapted from Table 10: Total Expenditure on Health, % GDP; 'OECD Health Data 2004', © OECD 2004.

The most clearly consistent and robust outcome of *econometric* studies is that per capita GDP is a major determinant and that the aggregate *income elasticity* of *demand for health* care is around +1.0 after allowing for *confounders*.

Experience Rating

The setting of insurance premia where the probabilities used are based on the historical risk, for example as revealed by past claims experience. Cf. *Community Rating*.

Experimental Arm

The group of people in a *clinical trial* receiving (or not receiving) a health care technology of interest whose experience will be compared with a *control group*. See *Clinical Trial*.

Experimental Event Rate

The proportion of patients in an experimental treatment group who are observed to experience the outcome of interest.

Explanatory Trial

A species of controlled *clinical trial*. Explanatory trials test whether an intervention has *efficacy*; that is, whether it can have a beneficial effect in an ideal situation. They yield understanding of the processes and pathways through which the procedure being tested has its effects. The explanatory trial seeks to maximize *internal validity* by assuring rigorous control for *confounding* variables. Cf. *Pragmatic Trial*.

Explanatory Variable

Same as *independent variable*.

Ex Post

A Latin tag indicating the value of a *variable* after a decision or event. Sometimes used to denote the outcome value of a variable as in 'ex post saving'. See *Ex Ante*.

Extended Dominance

An option that is dominated by another having the form of a linear combination of two other options. *Dominance* means that the combination option both is more effective and costs less than the simple option.

External Effects

These relate to the consequences of an action by one individual or group as they fall on others. There may be external costs and external benefits. Some are pecuniary, affecting only the value of other resources (as when an innovation makes a previously valuable resource obsolete); some are technological, affecting physically other people (communicable disease is a classic example of this type of – negative – externality; network externality is another, where it refers to any change in the benefit that an agent derives from a good when the number of other agents consuming the same kind of good changes; antimicrobial resistance is another: *herd immunity* from vaccination is a positive example); some are *utility* effects that impinge on the subjective values of others (as when, for example, one person feels sympathy and distress at the sickness of another, or pleasure at their recovery). This latter is sometimes known as a *caring externality*. When there are beneficial externalities of this kind, the standard maximizing behaviour assumed for individuals may not result in a *Pareto optimum*, notably if the *marginal benefit* received by the caring person is larger than the net marginal cost of the good or service to the consumer (that is, the *marginal cost* less the *marginal value* to the consumer). In the figure, a consumer has a *demand curve* (marginal valuation curve) shown by MV_1 and would, assuming that the price is equal to marginal social cost (here assumed constant for convenience), select output rate Q'. However, at that rate of consumption, some other caring individual or individuals also derive utility from this individual's consumption, as shown by the height of the curve labelled *EMV* (external marginal valuation) at this point. The optimal output rate is Q, beyond which the marginal cost to society exceeds the *marginal value* to society, as shown by the vertical sum of the two curves, D_1 *and EMV*. This is a Pareto-optimal

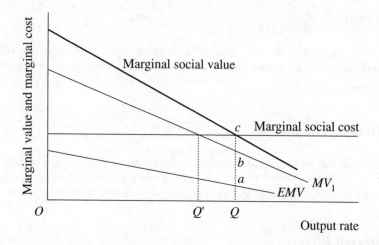

equilibrium, which might be obtained through subsidizing Q consumption, regulating it, or through direct exchange (as in charitable giving) between individuals (note here that, in the optimum, the marginal value placed by carers (Qa) is just equal to the difference between the marginal cost and the consumer's valuation (cb). Note also that the mere existence of an externality is not a ground either for predicting in*efficiency* or for subsidizing health care. If the *EMV* fell to zero at a rate of consumption lower than Q' there is still an externality but it is not 'Pareto-relevant', being entirely inframarginal. The analysis of external costs proceeds in a similar fashion, but summing internal and external costs vertically rather than the internal and external 'demands'.

External Validity

The extent to which the results of a study can be generalized beyond the setting in which they were derived without misleading. Cf. *Internal Validity*.

Externality

Same as *external effects*.

Extra Billing

Same as *balance billing*.

Extraneous Variable

Same as *confounder*.

Extra-welfarism

Extra-welfarism is an alternative way of doing *normative economics* to conventional *welfare economics*. Conventionally it is assumed that *utility* is the maximand, that sources of utility are goods and services, and that social welfare is derivable from (and only from) individual utilities. Thus health care constitutes the goods and services that may (amongst other things) enhance health. Health, in turn, is a source of utility, both directly and through the effects good health has on one's capacity to enjoy other goods and services.

Extra-welfarism has regard to a wider range of *attributes* than people's consumption of goods and services and might, for example, include changes in consumption or work patterns as direct sources of utility or disutility; or other states and changes in them (for example being divorced or getting divorced), participating in decisions, sharing sorrows, overcoming difficulties, feeling that one 'belongs', being 'private'. Extra-welfarism is 'extra' in enabling not only the consideration of other things that contribute to human flourishing beyond goods and services and the utility to be had from them, but also the effects on people of the processes and transitions of life.

In health, extra-welfarism commonly postulates health itself as the *maximand* of the health care sector, rather than the individual utility to which it may give rise. One specific advantage of the approach is that objectives cast in terms of *'health gain'* are commonly set by policy makers, and this approach fits well with the social decision-making approach in *cost–benefit analysis*. Another is that it makes no heroic assumptions about the ability of sick people to make rational *utility-maximizing* decisions on their own behalf, though it certainly assumes that collective decision making is improved by the use of 'rational' processes like *cost–effectiveness analysis*. Yet another is that indicators of value such as *willingness to pay* may be judged to be too contaminated by *abilities to pay* and imperfections in the *agency relationship* to be relied upon in the construction of health care priorities and the allocation of health care resources. A final advantage is that the method has proved valuable in laying bare the kind of *value judgments* that necessarily inhere in any concept of 'health'.

There is no scientifically 'correct' choice to be made between welfarism and extra-welfarism (though the ways in which costs and benefits are considered might vary radically between them). One's choice between them depends principally on either a direct value judgment or on a judgment about what is the most helpful way of setting up a problem in a particular circumstance. For example, if the agency on whose behalf some research is being undertaken wishes to discover the cost-effectiveness of a new diagnostic procedure, and that agency has clearly espoused 'health' as its maximand, it may be most appropriate to adopt an extra-welfarist approach, taking health gain as the maximand and considering pragmatically other factors deemed significant by the research clients (such as 'ease of implementation', short-term 'impact on waiting times', 'political acceptability' and the costs of achieving 'political acceptability').

The *quality-adjusted life-year* (QALY) is the most common entity chosen as maximand under extra-welfarism. In this context, however, it is probably best not to view the QALY as an index of (in some sense, average) preferences for health but as a representation of a collectively determined outcome measure explicitly posited by an authoritative agency; that is, an agency deemed to be a sufficient authority for the value judgments that are embodied in a QALY. These value judgments may, of course, accord a high place to respecting people's preferences. See *Welfare Economics*.

F

Face Validity

A judgment about the reasonableness of a measure based on its superficial examination preferably by people with relevant expertise/experience.

Factor Analysis

A multivariate statistical method of collapsing many (possibly) correlated variables into a smaller number of uncorrelated variables, and of exploring the structure of any relationships between these 'factors' or 'principal components'.

Factor Cost

Gross National Product and *Gross Domestic Product* become GNP at factor cost or GDP at factor cost when taxes are subtracted and subsidies added to these entities at *market prices*.

Factor of Production

An *input* in the production of goods or services. They are often classified into land, labour and *capital*.

Factor Substitution

The proposition that one *input* or *factor of production* (like labour) can, given sufficient time for adjustment and sufficient resources to effect the change, be substituted for another (like *capital*) to produce the same output. See *Isoquant*.

Fair Innings

A term borrowed from cricket but equivalent to the singular usage 'inning' of baseball. It is the name given to the idea that individuals who have not yet had a 'fair innings' (in terms of length of life in reasonable health) should receive a higher weighting in *cost–effectiveness analyses* than those who have had a fair innings (and even higher presumably than those who have already had more than a fair innings). It has proved possible to make empirical estimates of the weights through surveys, but the principle is controversial.

Fair Premium

An insurance premium is actuarially fair when it is equal to the monetary value of the benefit insured multiplied by the probability of successfully claiming that benefit.

Fairness

A general treatment of this topic from an economic point of view is under *Equity*. A famous concept of 'justice as fairness', which has much influenced economists, was developed by the US philosopher John Rawls (1921–2002). The foundation of what is probably the twentieth-century's most impressive contribution to political philosophy is a *veil of ignorance*. Rawls asks us to imagine ourselves to be the constructors of a just society, but being ignorant of our racial, social and economic position within that society, on the grounds that these are irrelevant to questions of justice. From this 'original position', he asserts that a rational person would select only two basic principles of justice. The first would be the liberty principle: a schedule of basic rights, including liberty of conscience and movement, freedom of religion, which ought to be equally distributed and as complete as is consistent with each having the same. The second would be the difference principle: social and economic inequalities are justifiable only if they are to the advantage of the least advantaged person. Economists (and others) have struggled to fit health into Rawls' scheme. Rawls himself explicitly excluded health from the operation of the difference principle, arguing that it was a 'natural good' like 'intelligence'. Many economists, philosophers and other analysts think that Rawls was wrong to exclude health in this way. See John Rawls (1971), *Justice as Fairness*, Cambridge: Harvard University Press. See *Entitlement Theory, Equity, Interpersonal Comparisons of Utility, Utilitarianism*.

False Negative

A test result indicating that a diseased individual is disease-free.

False Positive

A test result indicating that a disease-free individual is diseased.

FDA

Acronym for *Food and Drug Administration.*

F-distribution

Used for random variables which are constrained to be greater or equal to 0. It is often used in the *analysis of variance* to compare the ratio of the variance of the means from a number of groups to the expected variance of those means if all the groups were the same. Also called the variance ratio *distribution.* Named after the British statistician Sir Ronald Fisher (1890–1962).

Fee-for-service

A method of remunerating professionals (especially medical doctors) according to an agreed fee-schedule specifying what is payable for each item of service supplied. It is to be distinguished from (though it may be used in conjunction with) *capitation* and salaried means of remuneration.

Fee Schedule

A list of services or procedures together with the fee for each payable by a *third party payer* like an insurance company.

Fieller's Theorem

A parametric method of calculating *confidence limits* of cost differences and effectiveness differences in cost–effectiveness analyses. See E.C. Fieller (1954),

'Some problems in interval estimation', *Journal of the Royal Statistical Society*, Series B, **16**, 175–85.

Final Good

A good or service that yields direct *utility* to an individual.

Financial Appraisal

A procedure for assessing options that is similar to *economic appraisal* except that only the financial costs and benefits are considered, rather than *opportunity costs* and a wider set of benefits. See also *Discounting*. It is a vulgar error to confound financial appraisal with economic *appraisal*.

Financing Health Care

Typical aspects of finance that are examined by health economists include tax financing, subsidization of access to health care, income redistribution, insurance (public and private) and their consequences for *efficiency*, *equity*, total expenditure and patterns of use of services.

Finished Consultant Episode

A Finished Consultant Episode is a period of admitted patient care under a consultant within a National Health Service Trust in England. This is not always the same as a single stay (spell) in hospital.

Finnish Office of Health Technology Assessment

FinOHTA is an independent public assessment agency working as a part of Finland's National Research and Development Centre for Welfare and Health. It produces and disseminates health technology assessments. Its web address is www.stakes.fi/finohta/e/.

FinOHTA

Acronym for *Finnish Office of Health Technology Assessment.*

First-copy Cost

The cost of producing an early, experimental version of a drug.

First Fundamental Theorem of Welfare Economics

The proposition that, given particular assumptions, competitive markets are *Pareto-optimal.* The assumptions include these: markets are *complete*, property rights are well-defined and costlessly enforced, so that buyers and sellers can trade freely in all current and future goods; producers and consumers are selfish maximizers of their benefits and minimizers of their costs; that within these perfectly competitive markets prices are known by all individuals and firms; that the use of the price mechanism does not itself consume resources. Cf. *Second Fundamental Theorem of Welfare Economics.*

First Order Uncertainty

This is the idea in probability theory that, although you may not be in any doubt that a head is a head and a tail a tail, you will be in doubt as to which a throw of a fair coin will result in. If you doubt the fairness of the coin, then that is a type of *second order uncertainty.* See *Uncertainty.*

Fisher's Ideal Index

Fisher's ideal price index is the *geometric mean* of the *Laspeyres* and *Paasche* indices of price or quantity. Named after the British statistician Sir Ronald Fisher (1890–1962).

Fixed Cohort Study

A *cohort study* in which subjects are recruited and enrolled at a uniform point in the natural history of a disease or by some defining event and which does not permit additional subjects to be added subsequently. Cf. *Open Cohort Study.*

Fixed Costs

Costs that do not vary with output rates.

Fixed Effect Model

This is a statistical model in which treatments are chosen at fixed levels (cf. *Random Effect Model*). A fixed effect model is useful for studying the effect of treatment at a specified level but any conclusion derived from it cannot be generalized. It is limited to the range of treatment levels studied.

Floor Effect

Opposite of a *ceiling effect*.

Flow

A *variable* having an interval of time dimension: so much per period. Cf. *Stock*, which is a variable at a particular date.

Focus Group

A group chosen to discuss and comment on a topic being researched. The group may be informed by relevant witnesses. Common outcomes are the insights, opinions and conclusions which result from the interaction between the participants. Similar to *consensus panel*.

Follow-up Study

Same as *cohort study*.

Food and Drug Administration

An organization within the US Department of Health and Human Services with responsibility for the regulation of pharmaceutical and other food and medicinal products.

Forest Plot

See *Meta-analysis*.

Formulary

A list of drugs approved for prescription and reimbursement by a hospital, pharmacy or *third party payer.*

For-profit

A motive postulated for much economic behaviour. See *Hospital Economics*.

Foundation Trust

A type of *secondary care* provider introduced in the English National Health Service in 2004 having more local autonomy than other secondary providers. See *Trusts*.

Framing Effect

This is sometimes thought of as an 'irrational' (in terms of *expected utility theory*) response by subjects in experiments. It occurs when the same question, asked in somewhat different ways, elicits different answers. For example, people respond differently according to whether the choices presented to them are framed in terms of gains or in terms of losses. But, of course, this may not be irrational at all and, indeed, is not in the context of *prospect theory*. Cf. *Reflection Effect*. See *Regret Theory*.

Framingham

A town in Massachusetts whose residents have been studied by epidemiologists for more than 50 years, especially in connection with diseases of the heart, lung and blood. The data collected in this massive set of data have been enormously influential.

Free Good

In economics, a free good is not the same as a good that is offered free of charge. 'Free good' is a term used in economics to describe a good that is not *scarce*; it is one of which more is not demanded at a zero price than is available – as much is available as anyone wants at any price. It is not an *economic good*. It has no *opportunity cost*. Many goods and services that are offered free of charge are not 'free' in the economic sense, and health care is a classic example (for insured persons). An economic good that is offered free of charge will normally have required scarce resources in its production and there is likely to be an *excess demand* for it.

Free Loader

Same as *free rider*.

Free Lunch

The quip, 'There ain't no such thing as a free lunch', refers to the depressing fact that many of the best things in life are indeed not free (in the economist's sense of 'free').

Free Rider

One who consumes a good (especially a *public good*) without contributing to the cost of providing it.

Frequency

The number of times an event occurs over a period of time.

Frequency Distribution

A *distribution* of the frequencies with which an event or observation occurs. See *Beta Distribution, Gamma Distribution, Gaussian Distribution, Lognormal Distribution, Normal Distribution, Triangular Distribution, Uniform Distribution*.

Frequentist Approach

Essentially this is the approach to *probability* adopted by classical statisticians who would estimate the probability of an event, say, the probability that a given individual *x* will have disease *y*, by taking a suitable sample of the relevant population, discovering the *prevalence* of the disease in that sample, and then inferring that the chances of *x* having *y* were the same as the prevalence rate in the sample. Strictly speaking, the frequentist approach depends upon a 'large' number of samples being taken. This approach is to be contrasted with the *Bayesian approach*. Much heat has been generated as to which approach is most useful (there is agreement about the maths), as may be expected, given that each approach depends upon particular (subjective) assumptions being made and holding true, though the nature of these assumptions is not the same in each. Cf. *Bayesian Approach*.

Friction Cost

Friction cost is the name given in *cost–effectiveness* and *cost–utility analyses* to the loss of productive work time that is incurred between the time that an employee is absent from work through accident or sickness and their replacement by another. It is a form of *productivity cost*. Some studies in these genres, particularly early ones, used the *human capital* approach in assessing the benefits of health care and tended to assume that replacement took place only when the injured/sick employee returned to work. The friction cost approach recognizes that there is usually more than merely *frictional unemployment* in any economy (that is, there is *involuntary unemployment* too) and this pool of potential workers may have the effect of substantially reducing the time for which a job is vacant. These costs, it should be noted, do not include the expenses incurred by firms in paying 'sick pay' and the like, which are *transfers* and not *opportunity costs* in any sense.

Frictional Unemployment

That part of total unemployment in an economy caused as people change jobs, engage in job search from a position of not being employed (and therefore, perhaps, are freer to travel to interviews and so on). Frictional unemployment exists even when there is technically full employment because most people change jobs at some time and many do so frequently in dynamic economies. See *Friction Cost, Full Employment, Involuntary Unemployment, Natural Rate of Unemployment, Structural Unemployment*.

Frontier

A locus of combinations of *inputs*, *outputs* or *outcomes* that constitutes the boundary between what is possible with given technologies and resources and what is not. See *Health Frontier*.

F-test

The F-test can be used to test whether the *standard deviations* of two *populations* are equal.

Full Employment

A situation where all who wish to work at going wage and salary rates do so. This is not synonymous with zero unemployment thanks to *frictional unemployment*. Most governments seek to achieve a level of unemployment (to put it rather negatively) that is the lowest rate consistent with non-accelerating inflation, the so-called NAIRU. See also *Structural Unemployment*.

Full Profile Conjoint

A form of *conjoint analysis* in which the subjects prioritize the full range of the attributes of services. Cf. *Adaptive Conjoint Analysis*, *Pairwise Comparison*.

Funnel Plot

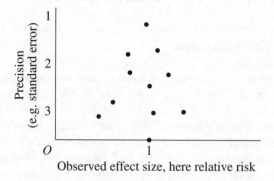

A graph of sample size plotted against effect size that is often used to investigate *publication bias* or the heterogeneity of studies in *systematic reviews*. Each blob in the *scatter plot* indicates the results of one study. The name arises from the fact that precision in the estimation of the true treatment effect increases as the sample size of the component studies increases. Because large studies estimate effect size more precisely than small studies, they tend to lie in a narrow band at the top of the scatter plot, while the smaller studies, with more variation in results, fan out over a larger area at the bottom, thus creating the impression of an inverted funnel. In the absence of *bias* the plot should resemble a symmetrical inverted funnel.

G

Gail and Simon Test

Used to explore quantitatively and qualitatively the homogeneity of the effects of treatment in a *clinical trial* amongst subgroups and to identify subgroups of patients with greater or lesser levels of treatment effect. See Mitchell H. Gail and R. Simon (1985), 'Testing for qualitative interactions between treatment effects and patient subsets' *Biometrics*, **41**, 361–73.

Gambler's Fallacy

The incorrect belief that the probability of an event occurring rises the longer the time that has elapsed since its last occurrence.

Game Theory

Game theory consists of models of strategic decisions, as the parties to the game move or propose moves and countermoves. The playfulness implied by the label is by no means a common characteristic either of the game in question (which may be a war) or of the players (who may be criminals). See *Expected Utility Theory*.

Gamma Distribution

A probability *distribution* often used to model individual heterogeneity, especially in *duration analysis*. The gamma distribution is related to the *beta distribution* and has two free parameters generally labelled α (alpha) and θ (theta). See *Frequency Distribution*.

Gastroenterology

The medical specialty concerned with diseases and abnormalities of the stomach and intestine.

Gatekeeper

A community-based provider (often a *general practitioner*) who in managed care plans and public health care systems coordinates the patient's diagnosis and treatment across the various possible disciplines and professions and who refers patients to *secondary care* for specialist treatment.

Gaussian Distribution

Same as *normal distribution*. Named after Karl Friedrich Gauss (1777–1855), the German mathematician and astronomer.

GDP

Acronym for *Gross Domestic Product*.

GDP Deflator

An index of the general price level in the economy: the ratio of GDP (Gross Domestic Product) in *nominal* (cash) terms to GDP at *constant prices*.

GE

Acronym for *general equilibrium*.

General Equilibrium

A state of an entire economy in which there is no excess demand or supply and no incentive for any actor to change their behaviour. It is modelled by multiple equations describing the relationships between *independent* and *dependent variables* in systems of equations that reflect the behaviour of the actors in the system, the technical possibilities open to them and the nature of any significant interactions between the various sectors. Cf. *Partial Equilibrium*. See *Arrow–Debreu Equilibrium, General Equilibrium Theory*.

General Equilibrium Theory

An extension of *partial equilibrium theory*, in which the feedbacks between sectors and other interactions are explicitly modelled. In general *equilibrium* theory, the consumer is envisaged as being endowed with a bundle of real *goods* rather than 'income'. See *Nash Equilibrium*.

General Practitioner

A doctor, dentist or other health care professional who diagnoses and treats the health problems of individuals and families in the community and who may refer more complex or technically demanding cases to a hospital specialist. See also *Gatekeeper*, *Primary Care*.

Generalizability

The extent to which the results or conclusions of one piece of empirical evidence may be validly transposed to other situations. In statistics the term 'exchangeability' is sometimes used.

Generalized Least Squares

A generalization of *ordinary least squares* which relaxes the assumption that the error terms are independently and identically distributed across observations.

Generic

Usually used to describe drugs that are no longer *patent* protected and that are generally sold under a name related to their chemical character rather than their *brand name*. Thus the generic name for the famous antidepressant Prozac is fluoxetine and the generic name for the world's best-selling (2004) patented anti-cholesterol medicine Lipitor is atorvastatin (global sales $10.3 thousand million).

Genetics

The science of heredity and inherited characteristics.

Geometric Mean

A measure of central tendency, the geometric mean is the nth root of n positive real numbers multiplied together.

Geriatrics

The medical specialty concerned with the diseases and care of elderly people.

Gerontology

The study (usually multidisciplinary) of old people and aging processes.

GHM

See *Groupe Homogène de Malades*.

Giffen Good

A type of *inferior good*. It is supposed to generate an upward-sloping *demand curve*, though the evidence for its empirical validity is contested.

Gini Coefficient

The Gini coefficient was invented by the Italian statistician Corrado Gini (1884–1965) as a measure of income inequality, though it can be (and has been) used to measure, say, the *distribution* of health or of health care resource consumption. The Gini coefficient is a number between 0 and 1, where 0 corresponds to perfect equality (everyone has the same income, health care and so on) and 1 is perfect inequality (one person has all the income, health care and so on). While the Gini coefficient is mostly used to measure income inequality, it can be used to measure wealth inequality as well.

The Gini coefficient is calculated using areas on a Lorenz diagram. Let the area between the line of perfect equality and Lorenz curve be A, and the area underneath the Lorenz curve be B; then the Gini coefficient is $A/(A+B)$. See *Lorenz Curve*.

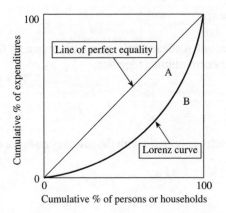

Global Budget

An overall financial allocation to a hospital or other health care provider, sector or region, out of which it is expected to provide or purchase health services. It is generally based on a previous year's global allocation with adjustments for inflation and special pleading.

GLS

Acronym for *generalized least squares*.

GNP

Acronym for *Gross National Product*.

Gold Standard

In health economics one is most likely to encounter this term in its sense of an instrument or procedure that is taken as a valid measure or example of good practice against which the validity of others can be tested.

Gompertz Function

Benjamin Gompertz invented a Law of Mortality to the effect that the mortality rate increases in a geometric progression. Hence, when death rates are plotted on a logarithmic scale, a straight line known as the Gompertz function is obtained. Benjamin Gompertz (1779–1865) was a self-educated (being denied access to English universities by virtue of being Jewish) English mathematician (of Dutch parentage).

Gompertz's Law of Mortality

See *Gompertz Function*.

Goodness of Fit

A measure of the extent to which the predicted values of a *variable* estimated in a model agree with the observed data.

Gross Domestic Product (GDP)

The total expenditure by residents and foreigners on domestically produced goods and services in a year.

Gross Investment

An economy's total investment before deducting *capital* consumption (or fixed capital formation) but including the value of any change in physical stocks of goods. See *Investment*.

Gross National Product (GNP)

GNP is *GDP* plus income earned abroad by residents and less income earned in the economy by foreigners: GDP plus 'net property income from abroad'.

Group Insurance

An insurance arrangement under which a group of people are covered by a common policy (as when employees are covered by their employer).

Groupe Homogène de Malades

The French equivalent of *Diagnostic Related Group*.

Guidelines

See *Clinical Guidelines*.

Guttman Scale

A method of scaling qualitative entities such that any point on the scale indicates an accumulation of characteristics. Also known as cumulative scaling or scalogram analysis. Suppose there are ten ordered statements. Then a score of six will indicate that a subject agrees with the first six statements and a score of ten indicates that there is agreement with all ten. *The scale is ordinal*. Named after Louis Guttman (1916–1987). See Louis Guttman (1944), 'A basis for scaling qualitative data', *American Sociological Review*, **9**, 139–50.

Gynaecology

Also 'gynecology'. See *Obstetrics and Gynaecology*.

H

Haematology

The medical specialty concerned with the *physiology* of blood. Also 'hematology'.

Halo Effect

The effect on recorded observations of the observer's perceptions of aspects that are not part of the study. Not the same as *placebo effect*.

Handicap

Disadvantages experienced by the individual arising from *impairment* or *disability*. The extent of handicap may be conditional on environment (for example, the nature of work) and may include general deleterious effects on the *quality of life*.

The Harvard Center for Risk Analysis CUA Database/CEA Registry

The Center maintains a catalogue of cost-per-QALY results scores obtained from published *cost–utility* and *cost–effectiveness analyses*. Its website is at www.hsph.harvard.edu/cearegistry/.

Hawthorne Effect

An improvement in productivity due to its observation. The effect was first noticed in the Hawthorne plant of Western Electric in Cicero, Illinois, where production increased, not as a consequence of actual changes in working conditions, but because there was a Harvard research team taking an active interest in working conditions in the plant and management was taking an interest. A type of *confounding factor* in experiments and trials that may lead to *bias*. The term is now used for any situation where the behaviour of the subjects being studied may be affected by the fact of their being studied. Also known as 'attention bias'.

Hazard

The probability of occurrence of an outcome: an estimate of the number of people experiencing the outcome divided by an estimate of the number at risk.

Hazard Function

Closely related to the *survival curve*, it shows the risk of dying in a very short time interval after a given time (assuming survival to that point).

Hazard Ratio

Same as *relative risk*.

HBG

Acronym for *Health Benefit Group*.

HCFA

Acronym for *Health Care Financing Administration*.

Health

According to the World Health Organization's charter, this is a state of complete physical, mental and social well-being and not merely the absence of disease or infirmity. Less star-gazing notions are usually embodied in practical work (including that of the WHO). See *Assessment Quality of Life, Disability-adjusted Life-year, EQ-5D, Health Gain, Health Status, Health Utilities Index, Healthy Years Equivalent, Quality-adjusted Life-year, SF-6D, SF-8, SF-12, SF-36.*

Health Benefit Groups

Health Benefit Groups are standard groupings of people who are expected to need similar health care interventions and to derive similar benefits from their treatment. HBGs focus on those at risk from a particular health condition or disease and on people with acute or continuing long-term needs. They are being developed to complement Healthcare Resource Groups (HRGs) in the National Health Service in England. The objective is to provide the NHS with a standardized presentation of relative needs for health care resources.

Health Benefit Plan

Any programme of directly provided health services or indemnification of medical expenses offered by service providers or third-party payers, such as a *health insurance* policy, a *health maintenance organization, preferred provider organization*, health service contract sponsor, or an approved employee welfare benefit plan. The term does not usually include medical coverage under *workers' compensation* or motor insurance.

Health Care

Goods and services provided to promote health, or prevent, alleviate or eliminate ill-health. Sometimes 'healthcare'.

Health Care Expenditures

Same as *expenditures on health care.*

Health Care Financing

Health care is typically financed from a number of sources in any jurisdiction, though the proportions vary greatly from one to another. The usual sources are *direct* and *indirect taxes* (including taxes on employers and employees and special taxes designated or earmarked for health care), social insurance contributions, private insurance premiums and direct payments for care (paid by patients or *third party payers*).

Health Care Financing Administration

The US federal body formerly responsible for the Medicare and Medicaid programmes. Now termed *The Centers for Medicare & Medicaid Services*. Its web address is www.cms.hhs.gov/default.asp?

Health Care Savings Account

Same as *medical savings account*.

Health Care Systems

Systems for financing and providing health care vary substantially across jurisdictions. They are commonly classified (by first-world writers) into four (not very well differentiated) types: sickness insurance (private insurance and care provision with often large public subsidies and governmental regulation, as in Austria, Belgium, France, Germany, Luxembourg and The Netherlands); national health insurance (public insurance with premiums either separate or embodied in the tax structure and mixtures of public and private provision, as in Canada, Finland, Norway, Spain or Sweden); national health services (public insurance mostly via the tax structure and mostly public provision, as in Denmark, Greece, Italy, New Zealand, Portugal, Turkey and the UK); mixed systems (having the foregoing in varying mixes, as in Australia, Iceland, Ireland, Japan, Switzerland and the USA). Some would dispute that the latter group (especially the USA) classifies as a 'system'. The greater part of humankind in the world does not live under any kind of health care 'system'.

Health Economic Database

HEED is a database of some 28 000 articles that are or purport to be *economic appraisals* of health care technologies. It covers 4500 journals and is produced by the Office of Health Economics. Its website is at www.ohe-heed.com.

Health Economics

The application of economic theory to phenomena and problems associated with health. Topics include, among others, the meaning and measurement of *health status,* the production of health and health services, the *demand for health* and *demand for health services, cost–effectiveness* and *cost–benefit analysis* in the health territory, health *insurance,* the analysis of markets for health services, health service financing, *disease costing, option appraisal* in health services, *manpower planning,* the economics of medical supply industries, *equity* and the determinants of inequalities in health and health care utilization, *hospital economics,* health care budgeting, territorial resource allocation, methods of remuneration of medical personnel, and economics of comparative health systems. See *Williams' Schematic of Health Economics.*

Health Economists' Study Group

The oldest of the professional associations for health economists, it celebrated its 25th anniversary in 1997. Its website is at: www.city.ac.uk/economics/research/HESG.htm.

Health Expenditures

See *Expenditures on Health Care.*

Health Frontier

A locus of the maximum health (or gain in health) possible for two or more individuals when resources and technology are given but the resources going to each individual may be varied. Cf. *Production Possibilities Curve.*

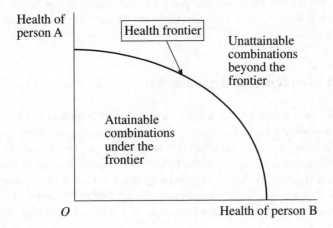

Health Gain

An increase in the *health* of an individual or a population.

Health Human Resource Planning

See *Manpower Planning*.

Health Impact Assessment

An approach to health service planning through which any policy, programme or project is judged in terms of its potential effects on the health of a population, the *distribution* of the health effects across the population and the steps that could be taken to enhance desired and reduce undesired consequences.

Health Indemnity Plan

Health insurance that reimburses the insured person retrospectively after paying their own medical expenses, minus any *deductible* or *copayment*.

Health Insurance

An arrangement by which the insurer pays contingent sums of money to the insured person or their service provider according to the terms of the insurance policy. A more accurate term would be 'health care insurance'. See *Insurance*.

Health Maintenance Organization

An HMO is a group of US health care providers which offers an agreed comprehensive package of care to a subscriber for a prepaid premium. They are a species of *managed care* plan. There is a great variety of forms of HMO organization and great variety in the form of remuneration for physicians, but two broad types of HMO are approved by the US Health Maintenance Organization Act. One is the closed panel HMO. Under this type, the HMO employs a group of medical professionals at a central location or contracts with a medical group to provide services exclusively for the HMO's members. Tight control of medical services is maintained because of the close affiliation between the employer HMO and its medical personnel. The other type is the *Independent Practice Association*. See also *Preferred Provider Organization*.

Health-related Quality of Life

See *Assessment Quality of Life*, *Disability-adjusted Life-year*, *EQ-5D*, *Health*, *Health Gain*, *Health Status*, *Health Utilities Index*, *Healthy Year Equivalents*, *Quality-adjusted Life-year*, *SF-6D*, *SF-8*, *SF-12*, *SF-36*.

Health Services/Technology Assessment Text

An internet search facility operated by the National Center for Biotechnology Information (NCBI) of the US National Library of Medicine (which is located at the National Institutes of Health in Bethesda, Maryland). The texts are books or reports.

Health Status

The measurement, via some form of *utility* measure, made up from *attributes* of a person's or group's state of health. Normally measured with respect to activities of daily living such as freedom from pain, anxiety, ability to feed, dress oneself. See *Assessment Quality of Life*, *Disability-adjusted Life-year*, *EQ-5D*, *EuroQol*, *Health*, *Health Gain*, *Health Status*, *Health Utilities Index*, *Healthy Year Equivalents*, *Quality-adjusted Life-year*, *SF-6D*, *SF-8*, *SF-12*, *SF-36*.

Health Technology

A widely used term conventionally relating to the ways in which health services can promote health or prevent/postpone ill-health. The 'ways' in question are in principle very broad and may, for example, extend well beyond the practice of medicine, for instance to embrace managerial arrangements, though it is more common for a narrower range of technologies to be embraced, even as narrow as drugs. Because we lack a suitable term for technologies that this narrow interpretation would exclude, it seems desirable to see its scope as even wider, to treat anything as a 'health technology' which promoted health or prevented ill-health, regardless of whether it was conventionally located in 'health services' conventionally understood.

Health Technology Assessment

Health technology assessment (HTA) usually addresses the following questions. Does the technology in question work? For whom does it work? How well does it work? At what cost does it work? How does it compare with other technologies deemed to be suitable comparators?

Health Technology Board for Scotland

The function of the HTBS is to perform original health technology appraisals for the Scottish *National Health Service*. These appraisals embody evidence on cost-effectiveness as well as clinical effectiveness. The Board works in conjunction with the *National Institute for Health and Clinical Excellence* and, for example, generally adopts NICE recommendations unless particular conditions in Scotland indicate otherwise.

Health Utilities Group

HUG is a group of Canadian economists and decision theorists who have developed the *Health Utilities Index*. Their website is at: www.fhs.mcmaster.ca/hug/.

Health Utilities Index

The Health Utilities Index (HUI®) is a generic, preference-scored, comprehensive system for measuring health status and health-related quality of life, and producing utility scores. It is sponsored by (and was essentially created by members of) the *Health Utilities Group* (HUG), which focuses on preference-based measures of health-related quality of life for describing treatment process and outcomes in clinical studies, for population health studies and economic evaluations of health care services. There are three versions of the Index: HUI Mark1 (HUI1), HUI Mark2 (HUI2), and HUI Mark3 (HUI3). HUI2 has seven 'attributes': Sensation on a scale of 1–4, Mobility (1–5) Emotion (1–5), Cognition (1–4), Self-care (1–4), Pain (1–5) and Fertility

(1–3). HUG's website is at: www.fhs.mcmaster.ca/hug/. Cf. *Assessment Quality of Life*, *Disability-adjusted Life-year*, *EQ-5D*, *EuroQol*, *Health Gain*, *Health Status*, *Healthy Year Equivalents*, *Quality-adjusted Life-year*, *SF-6D*, *SF-8*, *SF-12*, *SF-36*.

Healthcare Resource Groups

Healthcare Resource Groups (HRGs) are standard groupings of clinically similar treatments, which use common levels of health care resource in the *National Health Service* of England. They are intended to enable *case-mix* adjusted comparisons between institutions and underpin the national schedule of *reference costs*. They have also been used in setting targets for providers to reach. Cf. the US predecessor, *Diagnostic Related Group*.

Healthy Entrant Effect

A source of possible *bias* in *clinical trials* whereby the health outcome of the treatment under investigation is better than would be expected in the general population (or the population at risk) on account of the trial's subjects being healthier than average at the beginning of the trial.

Healthy Worker Effect

Workers generally experience lower mortality rates and better health than the general population on account of the fact that those who are severely ill or disabled are not usually in employment. This is the original 'healthy worker effect', but it applies to any subgroup from which those at relatively high risk of death or ill-health are excluded. Any sample based on the subgroup would give a biased picture of the general population from which it was drawn, unless this effect were compensated for.

Healthy Years Equivalent

The number of years of perfect health followed by instantaneous death that has the same *utility* as a profile of actual health states over an expected lifetime. The experimental method used to derive preference-based values of health states for use in *cost–effectiveness* and *cost–utility* analyses employs both the *standard gamble* and the *time trade-off* methods. The HYE was invented in order to overcome disquiet over some of the assumptions needed to base *quality-adjusted life-years* on individual preferences. In particular, HYEs do not depend on 'adding up' QALYs ascribed to periods within an overall period of time (such as a lifetime); they depend instead on an individual's ability to ascribe a health value to the profile of health states across the whole time period. Cf. *Assessment Quality of Life, Disability-adjusted Life-year, EuroQol, EQ-5D, Health Gain, Health Status, Health Utilities Index, HeaLY, Quality-adjusted Life-year, SF-6D, SF-8, SF-12, SF-36*.

HeaLY

The healthy life year (HeaLY) is a composite measure of health loss that combines the amount of healthy life lost owing to morbidity, plus that attributed to premature mortality. Cf. *Assessment Quality of Life, Disability-adjusted Life-year, EuroQol, EQ-5D, Health Gain, Health Status, Health Utilities Index, Healthy Years Equivalent, Quality-adjusted Life-year, SF-6D, SF-8, SF-12, SF-36*.

Heckit Model

A two-step estimator designed to deal with *sample selection bias*. Cf. the *Tobit* model, which is designed to deal with estimation bias associated with censoring. See James Heckman (1979), 'Sample selection bias as a specification error', *Econometrica*, **47**, 153–61.

Hedonic Prices

These are prices calculated on the basis that the value attached to any good is a function of its characteristics, both inherent (such as colour, quality) and external (such as location and environment). The hedonic prices are computed by regression techniques and indicate the price of a marginal change in one of the characteristics or the addition of another characteristic, *ceteris paribus*. They are commonly used in economic studies of the quality of goods and services or to adjust for changes in quality over time when calculating price indices.

HEED

See *Health Economic Database.*

Herd Immunity

The protection offered by vaccines is rarely 100 per cent. Any vaccine will be more effective at the population level if more people have been vaccinated because some diseases may be able to jump from a vaccinated person to a person who has not been vaccinated but is unlikely to jump from one vaccinated person to another who has been vaccinated. Empirically, when a particular percentage of a population is vaccinated, the spread of the disease is effectively stopped. This critical percentage varies according to the disease, the interactions between members of the population, and the vaccine, but 90 per cent is not uncommon. This is herd immunity: the fact that others in the herd or population have been vaccinated provides protection to all others, whether or not vaccinated themselves. An obvious implication is that 100 per cent vaccination is not normally a technically necessary target to obtain effective 100 per cent population protection. Of course, a *cost-effective* rate of vaccination will normally be even less than this, depending on the social value of the marginal reduction in risk and the cost of increasing vaccination from a lower to a higher percentage (but still lower than the herd immunity level) of the population at risk. The marginal costs of increasing vaccination rates may rise quite sharply as one seeks to immunize groups who are reluctant (for a variety of reasons, including religious objections, fear of the needle, imaginary risks, lack of contact with health care services, ignorance).

Herfindahl Index

The Herfindahl index is a measure of the degree to which an industry is concentrated. The formula for the index (H) is:

$$H = \sum_n f_n^2,$$

where f_n is the market share of the nth firm. It has a maximum value of $100^2 = 10\ 000$ (which indicates a *monopoly*) and a minimum value of zero. It is sometimes also termed the *Herfindahl–Hirschmann Index.* See *Concentration Ratio.*

Herfindahl–Hirschmann Index

Abbreviated to HHI. See *Concentration Ratio, Herfindahl Index.*

HES

Acronym for *hospital episode statistics.*

Heterogeneous

An entity is heterogeneous when there is variance in a relevant characteristic of an entity (note the four 'e's in this word). Cf. *Homogeneous.*

Heteroskedasticity

It is usually assumed in regression analysis (for example, *ordinary least squares*) that the *error term* has a constant *variance*. This will be true if the observations of the error term are assumed to be drawn from identical *distributions*. But if the error terms were not all to have the same variance, this assumption would be invalidated and there would be heteroskedasticity. Also appears as 'heteroscedasticity'. Its converse is 'homoskedasticity'.

Heuristic

Assisting in the process of learning or understanding. It is both noun and adjective.

HHI

Acronym for *Herfindahl–Hirschmann index.*

HIA

Acronym for *health impact assessment.*

Hierarchical Choice

A statistical procedure for deriving utilities in *conjoint analysis*.

Hierarchical Data

Data that are organized in classes, with subclasses beneath them and possibly further subdivisions of the subclasses.

Hierarchy of Evidence

A procedure for labelling the strength of the evidence in support of the use of drugs and other medical products and procedures. It is widely used in *systematic reviews*. A ranking might be as follows:

1. Evidence from at least one properly designed randomized controlled trial.
2. Evidence from several well-designed controlled trials but without randomization.
3. Evidence from several well-designed case-control studies by different authors.
4. Evidence from observational studies, time-series or uncontrolled experiments.
5. Expert opinion.

Histogram

A diagram consisting of (usually) vertical bars whose area is proportional to the relative frequency of the observations within the bounds of each bar. When each bar has the same width, the height is proportional to the frequency. Cf. *Bar Chart*.

Histology

The study of the structure of cells and tissues. It usually involves the microscopic examination of tissue sections. For example, the histology of a tumour is determined by a biopsy of it which is examined under a microscope.

Historical Controls

Patients who are not assigned to an arm of a *clinical trial* at its start but who received treatment at some time previously and are used as a comparison group.

HMO

Acronym for *Health Maintenance Organization.*

Holding Gain

The increase over time in the value of an asset merely by continuing to own it.

Hold-up

A rate of reimbursement by a purchaser at which the provider receives the lowest rate they are willing to accept to provide a service but which provides no incentive to invest. See *Purchaser–provider Split.*

Homogeneous

An entity is homogeneous when there is a lack of variance in a relevant characteristic of an entity. (Note the second 'e' in this word.) The opposite of *heterogeneous.*

Homoskedasticity

This exists when the variance of the *error term* is constant across observations. The *homogeneity* of *variance*. Cf. *Heteroskedasticity.*

Homotheticity

This is a property mainly used (in economics) when *utility* or *production functions* have a constant slope of the *isoquants* along any *expansion path.*

Horizontal Equity

Treating equally those who are equal in some morally relevant sense. Commonly met horizontal equity principles include 'equal treatment for equal need' and 'equal treatment for equal deservingness'. Cf. *Vertical Equity.* See *Equity.*

Hospital Behaviour

Theories of the behaviour of hospitals as institutions generally take their non-profit status as given (see *Hospital Economics*) and then explore models and their *comparative statics* for purposes of explanation and prediction. Despite the potentially complex interactions between the Chief Executive Officer, the Board (of 'trustees') and senior clinical staff, it is generally assumed that 'the hospital' can be characterized as an individual and that it maximizes a *utility function* defined over entities such as quantity of service, quality and net income. This function is maximized subject to a *budget constraint* and to a condition that the net residual ('profit') be zero, so that *average cost = average revenue* and there may be elements of *X-inefficiency* as decision makers work to ensure that average cost is sufficiently high for the purpose: the hospital is, to some extent, a 'conspicuous producer', using prestigious technologies that are not *efficient* from a societal *perspective* (for some people this may, of course, be an indicator of 'quality'). The limiting case when doctors' incomes are the only argument in the utility function produces a theory in which the hospital is assumed to maximize net revenue per (already on the staff roll) doctor.

Where there is *competition* in the market for hospital services, one predicts that all these utility-maximizing models tend to converge on the general profit-maximizing model of the firm, even though the ownership (shares) of the hospital is not tradable in *capital* markets. This is expected partly because price competition will drive out hospitals (or hospital managements) that inflate costs in order to generate sources of utility for management and partly because new entrants (if there are no significant *barriers to entry*) will tend to cause prices in established institutions to fall and income residuals, whether for spending on on-the-job or take-home sources of utility, will fall. In fact, there is a secular trend in the USA for non-profit hospitals to convert to for-profit status and, in other jurisdictions, private sector providers (whether for profit or non-profit) are increasingly being allowed to compete with public sector hospitals for contracts to provide services for publicly insured patients.

Empirically, it is hard to detect differences that would enable one to discriminate between these rival theories. This is particularly so in markets where competition is limited, where third party payers have considerable influence on case loads, *case-mix* and reimbursement rates, and where *exit barriers* may be strong. See *Hospital Costs*, *Hospital Economics*.

Hospital Costs

Hospital cost analysis has been mainly concerned with the use of routine data either to explain apparent differences in unit costs or to inform decisions about what the appropriate 'allowances' might be to compensate hospitals for 'teaching' or 'research'. All studies are beset with the problem of coping with varying degrees of technical inefficiency and X-inefficiency (as when hospitals are not located on *isoquants*), varying degrees of 'difficulty' of patient cases and dating of the end-point at which the health output is assessed (which is often after discharge from hospital), differences in *case-mix*, and imperfect specification of outputs which leads to problems of *omitted variable bias*. The literature is highly technical and considerable imagination is given to the solution of these and other difficulties. While carefully conducted econometric analysis of hospital costs can be of great value in practical decision making, to use it well requires sophistication and the ability to integrate it into a wider understanding of the hospital world.

The classic tour de force in this territory is undoubtedly Martin Feldstein (1967), *Economic Analysis for Health Service Efficiency: Econometric Studies of the British National Health Service*, Amsterdam: North-Holland.

Hospital Economics

Hospitals are characteristically (though not invariably) non-profit institutions which are often also registered charities (or have a similar status). The essential characteristic of a non-profit institution is that its owners (usually either 'trustees' when the hospital is privately owned, or publicly appointed non-executive directors when publicly owned) do not have the right to any residual profit, which may not be taken out of the business. Charitable status also grants them exemption from many of the obligations of for-profit organizations, including exemption from corporation tax. These (together with some other) characteristics give rise to the special treatment of hospitals in economics. A puzzle that arises is why this form of organization is so common, whether the hospital be privately owned non-profit (where the owners are effectively the trustees) or publicly owned non-profit (where the owner is a government). Embarrassingly there is no good answer to this question (in economics). Most attempts run along the lines that hospitals are there to internalize marginal (*Pareto-relevant*) *externalities* and produce services that have in many respects the character of *public goods*. However, while this suggests that hospitals (of any kind) are likely to underproduce without special incentives, it scarcely explains why (or justifies why) they should be publicly owned or be charitable, as distinct from being in receipt of a public subsidy in return for providing services of a kind and on a scale they would not otherwise choose.

Another explanation rests on the assertion that non-profit organizations are more trustworthy than for-profits. Yet other explanations arise from the historic context in which most hospitals began (as charitable foundations for the poor sick) but which then gradually became centres of expertise as medical science progressed, eventually becoming centres for the treatment of all without, however, having shed their legal status.

Besides the for-profit/non-profit issue there is the public/private issue. Why are hospitals such popular targets for being publicly owned? There exist popular beliefs that public ownership is somehow more *efficient* than private, or that public ownership in the specific case of medical care is more efficient than private (which is hard to pin down theoretically, desperately difficult to nail empirically and whose advocates – this is largely a world of advocacy rather than analysis – seem less concerned with *primary care* (general practitioners are almost universally private in all systems) than with *secondary*. Other explanations are managerial in nature, to the effect that it is easier (cheaper) to manage hospitals in accordance with a set of public objectives if they are directly line-managed from the 'ministry' than if they were private institutions under contract to the same ministry. Again the theory is unclear and the evidence is absent (which is not, of course, the same as saying the evidence exists and it supports the private production plus public subsidy argument).

One set of reasons for the evidence being so difficult to obtain in this area, in addition to the absence of any coherent theory, is that (a) there is a huge variance in the performance of hospitals (however judged) within the non-profit groups (and within the public or charitable sectors) as well as across them; (b) hospitals produce multiple outputs that are easy to oversimplify (for example, 'deaths and discharges' – as though the difference did not matter) but difficult to summarize in ways that are conducive to quantitative analysis; (c) hospitals also produce widely differing mixes of these outputs (notably varying in their *case-mix*); (d) hospitals are presented with human cases of widely varying 'difficulty' (in both *diagnosis* and treatment); and (e) hospitals also have a widely varying perceived 'quality' independently of the goodness of their clinical outcomes. In quantitative analysis it is consequently very easy to fall foul of the problem of *omitted variable bias*.

Amongst the more plausible partial theories of hospitals in economics is a theory that builds on the descriptive historical account alluded to above and sees them essentially as doctors' workshops. This approach utilizes a version of *interest group theory* in which being able to admit patients to hospital became a powerful right through which doctors increasingly acquired control over hospitals and, in particular, over other doctors and any threat their behaviour might constitute by way of impediment to the private practice of medicine. The non-profit mode suits this interest group by ensuring the dominance of their interests over those of shareholders. The public acquiesce in this arrangement partly because of *asymmetry of information* and partly because, unlike the doctors, they are diffuse and disorganized. See *Hospital Behaviour, Hospital Costs*.

Hospital Episode Statistics

Hospital episode statistics (HES) provide information on admitted patient care delivered by *National Health Service* (NHS) hospitals in England from 1989. This is used to provide wide-ranging analysis for the National Health Service, government and other organizations and individuals. The HES database is a record-level database of hospital admissions and is currently populated by taking an annual snapshot of a subset of the data submitted by NHS *trusts*. Quarterly information is also collected. A separate database table is held for each financial year containing approximately 11 million admitted patient records from all NHS trusts in England.

Hospital Separation

A discharge from hospital (alive or dead).

Household

Usually defined (pragmatically) as a single person living alone or a family group voluntarily living together, having meals together and having housekeeping shared in common.

HRG

Acronym for *Healthcare Resource Group*.

HRQoL

Acronym for *health-related quality of life.*

HTA

Acronym for *health technology assessment.*

HTBS

Acronym for the *Health Technology Board for Scotland.*

HUI

Acronym for *Health Utilities Index.*

HUI1

See *Health Utilities Index.*

HUI2

See *Health Utilities Index.*

HUI3

See *Health Utilities Index.*

Human Capital

The *stock* of human skills embodied in an individual or group. In value terms it is usually measured as the *present value* of the *flow* of marketed skills (for example, the present value of expected earnings over a period of time). It is determined by basic ability, educational attainment and *health status*, among other things. The 'human capital approach' in early *cost–effectiveness analy-*

ses tended to regard increases in human capital, or prevention of reductions in it, as the principal *outcome* of health care. This seemed to be the product of a distressing mental state in which the analysts were incapable of distinguishing people from carthorses – and is thankfully not an approach much taken today. When an outcome measure such as 'health' is also used there is also the risk of double-counting a benefit already included in the valuation placed upon an additional (quality-adjusted?) life-year. See *Capital, Value of Life.*

Human Resources

The treatment of human beings as *inputs* in the production of goods and services, in contrast to (though not to the exclusion of) their treatment as the ultimate end-purpose of health policies.

Hybrid Health Plan

Same as *Point of Service plan.* A health benefit plan in the USA that combines elements of *managed care* and traditional *indemnification* for medical fees. Members are encouraged to use a *health maintenance organization* or similar provider network but may also choose a doctor outside the network and be reimbursed for a part of the cost.

HYE

Acronym for *healthy-years equivalent.*

Hypothecation

Same as *earmarking.*

Hypothesis

A conjecture, preferably with a clear foundation in theory, that can be empirically refuted (at least in principle).

Hysteresis

This is a term in economics that has been borrowed from physics. It refers to a situation in which the past history of a *variable* can affect its current value. For example, the longer the period one has been off work through sickness, the less likely you are to find employment (regardless of your current state of health).

I

Iatrogenesis

An adverse condition induced in a patient through the effects of treatment by a health professional.

ICER

Acronym for *incremental cost–effectiveness ratio.*

ICF

Acronym for the *World Health Organization*'s *International Classification of Functioning, Disability and Health.* Its website is: http://www3.who.int/icf/icftemplate.cfm. See *Disability.*

Identification Problem

This arises in econometric attempts to estimate two or more relationships when each shares *variables* with another (for example, supply and demand share both price and quantity).

Impact Statement

A statement of all the identified and significant effects on the health care system of an option in *economic appraisal* and whom within the system they affect.

Impairment

An impairment is usually taken to be any loss or abnormality of psychological, physiological or anatomical functioning. Cf. *Disability*, *Handicap*.

Imperfect Competition

A market situation in which sellers need to search out the best price for their products. See *Competition*, *Price-searching*.

INAHTA

See *International Network of Agencies for Health Technology Assessment.*

In-area Emergency Services

Emergency medical care that is rendered within the service area of a *health maintenance organization*. A typical HMO plan provision covers members who are treated at any nearby emergency facility, rather than requiring them to go to a specific facility under contract with the HMO.

Incentives

The response of individuals (patients, doctors and so on) to anything that relaxes any of the various financial and other limits on their ability to act as they prefer. Positive inducements to act in particular ways. Disincentives are negative inducements.

Inception Cohort

A group of patients who are assembled at the onset of the disease being investigated.

Incidence

This has wholly different meanings in *epidemiology* and economics. In epidemiology, 'incidence' is the number of new cases of a disease identified during a time period. It is usually expressed as the proportion of those who are susceptible or at risk at the beginning or middle of the period.

In economics, 'incidence' is the ultimate distribution of the *burden of taxation*, after all effects arising from the *elasticities* of demand and supply have been allowed to work their way out and all tax shifting has occurred.

That the answer to the question 'who pays an indirect tax?' is not self-evident may be seen from the following diagram. Initially a price is established where supply S equals demand. When an excise tax is imposed (say a constant amount per unit of the good), the effective supply curve shifts to S' and a new, higher price is established. Since demand is relatively elastic, price rises by an amount that is plainly less than the tax, so it would be an error to assume that the 'burden' of the tax falls entirely on consumers (in the case shown here, sellers bear a larger proportion than consumers).

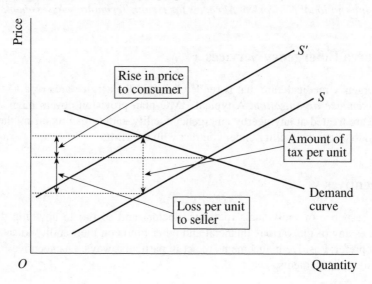

Inclusion/Exclusion Criteria

These have two common uses. One refers to the medical or social standards determining whether a person may or may not be allowed to enter a *clinical trial*. The criteria usually include age, gender, type and stage of a disease, previous treatment history and other medical conditions. The aims are to identify experimentally appropriate participants and to avoid harming them. The other relates to the scientific standards set to determine which items in a literature (journal articles, book chapters and so on) will be included in a *systematic review*. The criteria usually include quality and specific tests related to the purposes for which the review is being conducted.

Income Distribution

The way in which total income is divided amongst the households in an economy. Usually measured in terms of greater or lesser equality by a statistic such as the *Gini coefficient*.

Income Effect

The effect on the demand for a good or service that arises from the impact on *real income* of a change in its price, *ceteris paribus*. It may be positive or negative. For example, a fall in price means that the same rate of consumption can be maintained at a lower level of expenditure. This is equivalent to an increase in the real income (one can now buy more of everything) and this will lead to a rise in demand for all income-elastic goods. If the good whose price has fallen is an *income-elastic* good itself, then there will be a further boost to demand deriving from this 'income effect'. Cf. *Substitution Effect*.

Income Elasticity

The responsiveness of something (usually demand) to a change in income. See *Elasticity*.

Incomplete Data

It is common in clinical studies and *cost–effectiveness* analyses for the data to be incomplete. This may or may not be a significant problem. Examples of types of missing data include single missing items (such as failure to record a survey result for one item in an *EQ-5D* schedule), missing whole questionnaires, and missing data as a result of drop-out. Whether these omissions matter will depend partly on whether they are 'missing completely at random', in which case the sample remains representative, 'missing at random', in which case they can be imputed, or whether they are not randomly missing (sometimes termed 'non-ignorable non-response'). Ways of coping (which can hardly be commended) have included '*Last observation carried forward*', 'complete case analysis' (that is, using only complete cases with no imputed values, with the risk of *bias* if the sample with omissions is not representative); 'unconditional mean imputation' (that is, replacing missing data with the mean value of the data in the sample with omissions), with, again, evident risk of bias. Better methods include 'regression imputation', 'stochastic regression imputation' and 'multiple imputation' in which missing values are replaced by plausible alternatives in a process that takes account of the uncertainty about the right value to impute.

Increasing Returns to Scale

A feature of *production functions*. A production function exhibits increasing returns to scale if increasing all inputs in the same proportion increases outputs by a larger proportion.

Incremental Cost

Same as *marginal cost*.

Incremental Cost–effectiveness Ratio

The ratio of the difference between the *costs* of two alternatives and the difference between their *effectiveness* or *outcomes*.

IND

Acronym for *investigation of a new drug*.

Indemnification

The compensation or benefits payable under an *insurance* policy, or a principle of insurance, to the effect that an insured person should be retrospectively restored to the same financial position as before a covered loss.

Indemnity Insurance

Traditional private health care insurance which places few restrictions on the character of service covered or choice of provider.

Independent Practice Associations

An association of physicians and other health care providers, including hospitals, who contract with a *Health Maintenance Organization* (HMO) to provide services to its members but usually still see non-HMO patients and patients from other HMOs. Patients are usually seen in the physicians' own offices. The doctors maintain their own private practices and thus can contract with more than one HMO and see regular fee-for-service patients as well. The usual method of remuneration is *capitation*, though the other contracts may be *fee-for-service*.

Independent Variable

A *variable* that affects other variables but is not affected by them. See *Dependent Variable*.

Indifference Curve

A locus of points in a figure having two goods, one on each axis, such that an individual is indifferent between all points on the curve. The curve is usually axiomatically taken to be convex to the origin, reflecting a diminishing *marginal rate of substitution*, and indicating that both goods are *economic goods*. If an individual is indifferent between two options, this is generally taken in economics to be equivalent to the statement that the two options have equal *utility*. A family of indifference curves (an 'indifference map') shows successive curves like contours on a geographical map. As one moves in a north

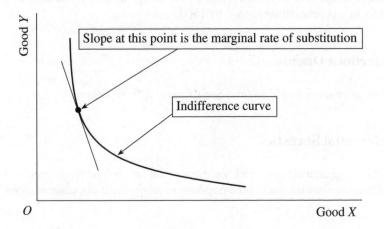

easterly direction, each indifference curve is associated with a higher utility number. An alternative name for an indifference curve is an 'iso-utility curve'.

Indirect Cost

In health economics, this refers usually to the *productivity costs* that may be the consequence of the use of a particular technology.

Indirect Tax

A tax on the production and sale of goods and services. Common taxes of this sort are Value-Added Tax (VAT), Sales Tax, Purchase Tax, Excise Tax, customs duty, stamp duty. Cf. *Direct Tax*.

Indivisibility

An input in a production process that cannot be physically subdivided into smaller parts. Given sufficient time, it may be possible to acquire smaller versions of an indivisible input (say, an ambulance) but they, in turn, cannot be physically subdivided without changing their character (as when they are disassembled and become 'spare parts'). Cf. *Fixed Costs*.

Infant Mortality Rate

Deaths in one year of infants under 1 year of age divided by number of live births in that year, all multiplied by 1000.

Infectious Disease

Same as *communicable disease*. See *External Effects*, *Vector*.

Inferential Statistics

The type of statistics in which *samples* are taken from which inferences are made about the character of the populations from which the samples came.

Inferior Good

A good for which a change in *income* causes an opposite change in *demand*. The income-*elasticity* is negative. In an extreme case and if money income does not change, it is possible to conceive of the demand for a strongly inferior good actually having a positive relationship to price, though alleged examples of this so-called 'Giffen good', named after the British statistician Sir Robert Giffen (1837–1910), are hotly contested and none are known in the health care literature. Cf. *Normal Good*.

Informatics

The study of information and its management, processing and dissemination.

Information Asymmetry

The usual asymmetry relates to the difference in the information known to a patient, or member of the public, and that known to a professional such as a doctor or nurse. Another asymmetry is that between insurers and those insured. The information asymmetries in health care have deep-reaching consequences for its organization, regulation and financing, mainly in order that the lay person (patient, potential patient, carer) is not exploited. For a fuller discussion, see *Asymmetry of Information*.

Information Bias

A form of *bias* that occurs when subjects' responses are affected by beliefs and values that colour their responses to questions that are not about such beliefs and values. Also known as 'observational bias'.

Information Cost

A form of *transaction cost* that relates to the cost of acquiring and interpreting information (for example, about the quality of locally provided doctors' services).

Informational Rent

The surplus over and above the minimum required by a provider to supply a service that arises because of an informational advantage (say, about costs) that they have but to which the purchaser is not privy. See *Purchaser–provider Split, Rent*.

Input

Same as *factor of production*. The resources that are used in production processes. See *Production Function*.

In Situ

A Latin tag meaning 'in a particular location' or 'in its original place'. In the treatment of cancer it refers to the original location of a cancer before it has metastasized. When interventions on cells or tissue take place on the living tissue, cells and so on in the body rather than in the laboratory, the tissue and so on is said to be 'in situ'.

Instantaneous Rate

A term used by some epidemiologists to mean what economists simply call 'rate'.

Instrumental Variables

A method of statistical estimation of models with *endogenous* regressors (that is, regressors that are correlated with the error term). It relies on *variables* ('instruments') that are good predictors of an endogenous regressor but that are not related to the *error term*. These can be used to purge *inconsistency* caused by *endogeneity*.

Insurance

Health insurance consists of a contract between the client and the insurer to the effect that, in the event of specified events occurring, the insurer will pay certain sums of money either to the insured person or to the health service agency. By pooling risks the insurer is able to select premiums that actuarially (after allowances for other expenses and so on) make it worthwhile for the purchaser. For the insured person, the advantage of insurance is that the probability of a large financial loss through lost earnings or expenses of medical care is exchanged for the certainty of a smaller loss (the payment of a premium). The standard *expected utility* explanation for people insuring is as follows. The figure shows how utility varies with income. Diminishing *marginal utility* of income is assumed. When income is $30 000, utility is *Oa*, when income is $5000, utility is *Ob*. Suppose that an uninsured individual would have to pay out $25 000 if they fell ill. Let the probability that this will occur be taken as 0.4. The expected value of income is therefore 0.4 × $5000 + 0.6 × $30 000 = $20 000. The expected utility of this expected income is *Oc* (0.4 × *Ob* + 0.6 × *Oa*), assuming that the utility function stays where it is in sickness or in health. Now, however, suppose that insurance can be bought at an actuarially fair premium of $10 000. Paying this sum (for certain) leaves an income of $20 000, whose (certain) utility is *Od*. Since *Od* > *Oc*, plainly the expected utility-maximizing individual will prefer *Od*, the insurance choice. Such an individual will also still choose to insure even when the premium is actuarially unfair, so long as it is not too unfair. See also *Adverse Selection, Copayment, Creaming, Deductible, Dumping, Loading, Moral Hazard, Skimping.*

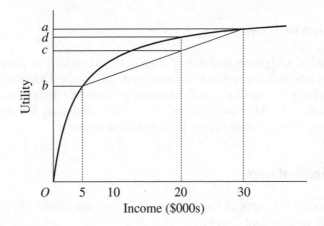

Intangibles

The literal sense of 'not capable of being touched' is not the general sense in which this term is used in economic analyses. Often misnamed 'intangible costs' in some *cost–effectiveness analyses*, these effects are usually undesired states or consequences of decisions such as pain, disutility and disappointment that have it in common that they are not quantified or measured. It is not a satisfactory term since few, if any, consequences are truly intangible in this sense. There are, in fact, many quantifying measures of pain, disutility and so on. See *Tangibles*, *Utility*.

Integrated Care

A medical benefit programme in the USA that is provided by an employer and which coordinates *workers' compensation* insurance with group health coverage to provide seamless medical care to the employee. Two separate insurance policies are issued: one for workers' compensation and one for *health insurance*.

Intellectual Property Right

These (IPRs) are exclusive private property rights such as copyrights, trademarks or *patents* to use ideas in particular ways and for particular purposes which deny their use to others without agreed compensation of the owner.

Intention to Treat

A method of analysis in randomized *clinical trials* in which all patients who are randomly assigned to one of the treatments are analysed together, regardless of whether or not they actually received or completed that treatment. One of the reasons for this type of analysis is to guard against any bias that might be introduced when dropping out is related to the outcome.

Interdecile Range

The central 80 per cent of (ordered) observations (that is, excluding the first and tenth *deciles*). See *Quantile*.

Interest

A payment for the use of borrowed money denoted as a percentage of the sum borrowed. See *Discounting*, *Internal Rate of Return*, *Time Preference*.

Interest Group Theory

The basic theory comes from the economic approach to political decision making, in which government activities are viewed as processes through which *wealth* or *utility* is redistributed between individuals and groups. For some, the unit cost of collectively organizing so as to procure a transfer from others is less than the value of the transfer; for others, the contrary is the case. People can thus be seen as demanders and suppliers of transfers. Representative democracy and its agents are seen as the mechanisms through which these interests are played out and equilibria established.

Interior Solution

An *equilibrium* that is not a *corner solution*. For example, in the figure, the tangency of the *indifference curve* with the *budget line* is an interior solution. Cf. *Corner Solution*.

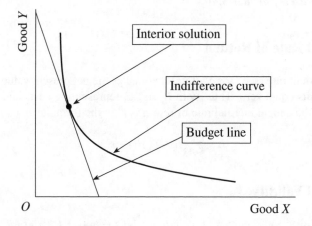

Intermediate Good

A good or service that does not itself yield *utility* to an individual but that might be used to create another good or service that is a *final good* or be used in conjunction with other goods and services to yield utility. Although it is sometimes said that health care does not yield utility (apparently on the ground that illness has negative utility), cost-effective health care does: that is (expected) utility is higher with it than without, even though utility might have been even higher had the *need* for health care not arisen in the first place.

Internal Cost and Benefit

A cost or benefit that accrues to the decision maker in question rather than being thrust upon an external party. Cf. *Externality*.

Internal Market

Market-like arrangements used within publicly provided services like health care. The central characteristic of internal markets is that the players are divided functionally into purchasers (sometimes called 'commissioners') and providers with the former contracting with the latter to provide services of specified types to a specified group of clients (usually defined on a geographical basis) at an agreed cost and to agreed standards. The UK's *National Health Service* is essentially organized as the world's largest internal market, in which *Primary Care Trusts* commission (they are also providers of *primary care* services) hospitals to provide *secondary care*. See *Purchaser–provider Split*.

Internal Rate of Return

That discount rate (see *Discounting*) that makes the net present value of costs and benefits equal zero. Thus, with B_t and C_t representing costs and benefits in year t, the annual internal rate of return is r^* in the formula:

$$0 = \sum_t (B_t - C_t)/(1 + r^*)^t.$$

Internal Validity

The reliability and accuracy of a *clinical trial*'s results. Cf. *External Validity*.

International Classification of Diseases

The *International Classification of Diseases* (ICD) is designed to promote international comparability in the collection, processing, classification and presentation of mortality statistics and is published by the World Health Organization. The current classification is the tenth edition (ICD-10). The codes are as follows:

I	Infectious and parasitic diseases
II	Neoplasms
III	Diseases of the blood and blood-forming organs
IV	Endocrine, nutritional and metabolic diseases, and immunity disorders
V	Mental and behavioural disorders
VI–VIII	Diseases of the nervous system and sense organs
IX	Diseases of the circulatory system
X	Diseases of the respiratory system
XI	Diseases of the digestive system
XII	Diseases of the skin and subcutaneous tissue
XIII	Diseases of the musculoskeletal system and connective tissue
XIV	Diseases of the genitourinary system
XV	Complications of pregnancy, childbirth and the puerperium
XVI	Certain complications originating in the prenatal period
XVII	Congenital malformations, deformations and chromosomal disorders
XVIII	Symptoms, signs and ill-defined conditions
XIX	Injuries, poisonings and certain other consequences of external causes
XX	External causes of morbidity and mortality

International Classification of Functioning, Disability and Health

The *World Health Organization*'s comprehensive definition of *disability*. ICF's website is http://www3.who.int/icf/icftemplate.cfm.

International Network of Agencies for Health Technology Assessment

An international network of health technology assessment agencies. The Network aims to accelerate exchange and collaboration among agencies, promote information sharing and comparison, and prevent unnecessary duplication of activities. Its website is at www.inahta.org/inahta_web/index.asp.

International Society for Pharmacoeconomics and Outcomes Research

ISPOR is a multidisciplinary and multiprofessional international organization for promoting pharmacoeconomics and health outcomes research. Its website is www.ispor.org.

Interpersonal Comparisons of Utility

An influential book by Lionel (later Lord) Robbins (1898–1984) entitled *An Essay on the Nature and Significance of Economic Science* (London: Macmillan, 1932) provided not only the most commonly met definition of economics that is still in use (see *Economics*) but also introduced into economics the highly influential distinction between *normative* and *positive*. In positive economics, making interpersonal comparisons of *utility* has been regarded, at least by economists influenced by *logical positivism*, as 'meaningless' partly on the grounds that one person's utility is not observable to anyone else and partly because making such interpersonal comparisons was held to involve ethics – and ethics, according to logical positivism, is scientifically meaningless. In *welfare economics* a similar ban on making interpersonal comparisons exists amongst staunch users of the *Pareto criterion* but on less clear grounds, since this seemed to deny welfare economics the possibility of addressing most practically relevant ethical issues in public policy (even Pareto himself did not hesitate to make them when necessary, as in policy judgments). Interpersonal comparisons are explicitly disallowed in the *Arrow social welfare function*, and Arrow himself described interpersonal comparisons of utility as having 'no meaning'. Thus, for example, policy measures to alleviate extreme poverty might be agreed to be highly desirable but they could not be *Pareto improvements* if they were to involve involuntary sacrifices by the rich (they might be actual improvements but the criterion could not say whether that was so).

Yet people plainly have empathy and make interpersonal comparisons of subjective feelings and experiences all the time, especially within families and other groups having important things in common, and the 'states of mind' of others are not invariably invisible, though we may sometimes be deceived about them, nor is our objective behaviour uninfluenced by what we perceive others to feel. While several very distinguished economists (some of whom are mentioned in the Preface) have provided penetrating analyses involving interpersonal comparisons of utility, many still do their best to avoid analysis involving them.

Health economists have tended to be far less squeamish regarding interpersonal comparisons than other economists, especially those adopting the *extra-welfarist* position, largely because *health* and the *equity* of its *distribution* lie at the heart of so much public policy and a concern on the economists' part that economics be able to contribute to the solution of the enormous resource allocation issues that arise in the field of health. This is not to suggest that it is any economist's business to make distributional value judgments; rather it is to suggest that their orderly discussion (by economists among others) in public policy debate is highly desirable and to the benefit of those whose business it is to make such judgments. See also *Arrow Social Welfare Function, Perspective, Quality-adjusted Life-year, Social Welfare Function, Utility*.

Interquartile Range

The central 50 per cent of (ordered) observations, that is, excluding the first and last 25 percentiles.

Interrater Reliability

An indicator of the consistency of the rating or score assigned to an entity by different judges. Cf. *Intrarater Reliability*.

Interrupted Time Series

A study design in which measurements are taken over time, interrupted by occasions of treatment.

Interval Regression

A variant of the *ordered probit model* that can be used when *threshold* values are known.

Interval Scale

A scale of measurement in which, like temperature measurement, the ratios of intervals between the points on the scale are the same for each set of possible numbers and the zero point is arbitrary. Each set of possible numbers is a *linear transformation* of another. See *Utility*.

Interviewer Bias

A form of *bias* that arises in social surveys when the expectations or prejudices of the interviewer colour the respondents' responses.

Intrarater Reliability

An indicator of the stability of the rating or score assigned to an entity by the same judge on different occasions. Cf. *Interrater Reliability.*

Investigation of a New Drug

A formal stage of testing a new drug in the USA for which approval from the Food and Drug Administration is required before trials on human subjects may proceed.

Investment

Investment is the change in the *stock* of *capital* over a period. In national income accounting, investment (descriptively) consists of expenditures on house building, plant and equipment, and stocks (inventories). In each case, it is only new output produced during the accounting period that is included. See *Gross Investment, Net Investment.*

Investment Appraisal

Same as *option appraisal.*

Invisible Hand

Describes the way in which markets apparently coordinate the activities of thousands of people without any evident 'steering'. See *Price Mechanism.*

Involuntary Unemployment

Unemployment that exists when workers are willing to accept jobs at the going wage but cannot find vacancies.

IPA

Acronym for *Independent Practice Association.*

IPR

Acronym for *intellectual property right.*

Isocost

A line in a two-input diagram along which costs are constant. Similar to a *budget constraint*. See *Isoquant.*

Isoproduct Curve

Same as *isoquant.*

Isoquant

A contour in a two-input diagram showing the lowest combinations of the two necessary in order to produce a given rate of output. Being 'on' an isoquant implies that the organization in question is technically *efficient.* Selecting an appropriate point on the isoquant will produce *cost-effectiveness* (the *opportunity cost* of producing that rate of output will be minimized). To achieve this one needs to know the prices (ideally the marginal *opportunity costs*) of the two inputs. The cost-minimizing combination of inputs at each rate of output is where the isoquant for that output rate is tangential to an isocost line. Selecting the appropriate isoquant (and, of course, the appropriate point on it) will produce general *efficiency* in the sense of *marginal cost* equals *marginal value.* To achieve this one needs to know the *marginal social value* of the output in question. See *Cost–effectiveness Analysis.*

Iso-utility Curve

Same as *indifference curve*.

Item Non-response

Occurs in surveys when a respondent does not provide data for a particular *variable*.

J

Jarman Index

An index of social deprivation that is used mainly in the UK. See Brian Jarman (1983), 'Identification of underprivileged areas', *British Medical Journal*, **286**, 1705–8. Cf. *Townsend Index*.

JCAHO

Acronym for *Joint Commission on Accreditation of Healthcare Organizations*.

Job-lock

Reductions in labour mobility that may arise in systems of employment-based health insurance.

Joint Commission on Accreditation of Healthcare Organizations

An independent, not-for-profit US organization, JCAHO is a major standard-setting and accrediting body in health care. It evaluates and accredits nearly 16 000 health care organizations and programmes in the United States. Its mission is 'To continuously improve [*sic*] the safety and quality of care provided to the public through the provision of health care accreditation and related services that support performance improvement in health care organizations.' Its web site is http://www.jcaho.org/.

Joint Costs

'Is the cost of the animal's feed the cost of the mutton or of the wool?' This is the problem famously posed when a production process (in this case sheep farming) produces *joint products*. The question as posed is unanswerable (sensibly), though the question 'what is the cost of extra feed?' is answerable when one is considering increasing meat or wool production or changing the combination of the two by slaughtering later or earlier. Fortunately there are few (if any) practical situations which can be usefully informed by asking (let alone trying to answer) the opening question in this entry. In health economics, the classic context for this question has been teaching hospitals, which produce health care services and medical education (and some even produce research output). See also *Overhead Costs, Sunk Costs*.

Judgment

To exercise one's judgment is to bring to bear on a matter one's experience, knowledge, powers of discernment and discrimination in order to make a decision or to determine the merit of something (like an argument). In health economics, judgments are frequently required in deciding (for example) whether the data that are available are good enough for one's purposes, whether a likely *bias* in one's empirical work is sufficiently important to warrant detailed investigation, whether the literature has been thoroughly enough searched, whether the claims for or against a particular course of action are warranted, or partly warranted, or not at all warranted by the available evidence base and the arguments put up. A particular type of judgment has been much discussed in economics: judgment of value (usually termed *a value judgment*), which has nothing to do with value in the sense of the price of something but refers instead to the ethical or moral merit in something. *Welfare economics* concerns itself principally with such value judgments.

K

Kakwani Index

A measure of the *progressivity/regressivity* of health care payment systems. It is the difference between a *concentration index* for payments and the *Gini coefficient* for prepayment incomes, equivalent to twice the area between the payments *concentration curve* and the *Lorenz curve*. A positive value indicates progressivity, a negative value regressivity and zero indicates *proportionality*. See Nanek C. Kakwani (1977), 'Measurement of tax progressivity: an international comparison', *Economic Journal*, **87**, 71–80.

Kaldor–Hicks Criterion

This is a criterion (*compensation test*) for judging whether a proposed change (say, the introduction of a new drug or the demolition of an old hospital) is *welfare*-enhancing. It is named after Nicholas (Lord) Kaldor (1908–1986) and Sir John Hicks (1904–89). The Kaldor criterion says that, if the minimum the gainers from the change are willing to pay is more than enough to compensate the losers fully, then the project is welfare-enhancing. The Hicks criterion says that, if the maximum amount the losers are prepared to offer to the gainers in order to prevent the change is less than the minimum amount the gainers are prepared to accept as a bribe to forgo the change, then the project is welfare-enhancing. The Kaldor compensation test takes the gainers' point of view; the Hicks compensation test is made from the losers' point of view. If both conditions are satisfied, both gainers and losers will agree that the proposed activity will move the economy toward *Pareto optimality*. There is the possibility that the Kaldor–Hicks criterion might sanction a move from state A to state B and then from B to A (*ad infinitum* and, probably, *nauseam*). This has led to the explicit ruling out of the reversal possibility, known as the *Scitovsky Criterion*, which also needs to be satisfied if a change is to be judged to be welfare-enhancing. Note that the compensation does not actually have to be paid. Note also that there is an implicit assumption that everyone has the same *marginal utility of income*. For true Pareto-optimality, compensation must actually be paid. See John H. Hicks (1939), 'The foundations of welfare economics', *Economic Journal*, **49**, 696–712; Nicholas Kaldor (1939), 'Welfare propositions in economics', *Economic Journal*, **49**, 549–52; Tibor Scitovsky (1941), 'A note on welfare propositions in economics', *Re-*

view of Economic Studies, **9**, 77–88. See *Compensating Variation, Equivalent Variation, Interpersonal Comparisons of Utility*.

Kaplan–Meier Method

The Kaplan–Meier method is a method of estimating the proportion of patients still surviving by any given date. See E.L. Kaplan and Paul Meier (1958), 'Nonparametric estimation from incomplete observations', *Journal of the American Statistical Association*, **53**, 457–81. See *Survival Curve*.

Keeler–Cretin Paradox

This is the argument in *cost–utility analysis* that, if health benefits are *discounted* at a lower rate than costs, the *cost–effectiveness ratio* can be improved by delaying the introduction of the technology in question and continue to be improved by further delays *ad infinitum*. See Emmett B. Keeler and Shan Cretin (1983), 'Discounting of life-saving and other non-monetary effects', *Management Science*, **29**, 300–306.

Kendall's Coefficient of Concordance

A measure of the degree of agreement (concordance) between different rank orderings of the same set of entities. Cf. *Spearman's Rank-order Correlation Coefficient*.

Kinesiology

The *physiological* study of muscles and the movement of the human body.

Kurtosis

A measure of the peakedness or flatness of a *frequency distribution* compared with a *normal distribution*. Cf. measures of *skewness*.

L

L'Abbé Plot

This is a convenient visual scatter diagram used in *meta-analysis* that compares the outcomes (say) of an experimental group with those for a control group in a set of *clinical trials*. Each trial is located in the space of a figure such as the one here, where the size of the circles indicates the size of the trial. It is often used as an indicator of heterogeneity and hence as an indicator of the likelihood that results from different trials can be validly combined. Named after Kristin L'Abbé. See Kristin A. L'Abbé, Alan S. Detsky and K. O'Rourke (1987), 'Meta-analysis in clinical research', *Annals of Internal Medicine*, **107**, 224–33.

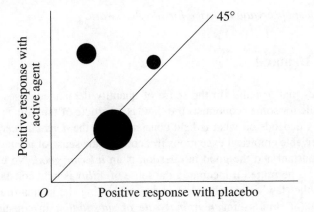

Labour Force Participation

The proportion of a population (perhaps a subgroup of the total non-institutionalized population of a jurisdiction) that is above a certain age (usually 16) and willing to work (that is, either in work or actively looking for work).

Laspeyres Price Index

An index number where prices and quantities of goods and services over time are weighted according to their values in a specified base period:

$$P_L = \sum P_n Q_0 / \sum P_0 Q_0,$$

where P_L is the Laspeyres index, P_n is the price per unit in period n and Q_0 is the quantity produced in period 0. The Laspeyres index measures the change in cost of purchasing the same basket of goods and services in the current period as was purchased in a specified base period. Named after Etienne Laspeyres (1834–1913). Cf. *Paasche Price Index*.

Last Observation Carried Forward/Backward

A (not very good) method of dealing with *incomplete data*. Sometimes termed 'last value carried forward/backward'.

Last Value Carried Forward/Backward

Same as *last observation carried forward/backward*.

Law of Demand

This states that *demand* (in the sense of quantity demanded) rises as price falls. While for some economists the 'law' is an article of faith, its interpretation really depends on what is held constant along the *demand curve*. There are conceivable empirical exceptions if income in the sense of money income is held constant and the good in question is an *inferior good*. No empirical exception is permitted if income in the sense of *utility* is held constant for in this case the 'law' is merely another way of putting the standard axiom of convexity (or diminishing *marginal rate of substitution* in consumption). These *ceteris paribus* notions are precisely that, of course: notions. In empirical work they are included amongst the *determining variables* but they still need careful definition (the concept of 'real' income to be used particularly needs definition). See *Demand Function*.

Law of Diminishing Returns

A somewhat less satisfactory term than an alternative: *Law of Variable Proportions*.

Law of One Price

A regularity that is often predicted by economic theory, though less frequently observed in practice, to the effect that a good which can be cheaply transported (like pharmaceuticals) and which is sold in international markets (like pharmaceuticals) will sell at the same price in all markets. Pharmaceuticals notoriously are not sold at uniform prices, despite their trivial transport costs.

Law of Variable Proportions

This 'law' is a generalization about the nature of technology when *factors of production* are substitutable. It states that, as the rate of use of one factor is increased, the others remaining constant, the *marginal product* (increase in output) will eventually fall and the *average product* too will eventually fall. While this is suggested as a general characteristic of *production functions*, it is particularly applicable in the *short run*. The term 'law of diminishing returns' is sometimes met but ought probably to be discarded in that it focuses attention on the 'constancy' or otherwise of factors of production rather than what is critical: the proportions in which the different factors are used. The element in the definition that runs 'the others remaining constant' is not a literally descriptive characterization but rather an analytical one, describing one essentially mathematical property of a production function. See *Diminishing Returns to Scale*.

Lead-time Bias

A *bias* in screening programme evaluation taking the form of increased survival times arising solely from making a diagnosis earlier in the history of the disease.

League Table

The relative *cost-effectiveness* of various health care technologies is frequently presented in the form of 'league tables' based upon literature reviews. A common reason for doing this is the maximizing idea that, provided the data reflect the true *incremental* cost-effectiveness of each technology and the effectiveness measure is appropriate, then the health budget will have its maximum impact by working down the table until the budget is exhausted (and by not funding anything else). Amongst the dangers in using such tables in other than a broadly indicative way are the following: the list is probably incomplete (and omits some cost-effective technologies); the data are not actually marginal (*incremental cost–effectiveness ratios*) but averages; the *perspective* on cost and benefit may vary from one technology to another; the literature reviews may have had inappropriate *inclusion* or *exclusion criteria*; the cost–effectiveness ratios may be dependent on the scale of use of each technology; the circumstances of the evidence collection in the reviewed studies may make the transfer of conclusions to other settings and circumstances inappropriate. A (famous) example is the table.

League table

Technology	Cost per QALY (£ sterling)
Pacemaker for atrioventricular heart block	700
Hip replacement	750
Valve replacement for aortic stenosis	900
CABG (severe angina; left main disease)	1 040
CABG (severe angina; triple vessel disease)	1 270
Coronary artery bypass graft (moderate angina; left main disease)	1 330
CABG (severe angina; left main disease)	2 280
CABG (moderate angina; triple vessel disease)	2 400
CABG (mild angina; left main disease)	2 520
Kidney transplantation (cadaver)	3 000
CABG (moderate angina; double vessel disease)	4 000
Heart transplantation	5 000
CABG (mild angina; triple vessel disease)	6 300
Haemodialysis at home	11 000
CABG (mild angina; double vessel disease)	12 600
Haemodialysis in hospital	14 000

Source: Alan Williams (1985), 'The economics of coronary artery bypass grafting', *British Medical Journal*, **291**, 326–9. Reproduced with permission of The BMJ Publishing Group.

Least Squares

A method for estimating *parameters* in a *regression analysis*, so called on account of its minimizing the sum of the squared differences between each observation and its estimated value.

Left-censored Data

Data from patients for whom follow-up did not begin at the same time as for other patients in a trial.

Length Bias

The mistaken attribution of increased *survival* times to a *screening* programme that arises from a tendency for insidious, slow-developing diseases to be more easily detected by screening than fast-developing, aggressive diseases. See *Bias*.

Length of Stay

A term usually referring to the time a patient of a particular type (or patients in general) spends in hospital. Mean length of stay (say, by *diagnostic related group* – DRG) is calculated by dividing the sum of inpatient days by the number of patients within the DRG. People entering and leaving a hospital on the same day have a length of stay of zero.

Liberty Principle

A principle of social justice associated with the name of John Rawls. It is a schedule of basic rights, including liberty of conscience and movement, and freedom of religion, which ought to be equally distributed and as complete as is consistent with each having the same freedom. See *Fairness*.

Licence

The legal (or other formal) permission granted to a professional person to practise their profession or for a pharmaceutical company to manufacture a product whose *patent* or other *intellectual property right* is owned by someone else.

Life Expectancy

The statistically expected remaining years of life for a representative person (usually in a specific jurisdiction and by subgroup: male, female, ethnicity and so on) at a given age (say, at birth, or having already reached 65). The World Health Organization publishes variants called 'Healthy Life Expectancy' which includes an adjustment for time spent in poor health. Healthy Life Expectancy at birth measures the equivalent number of years in full health that a newborn child can expect to live based on the current mortality rates and prevalence distribution of health states in the population.

Unadjusted life expectancy data show enormous variations across the world. A child born in Japan in 2002 had an expectation of life of 81.9 years (85.3 if female) whereas one born in Sierra Leone had an expectation of life of 34.0 years (35.7 if female). In general, females have a longer expectancy than males. Much of the disparity is attributable to high infant mortality rates. In Africa around 40 per cent of deaths occur amongst infants under five years of age. Poor sanitation and associated disease characteristics of grinding poverty – malnutrition, diarrhoea, malaria and infections of the lower respiratory tract – are principal causes. While the past decades have seen a general rise in expectation of life in all countries, in some regions, especially in Africa (for example Botswana, Lesotho, Swaziland and Zimbabwe) life expectation is actually falling thanks to HIV/AIDS. See *The World Health Report 2004 – Changing History*, Geneva: World Health Organization.

Life Table

A table showing how many people survive for a variety of periods of time. 'Survive' need not mean 'merely remain alive' (the table may be about surviving in a particular condition) and the periods do not have to be years, though life tables frequently embody both. Another name for them is *survival tables*.

Likelihood

Same as *probability* in the *frequentist* sense.

Likelihood Function

A function that represents the joint *probability* of all the points in a data set.

Likelihood Ratio

The likelihood that a particular test result is expected in a patient with the target condition compared with the likelihood that this same result would be expected in a patient without that condition. The link between the likelihood ratio (LR) and *sensitivity* and *specificity* is as follows:

Positive LR = sensitivity/(1-specificity)
Negative LR = (1-sensitivity)/specificity.

Likert Scale

An *ordinal* scaling of health states based upon ordinal rankings derived from surveys. A typical approach will pose a statement and ask the respondent whether they Strongly Agree, Agree, are Undecided, Disagree or Strongly Disagree. See Renis Likert (1932), 'A technique for the measurement of attitude scales', *Archives of Psychology*, **140**, 44–53.

Line Item Budget

Same as *global budget*.

Line of Equality

A line in a graph that indicates a completely equal distribution of whatever is measured on the vertical axis. See *Concentration Curve*, *Lorenz Curve*.

Linear Probability Model

A model of binary *dependent variables* based on the linear regression model. See *binary variable* and *multiple regression*.

Linear Programming

A mathematical technique for finding the maximum or minimum value taken on by a given function (the *objective function*) that satisfies a set of linear constraints in the form of equalities and inequalities.

Linear Transformation

The transforming of a *variable*, A, into another, B, by use of a linear equation of the form:

$$A = a + bY.$$

Linearity

A process or equation that can be expressed in a linear equation having the form

$$X = a + bY,$$

where b, the slope of the straight line relating X and Y, is a constant and a is a constant intercept.

Loading

A term indicating that an insurance premium has administrative and other costs 'loaded' onto it over and above the actuarially fair premium, which in principle is the expected cost of health care multiplied by the probability of that care being utilized. Because loading is unlikely to be systematically related to the risk of events, one of its consequences is that for-profit free market insurers are unlikely to offer policies for either very likely or very unlikely adverse events, where potential insurance clients' willingness to pay to avoid the consequences of risk is relatively low and the fraction of the premium taken up by loading is consequently higher. See *Insurance*.

LOCF/B

Acronym for *last observation carried forward/backward*.

Logical Positivism

A twentieth-century philosophical movement in which, in its most extreme form (which had considerable impact on economics), the only statements deemed to be meaningful are those that (a) are analytically true or (b) can be empirically verified (sometimes, which is not, of course, the same thing, 'refuted') by the evidence of one's senses as in controlled scientific experiments.

Logistic Distribution

A continuous probability *distribution* that is the basis of the *logit* model of binary choice.

Logistic Regression

Regression between a *binary dependent variable* and one or more *independent variables* using a *logit model*. Cf. *Discriminant Function Analysis*.

Logit Model

A model with binary *dependent variables* based on the *logistic distribution*.

Lognormal Distribution

A variable has a lognormal *distribution* if the log of the variable has a normal distribution. It is a distribution that is skewed to the right (so the *mean* is larger than the *median*). Like the normal distribution, the lognormal is characterized by two *parameters*: the mean and standard *deviation*. Values cannot be negative.

Long Run

A theoretical idea that has to do with the speed with which factors of production can be adjusted. A context for decision making (rather than a time period) in which all the *inputs* in a process can be treated as variable. In reality, nearly all inputs can be varied within any time period but the costs of doing so rise as the period shortens or is to begin at an earlier date, so whether to treat an input as fixed or variable is actually a choice for a decision maker rather than something fixed by 'nature'. Inputs treated as *fixed* may not necessarily be literally fixed in any technological sense (for example, the organization may be bound by a contract not to vary them). In general, the faster one seeks to make any change in input use, the more costly such changes will be. Some inputs are costlier, for many reasons, than others to alter and those that are costliest will tend to number amongst those most frequently treated as fixed. The real point, however, is that what to treat as fixed and what as variable is itself a question of choice and any decision about this will confine the scope of inputs to be varied. See *Production Function, Short Run, Time*.

Longevity

Length of life.

Longitudinal Data

Data that relate to successive periods of time. Cf. *Cross-sectional Data*.

Longitudinal Study

Any study using time series data. In econometric studies, the object is often to analyse the determinants of (the growth of) income, expenditure (for example, national health care expenditures) or consumption. Increasingly there are *micro* data sets available as well as *macro* data sets. *Clinical trials*, when individual people are followed, are called longitudinal *cohort studies* or *follow-up studies* (the two terms are substitutable). If individual people are not followed, but classes of people (usually age classes) are restudied, one has a longitudinal cross-sectional study.

Lorenz Curve

The Lorenz curve was developed by Max Lorenz (1880–1962), a US economist who developed it to describe income inequalities. It shows the cumulative percentage of income, health care expenditures and so on held by successive percentiles of the population. The percentage of individuals or households is plotted on the horizontal axis, the percentage of income, health care expenditures and so on on the vertical axis. A perfectly equal *distribution*, where each has the same, appears as a straight line, called the 'line of equality'. A completely unequal distribution, where one person has everything, appears as a mirror *L* shape. This is a line of perfect inequality. See *Concentration Index, Gini Coefficient*.

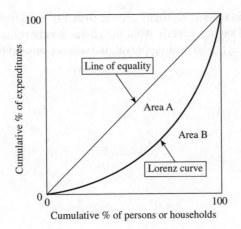

Cumulative % of persons or households

LOS

Acronym for *length of stay*.

Loss Function

Also known as 'criterion function'. It is a *function* that is minimized to achieve a desired objective. For example, econometricians minimize the sum of squared errors in making an estimate of a function or a slope; in this case the loss function is the sum of squared errors.

Loss to Follow-up

A common cause of missing data, especially in long-term studies, loss to follow-up occurs when researchers lose contact with participants in a trial through death, migration or any other cause. Planned data collection efforts are incomplete as a result.

Luxury Good

An *economic good* with an income-*elasticity* greater than 1.0. Because the term has pejorative overtones and also because the elasticity condition defines as 'luxuries' many things (apparently including many forms of health care) that are not generally regarded as luxuries, it is a term better avoided and 'good with an income elasticity greater than 1.0' used instead, which has the advantage of saying directly what the characteristic is that matters without overtones of approval or disapproval, importance or unimportance.

M

Macroeconomics

The study of aggregate entities in the economy, like money supply, income, exports or unemployment, and the links between them.

Magnitude Estimation

A method of deriving a *ratio scale* by asking raters of alternative states of health to think of them in terms of multiples (for example, state *A* may be 'twice as bad' as state *B*).

Malpractice

Mistaken, careless or unethical (legally negligent) medical practice for which the practitioner may be sued.

Managed Behavioral Health Care

A form of *managed care* provided in the USA for mental health and substance abuse care.

Managed Care

In the USA, managed care refers to a system of health care in which services are delivered through a network of contracting hospitals, physicians and other providers, and financed through a set fee. Some forms of managed care, such as *Preferred Provider Organizations* (PPOs) and *Point of Service plans* (POSs), allow patients to receive services outside the network but at a higher *out-of-pocket price* than for in-network services. *Health Maintenance Organizations* (HMOs) do not allow this. Ideally the managed care organization monitors the quality and appropriateness of care to guard against both over- and under-*utilization*, although sometimes *cost containment* or *dumping* the patient on another cost centre are said to be the most tangible motivations.

Typically *primary care* physicians are either salaried or paid *capitation* rates in HMOs and POSs, but in PPOs they generally are paid on a *fee-for-service* basis. HMOs and POSs usually require that patients first see a primary care *gatekeeper* for *referrals* but this is rarely the case in PPOs. Managed care organizations rely more on supply-side than on demand-side controls (such as the provision only of services for which there is evidence of *cost-effectiveness*), although recent years have seen substantial increases in patient cost-sharing requirements.

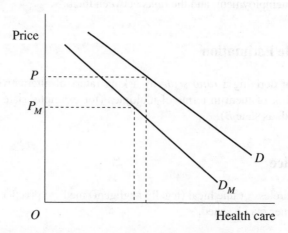

In idealized form, managed health care will effectively control both the demand and the supply side of a local market, acting as *agent* for members, eliminating demand for ineffective care on the one hand, and negotiating lower prices and restricting provision to services deemed to be cost-effective on the other. In the figure, for example, the 'normal' *demand curve D* is shifted to the left (D_M) and the price negotiated down from P to P_M so that total expenditure falls from the amount indicated by the larger rectangle to that indicated by the smaller one. Although the figure does not show the (hoped for) impact on health, it indicates the potential that managed care has for cost control. Essentially the same reasoning often lies behind arguments for '*socialized*' medical care.

Mandated Cover

Insurance benefits that are made compulsory by a regulatory or other governmental body.

Manpower Planning

The art of projecting the future demand and supply of particular types of labour so that appropriate policies may be adopted in the short term as regards training and education to ensure that future supplies are adequate for the demands that are to be met. Also known as 'health human resource planning'.

Mantel–Haenszel Test

A form of χ^2 test. See *Chi-squared Test*.

Marginal Benefit

The additional *benefit* from increasing the rate or volume of an activity. Mathematically it is the first derivative of benefit with respect to the (continuous) *variable* in question.

Marginal Cost

The additional *cost* from increasing the rate or volume of an activity. Mathematically it is the first derivative of cost with respect to the (continuous) *variable* in question.

Marginal Cost–effectiveness Ratio

Same as *incremental cost–effectiveness ratio*.

Marginal Intertemporal Rate of Substitution

The rate at which present consumption will be traded for an increase in future consumption. See *Time Preference*.

Marginal Product

The increase in *output* rate obtained by increasing the rate of use of one *input*. See *Production Function*.

Marginal Rate of Return

The incremental gain over time (conventionally a year) from sacrificing a little more current consumption or resource. Cf. *Rate of Return*.

Marginal Rate of Substitution

The marginal rate of substitution in consumption is the (negative) slope of an *indifference curve*. It is the ratio of the *marginal utilities* of two goods as one is substituted for the other such as to leave the individual in question indifferent (*ceteris paribus*).

The marginal rate of substitution in production is the (negative) slope of an *isoquant*. It is the ratio of the *marginal products* of two inputs as one is substituted for the other such as to leave the output rate constant (*ceteris paribus*). Also known as the *marginal rate of technical substitution*.

Marginal Rate of Transformation

The slope of a *production possibilities curve*.

Marginal Social Cost

The sum of marginal private *cost* (costs internal to the decision maker) and *marginal external costs*.

Marginal Social Value

The sum of individual *marginal values* placed upon a good or service that all must consume if anyone does. See *Public Goods*.

Marginal Utility

The increase in *utility* gained from a small increase in the rate of consumption of the good yielding it. See *Diminishing Marginal Utility, Utility*.

Marginal Utility of Income

The *marginal utility* to be had from an increment in income.

Marginal Value

The maximum value attached to a little more or less of a good, service or desired characteristic. See *Demand Curve.*

Market Failure

Markets in health care are notable, not because they fail to satisfy any one of the standard assumptions required for competitive markets to achieve *Pareto optimality*, but because they fail every single one of them: there is enormous *asymmetry of information* between producers (medical professionals of all kinds) and consumers (patients actual and potential); the *agency relationship* works imperfectly and can be distorted by systems of physician pay; there is little evidence that patients behave in accordance with the axioms of *rational* choice theory; markets, especially those for risk, are extremely *incomplete*; the medical care industry is riven with monopolistic organizations, from those in the *pharmaceutical industry* through those in the medical professions themselves, to the local monopolies held by hospitals and community-based primary care practices. In addition, much of health care has the character of a *public good* and generates *externalities* both physical (as with communicable disease) and psychic (as when you derive comfort from knowing that your neighbours are insured). Health care is also a field in which *equity* has always been regarded as of at least equal importance to *efficiency* (even if that is not how economists have allocated their effort).

This accounts for the extensive public intervention in health care and for the development of more or less economically informed methods of professional and other regulation, allocating resources to regions and institutions and conducting health technology *appraisals*. It also accounts for the substantial demand for health economists in both the private and the public sector beyond secondary and tertiary education.

Market Forces Factor

An adjustment made to the *national tariff* in the *National Health Service's* commissioning arrangements to allow for local variations in wages and prices. See *Purchaser–provider Split*.

Market Imperfections

Broadly, the reasons for *market failure*.

Market Mechanism

Same as *price mechanism*.

Market Prices

In national income accounting, *Gross Domestic Product* or *Gross National Product* at market prices means that the measure of each includes the effect of taxes and subsidies. Cf. *Factor Cost*.

Market Segmentation

The act of dividing an overall market into groups, or segments, of consumers with similar characteristics such as age, region of residence or average health status. It is usually done in order to engage in *price discrimination* in *price-searchers'* markets. Prices in the markets with less *elastic* demand tend to be higher. In order to work effectively, the segments need to be such that resale is not possible from low-price to high-price segments (*parallel trade*) so segmentation is likely to be seen when there is price-searching and the product is highly perishable, transport costs are high, or, where segments correspond to jurisdictions, suppliers have managed to 'capture' regulatory agencies.

Markov Chain

A Markov chain is a sequence of events whose probabilities at any one time interval depend upon previous values in the *decision tree*. See *Markov Model*.

Markov Model

A type of model used much in *cost–effectiveness* and *cost–utility* analyses in which the progress of a disease with and without interventions is modelled in a sequence of time periods, each being associated with a particular measure of health, and each having a probability of moving from it to the next state. The method is an extended form of the *decision tree* that is particularly suited to the analysis of chronic conditions when a normal decision tree might become uncontrollably complex. Named after the Russian mathematician Andrei Andreyevich Markov (1856–1922).

Markov Node

Decision points in a *decision tree*.

Markov System

Same as *Markov model*.

Masking

Same as *blinding*.

Matching

A process through which pairs of individuals are brought together in order to trade, share or otherwise engage in some mutual activity. There is also matching in biostatistics: selecting a control population that is matched on some characteristics that may influence the outcome of interest independently of the disorder in question.

Maternal Mortality Rate

The number of deaths in a year from puerperal causes divided by the number of live births in the same population in that year, all multiplied by 1000.

Matrix

An array of numbers (called 'elements') displayed in *vectors*: rows and columns. There is a special algebra for manipulating matrices.

Matrix Approach

A term sometimes used to describe the way in which the costs and benefits of an option are presented.

Maturation Effect

A change in a *dependent variable* that is due to the passage of time.

Maxillofacial Surgery

A branch of dentistry specializing in the surgery of the jaw and mouth.

Maximand

That which is to be maximized: for example, *health*, *profit*, *utility* or *welfare*.

Maximin

An ethical rule of distributive *fairness* which stipulates that one should maximize the *welfare* of the least well-off person in a society.

Maximum Likelihood Estimation

A method of estimation in which joint *probability* is reinterpreted as a *likelihood function* that depends on the model's *parameters*, given the observed set of data. The parameter values that maximize this function are used as estimates.

Maximum Price Law

A system established in 1966 in The Netherlands whereby a maximum price is set for pharmaceuticals of a particular class, based on comparisons with a selection of other European countries.

MBHC

Acronym for *managed behavioral health care* in the USA.

MBHO

Acronym for *managed health care organization* in the USA. See *Managed Behavioral Health Care*.

McCarran–Ferguson Act

The US McCarran–Ferguson Act was adopted in 1945 after extended controversy over the jurisdiction of state and federal governments in regulating the business of insurance. The principal objective of the Act was to establish the primacy of the states in regulating the industry. The purpose clause of the Act states that the continued regulation and taxation of the business of insurance by states are in the public's best interest and the Act explicitly empowers states to regulate and tax insurance.

Mean

A measure of the central tendency of a set of numbers. The average of a set of numbers. The sum of the observations divided by their number. Arithmetic mean = $\Sigma X_i/N$, where the X_i are the values of X and N is the total number of observations. The qualifier 'arithmetic' is usually dropped. See *Geometric Mean*.

Mean Survival

The average period for which a person having particular characteristics survives. See *Survival Analysis*.

Measurement

Assigning numbers to entities according to a rule in order to indicate order, size or other characteristics of interest. Cf. *Cardinal Scale, Ordinal Scale, Utility Measurement.*

Measurement Bias

Bias arising from inaccuracy in measurements, coding or classification in *clinical trials.*

Median

The middle value of an ordered set of numbers.

Median Voter Model

A theorem in *public choice theory* states that the median voter determines the rate of output chosen for *public goods* that are publicly produced (or privately produced but publicly financed). In the figure there are five *demand curves* for a community of five taxpayers, who each pay the same amount of tax. Public output decisions are taken by simple majority vote. The marginal tax rate is indicated by *MT* and the demand curves, D_1, D_2 and so on are the marginal value curves for the five voters. Voter 1's preferred output is Q_1,

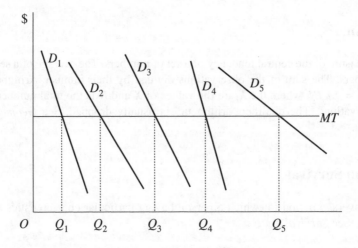

voter 2's is Q_2, and so on. If Q_1 is proposed, only voter 1 will support it, the others all preferring larger output rates. If Q_2 is proposed, voters 3, 4 and 5 will outvote voters 1 and 2, preferring more. If Q_4 is proposed voters 1, 2 and 3 will outvote voters 4 and 5 and voters 1, 2, 3 and 4 will outvote voter 5 in opposing output rate Q_5. The rate that commands the majority is Q_3, which just happens to be voter 3's preferred rate, and voter 3 is the median voter.

Medicaid

Medicaid is a US health plan developed by the federal government in 1965 as a companion to the *Medicare* programme. The programme is intended for low-income residents and is addressed particularly to families with children, pregnant women, children, the aged, the blind and the disabled. To be eligible for Medicaid, a person must belong to one of these groups and meet the financial criteria for that group. There are optional groups also, such as the 'medically needy'. Eligibility for the programme is through a means test that reviews the income and resources of the individual or family applying for coverage. Federal law provides that a state may qualify for federal Medicaid matching funds only if it designs its programme within specific federal re-quirements. These include eligibility for specific population groups, coverage for certain medical services and medical providers, and adherence to specific rules relating to payment methodologies, payment amounts, and cost sharing for Medicaid beneficiaries. To qualify for federal Medicaid matching funds, a state must obtain approval of its Medicaid State Plan.

Medicaid provides open-ended federal contributions according to a statu-tory formula to participating states with approved plans. The State Medicaid Agency will be reimbursed for a portion of actual expenditures made under the provisions of the state plan. Provided that the state plan meets the basic eligibility criteria, the portion is computed from a formula that takes into account the average per capita income for each state relative to the national average. By law, the portion (known as Federal Medical Assistance Percent-age) cannot be less than 50 per cent. See *Medicare*.

Medicaid Notch

A discontinuity in the leisure–income trade-off for Medicaid beneficiaries that provides a disincentive to work more than a given amount (beyond which substantial benefits are lost).

Medical Savings Account

A trust account established for the benefit of an employee (or, in some places, established by an individual) to pay for qualifying medical expenses. Where such trusts are permitted, contributions, interest accumulations and withdrawals applied to health costs are exempt from income tax. The employer is usually required to purchase catastrophic health insurance coverage with a high *deductible* which results in a reduced premium. The employee may also contribute up to a maximum equal to the health insurance deductible. Also known as a *Health Care Savings Account* in some jurisdictions.

Medical Services Advisory Committee

An Australian agency that advises the Minister for Health and Ageing on evidence relating to the safety and *cost-effectiveness* of medical technologies. Its web site is http://www.health.gov.au/msac/. See also *Pharmaceutical Benefits Advisory Committee*.

Medicare

A term used generally to describe publicly funded and provided health care in Australia, Canada and the USA. Medicare is the term used in Australia to describe its universal health insurance scheme. Introduced in 1984, it provides access to free treatment in a public hospital and free or subsidized treatment by primary practitioners (specified services only). It is funded through taxes and a special Medicare levy based on taxable income. In Canada, the term is used loosely to describe the provincially provided (but largely federally controlled) systems of public health care insurance, providing free access to hospital and doctors' (specialists and general practitioners) services. It is funded through provincial health insurance premiums and through provincial and federal general taxation.

In the USA the term refers explicitly to a federal programme that is the main health insurance programme for people aged 65 and older, the disabled and people with end-stage renal disease, regardless of income. People who qualify for social security benefits are automatically eligible for Medicare. It is funded via payroll taxes and members' payments: premiums, *deductibles* and *coinsurance*. Medicare coverage provides for acute hospital care, physician services, brief stays in skilled nursing facilities, short-term skilled home care related to a medical problem and prescription drugs. There are two major programmes: Hospital Insurance (Part A) and Supplementary Medical

Insurance (Part B). The Medicare coverage for Part A has no premium and pays 100 per cent of hospital costs for the first 60 days after payment of a deductible (currently about $876). Medicare Part B pays up to 80 per cent of doctors' bills for a monthly premium of about $66. Doctors may bill benefici-aries for an additional amount (the 'balance') not to exceed 15 per cent of the Medicare approved charge (see *Balance Billing*). Medicare currently has about 39 million beneficiaries. See *Medicaid*.

MEDLINE®

MEDLINE® (Medical Literature, Analysis and Retrieval System Online) is the US National Library of Medicine's (NLM) premier bibliographic data-base, containing over 12 million references to journal articles in life sciences with a concentration on biomedicine. MEDLINE is available on the Internet through the NLM home page at www.nlm.nih.gov and can be searched free of charge. No registration is required.

Merit Good

A good or service whose consumption is regarded (by someone influential) as being unusually meritorious. It is generally associated with the idea that people are not consuming enough of something and that it would be good for them (or society) if they consumed more. But the claim is not being made on *externality* grounds or because of *market failure* and seems inherently paternalist (for example, a belief that people are myopic or ignorant). Educa-tion is often cited as an example of a merit good; health care is rarely so cited. The grounds for this asymmetry are obscure.

Meta-analysis

'Meta-' has a Greek origin and indicates, amongst other things, that the subject matter (in this case 'analysis') has a second-order character: an analysis of analyses. A meta-analysis is a form of systematic review of literature in which the quantitative results of several studies are systemati-cally combined to generate more precise estimates of the effects under investigation, improve on the power of individual studies to detect effects, and to raise and discuss matters that may not have been evident in the individual studies. Of course, meta-analysis cannot correct for any defects that run throughout a literature (for example, the use of the potentially less valid outcome 'change in tumour size' rather than 'postponed death' as the outcome of a screening programme).

Meta-analyses are usually presented in the form of a forest plot. This is constructed as follows. The horizontal axis in the figure measures the treatment effect, for example the probability of death, so that to the left of the vertical axis death is less likely and to its right it is more likely. Where the vertical axis meets the horizontal corresponds to a probability of 1 (better outcomes are usually but not always to the left.) The line *ab* shows the result of a single research study. The solid square in the middle of the line is the point estimate of the mean effect in this study. This is a measure of the effect of the treatment compared to a control group and is most often represented as an *odds ratio*. The square is small or large depending on the weight this study is to be given in the combined analysis. The length of the line around the point estimate is the *confidence interval* for the result. When a study has only a few patients, the line will be long and the size of the square in its middle will be small.

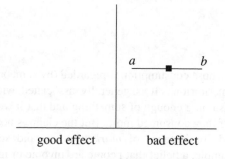

good effect   bad effect

Suppose there are two other studies, shown by the lines *cd* and *ef*. The study represented by *cd* shows the opposite effect to that in the previous study (in this study, the experimental group does better than the control) and the confidence interval is narrower and the weight this study receives will be

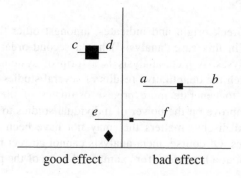

good effect   bad effect

larger. There is a third study also, which has relatively low *statistical significance* and a small weight. Taking all three together, the summary is represented by the diamond, whose height locates the best estimate of effect and whose width indicates its confidence interval. Its position relative to the vertical axis shows what the conclusion is, on balance, taking the whole literature (in this case a forest plot of three items) into account. If the diamond crosses the vertical line, the conclusion is that the literature as a whole does not yield a clear answer about the relative *effectiveness* of the procedure in question (conventionally at the 95 per cent confidence level).

MEWA

Acronym for *multiple employer welfare arrangement.*

MFF

Acronym for *market forces factor.*

Microeconomics

The economic study of individual units in society like persons, households and firms. Cf. *Macroeconomics.*

Mixed Economy

An economy in which the ownership of productive enterprises is variously private, charitable or public.

Mode

The most frequently occurring value of a single *variable* in a data set.

Modelling

Two broad kinds of modelling are done in health economics. One is the general kind employed throughout economics, which might be termed 'theoretical modelling', in which empirical characteristics are assumed (like *transitivity* of preferences) and general implications derived from an essentially analytical process of reasoning. The use of utility theory to model individual choices is a good example, from which is derived the implication that *demand curves* have a negative slope. The other is empirical modelling, where empirical relationships are postulated and interest focuses on simulating and quantifying the cause-and-effect relationships, elasticities and the like. Some modelling is relatively theory-free and is mainly concerned to forecast by the extrapolation of past trends, with due allowance for interaction between determining variables but without necessarily any prior notion of the nature of such interactions.

In health economics, modelling has assumed considerable importance in *cost–effectiveness analysis* (CEA) and related techniques. A distinction can be made between cohort modelling (where all modelled individuals share similar characteristics at the outset) and micropopulation simulation modelling (which can represent the mixed nature of real populations or communities).

Critical issues in modelling are that it should relate to relevant issues (for example, embody appropriate comparators), have an appropriate time horizon (for example, consequences should be modelled over a realistic time horizon), take a relevant *perspective* (for example, one relevant for decision makers), embody relevant outcomes (for example, final, not intermediate or surrogate), make realistic assumptions (for example, concerning adverse events) and have robust mathematical descriptions and appropriate modelling techniques (for example, use sensitivity analysis, discounting).

It is often necessary to construct an analytical framework within which to synthesize the available evidence in order to estimate both clinical effectiveness and cost-effectiveness. This framework will, in turn, usually require the development of a model. This may be a theoretical decision-analytic model using aggregated data or an empirical model using patient-level data.

Monopolistic Competition

A form of market in which sellers have to search out the best price for them. See *Competition, Price-searching.*

Monopoly

A market in which there is a single seller. See *Competition, Price-searching.*

Monopsony

A situation in which a resource user is sufficiently dominant in the market for the price of resources to be affected as this user's demand rises or falls. See *Competition*.

Monotonicity

The general property of a sequence of numbers that each successive number is greater than or equal (increasing monotonicity) or smaller than or equal (decreasing monotonicity) to its predecessor. The ordering is 'strong' if ties are not allowed. In economics, this property of choices generally means that if, x is preferred to y, then the *utility* of x > utility of y. In health economics, a special usage is that, if the health of one person increases, then the level of the community's health (or welfare) also increases (*ceteris paribus*). A weaker form of monotonicity requires only that the transformed entity does not fall, rather than that it should actually increase.

Monte-Carlo Simulation

A form of simulation, frequently used in *cost–effectiveness* and *cost–utility* analyses, in which random numbers drawn from a given probability *distribution* repeatedly stand for the values of uncertain *variables*. *Confidence limits* are placed on the most likely value after a large number of such *simulations*. Monte-Carlo simulation is named after Monte-Carlo, Monaco, where roulette wheels, dice, cards and slot machines replace the soberer games of economic modellers. See *Simulation*.

Moral Hazard

This is of two main types. *Ex ante* moral hazard refers to the effect that being insured has on behaviour, increasing the probability of the event insured against occurring. *Ex post* moral hazard derives from the price-*elasticity* of demand: being insured reduces the patient's price of care and hence leads to an increase in demand by insured persons. The basic economics of ex post moral hazard can be elucidated by considering the figure. The vertical axis shows the price of health care P (assumed – implausibly – to be set equal to *marginal cost*) and the *marginal value* placed upon health care consumption by an individual. The horizontal axis indicates the rate of consumption of

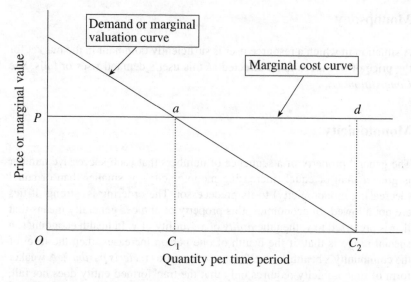

health care (so much per week, month and so on). The *demand curve*, or marginal value curve, is not perfectly inelastic, indicating that at lower prices more care (longer inpatient stays, for example) is demanded. The horizontal line is the (constant) *marginal cost* curve. In a world of no insurance, the individual faces a price OP at which OC_1 care will be consumed when ill. Let the individual (while healthy) consider buying insurance. Suppose neither the individual nor the insurer is in any doubt about the probability, p, of illness striking in any period (another tall order). Given that the insured, when uninsured, would consume $OP \times OC_1$, the actuarially *fair premium* (sometimes termed 'risk premium') is p times the cost of this amount of care. We assume also that there is zero *loading*: that is, the insurer adds nothing to the premium to cover the administrative costs of operating the insurance service. Now let the event insured against occur. Assuming that the premium payment has not had an effect on the individual's income sufficient to shift the demand curve, the amount demanded will now be OC_2: being insured reduces the price of consuming care to zero. Expenditure by the insurer will be $OPdC_2$, much larger than the amount upon which the premium was based. This is *ex post* moral hazard. It is held to be inefficient because the cost of producing C_1C_2 care is much larger than its value to the consumer: there is an *excess burden* or *deadweight loss*, or 'waste' of adC_2. However, before rushing to the conclusion that moral hazard must be controlled through *coinsurance*, *copayments* and other forms of rationing, it needs to be borne in mind that there may be reasons for wanting individuals to consume more care than, given their personal circumstances, they would normally choose (see, for example, *externality*). If such grounds exist, then a *second best* optimum may entail the need to do less to constrain demand (and even to encourage it further). Even more fundamentally, there may be reasons for entirely eschewing the idea that the demand curve reveals anything worth knowing about the value placed on health care. In that case, even if the behavioural account given of moral hazard may still stand, the ethical accusation of 'waste' entirely fails.

One behavioural effect of moral hazard in a market-based system is evidently to cause premiums to rise: in the example just considered, the increase in the premium is $p(C_1adC_2)$. Premiums thus reflect both the inherent element of risk (the fair premium) and the additional costs generated through moral hazard. This may be sufficient not only to cause the insured to withdraw from insurance and self-insure; it may, as in the figure, actually exceed the cost of purchasing out-of-pocket the original planned consumption of care at price P. The welfare effects of moral hazard ought thus to be considered in terms of its impact both on health care *utilization* and on the take-up of health care *insurance*.

Another form of moral hazard has been held to be the effect that being insured in public programmes like the US *Medicaid* has on savings: because Medicaid will pay for, say, the nursing home care of the elderly with few savings, the poor have a smaller incentive to save. As with other forms of moral hazard, one needs to ask, of course, whether the consequence is intended or unintended, desirable or undesirable. See *Market Failure*.

Morbidity

A synonym for illness, often proxied by a patient's contact with a physician and the resultant *diagnosis*. Morbidity rates are calculated in a manner similar to that for *mortality rates*, especially cause- (or disease-) specific mortality rates.

Mortality Rate

The crude mortality rate is often described as the total number of deaths per year divided by the population at mid-year times 1000 (that is number of deaths per 1000 person-years of observation). The age-specific mortality rate is the mortality rate for a specific age group (such as '65 years and older'). The sex-specific mortality rate is the mortality rate for males or females. The age- and sex-adjusted rates are weighted according to the proportion of each group in the population. The disease- or cause-specific mortality rate is the annual number of deaths from the particular disease divided by the mid-year population times 1000.

MOS-20

Derives from Medical Outcomes Study, a RAND project. Better known as *SF-20*.

MTU-FSIOS

See *Swiss Network for Health Technology Assessment*.

Multi-attribute Valuation

The method commonly used to calculate *quality-adjusted life-years*. It is multi-*attribute* by virtue of the essential concept ('health') being considered to be a function of several attributes (absence of pain might be one such). The valuation part relates to the process of combining and scaling the attributes using the principles of *utility* (or *expected utility*) theory. The measurements involved are usually derived from sample surveys or formal experiments involving groups of the public deemed to be relevant for the purposes of the study in question.

Multicollinearity

When two or more *independent variables* are very closely linearly related, they convey essentially the same information in *multiple regression* analysis. When this happens, the independent variables are said to be highly collinear and the phenomenon is called multicollinearity. If two or more variables are highly correlated, one is not likely to contribute significantly to the model in the presence of the other(s). Also spelled 'multicolinearity'.

Multilevel Modelling

The analysis of data that have a *hierarchical* structure.

Multinomial

Having the character of a polynomial, with a form like $y = a + bx + cx^2 + dx^3 + ex^4 + ...$, where a, b, c and so on are constants and x and y are variables.

Multinomial Logit Model

A statistical model for unordered *multinomial* outcomes.

Multiple Correlation

The correlation between a variable and more than one other variable. Cf. *Partial Correlation*.

Multiple Employer Welfare Arrangement

A US trust arrangement for self-funding a corporate group benefit plan covering medical and dental insurance and pensions. Generally MEWAs are created by small employers.

Multiple (Linear) Regression

A statistical technique based on an assumed *linear* relationship (that is, of the form $y = a + bx + cz + \ldots + \varepsilon$) between a *dependent variable* and a variety of explanatory or *independent variables*; ε (epsilon) is an error term generated by the fact that the independent variables are unlikely to account for all the changes in the dependent variable. The parameters a, b, c can be estimated by finding the line that best fits the data to the hypothetical linear structure. The *least-squares method* does this by minimizing the sum of squares of the vertical distances of each actual observation from the fitted line (assuming the dependent variable to be on the vertical axis). The coefficients give a quantitative account of the relationship between y and x. Thus, if $b = 7.4$, this means that a one-unit increase in x (any other variables constant) is associated with a 7.4 increase in the mean or expected value of y.

Multi-task Agency

The *agency relationship* in medicine is typically multi-task in nature (as is, for example, vividly revealed in physician fee schedules) and different methods of remuneration tend to produce different mixes of these various tasks and different mixes of quality. The optimum solution is elusive and methods of payment (such as *fee-for-service* or *capitation*) tend to be complemented by organizational, legal and social assumptions and values that reinforce the agency relationship.

Multivariate Analysis

An analysis in which there is more than one *independent variable*. Non-economists often reserve this term for systems that have multiple *dependent variables* and use 'multivariable' for the case of multiple independent variables.

Multivariate Sensitivity Analysis

A form of *sensitivity analysis* that allows for the possibility that factors affecting incremental cost–effectiveness ratios are not independent of one another. Same as *scenario analysis*.

Mutatis Mutandis

A Latin tag meaning 'making the necessary changes'. Allowing for the impact on a *variable* of indirect consequential changes which might otherwise have been ignored or assumed to be unimportant. So a cost curve might be constructed either on the assumption that the activity of the firm whose cost curve it is does not affect anything going on in the outside world (*ceteris paribus*) or on the assumption that it affects local wages and the behaviour of other local employers with those consequences (*mutatis mutandis*) built into the cost curve.

N

n-of-1 trials

A type of *clinical trial* in which the patient undergoes pairs of treatment periods such that one period involves the use of the experimental treatment and the other involves the use of an alternative. Treatment periods are replicated until the triallist is convinced that the treatments have different outcomes (or not, as the case may be).

NAS

Acronym for *new active substance*.

Nash Equilibrium

A concept used in *game theory* and, in particular, non-zero-sum games. A Nash *equilibrium* is a set of strategies such that no player can benefit by changing their strategy while the other players keep theirs unchanged. Named after John Nash, the mathematician and *game theorist* (b. 1928), he of the 'beautiful mind'.

National Coordinating Centre for Health Technology Assessment

The (England and Wales) centre through which the Health Technology Assessment Programmes of the government's Department of Health are coordinated. Its website is at www.ncchta.org/.

National Health Service

The common name given to the health care systems of the four countries in the United Kingdom (England, Wales, Scotland and Northern Ireland). Although broadly similar, there are variations in the administrative and managerial arrangements between them and in their funding levels.

National Income

Same as *net national product*.

National Institute for Health and Clinical Excellence

The Institute (NICE) is a statutory *National Health Service* (NHS) organization for England and Wales whose principal jobs are to identify and recommend
cost-effective health care technologies and develop authoritative *clinical guidelines* which include economic criteria. It also conducts confidential enquiries
into deaths of people in the care of the NHS. It is probably unique in living
up to the promise of its acronym. It acquired 'Health and' in its title in 2005
but its acronym remains NICE. Its web site is http://www.nice.org.uk/.

National Service Framework

This is a planning mechanism used in the UK *National Health Service* to set
national standards and define service models for a service or care group, to
put in place programmes to support implementation and to establish performance measures against which progress within agreed timescales can be
measured. They currently (2004) cover five key areas: cancer, coronary heart
disease, diabetes, mental health and older people.

National Tariff

A list of prices per *Healthcare Resource Group* used in *commissioning* health
care in the *internal market* of the English *National Health Service*.

Natural Rate of Unemployment

The rate of unemployment that is (just) consistent with a zero inflation rate.
Although there may be nothing 'natural' about it, it does appear to be determined by factors outside the conventional fiscal and monetary instruments of
government (for example, customary employer and trade union practices).
Deregulation and greater flexibility of working practices are argued to be some
means by which the natural rate might be reduced. Also sometimes called the
'non-accelerating inflation rate of unemployment' (NAIRU), which does not
carry the unfortunate implication of inevitability suggested by 'natural'.

NCCHTA

See *National Coordinating Centre for Health Technology Assessment.*

NCE

Synonym for *new chemical entity.*

NDA

Synonym for *new drug approval.*

Need

Arguably the most used and the least properly comprehended word in discussions of health. The meanings that attach to it are legion. Its persuasive power probably derives from a combination of two factors: one, the embodied implication that the entity asserted to be needed is actually necessary; the other, that this needed entity ought to be received. To elucidate what any particular writer may be getting at, it is often helpful to ask what the thing said to be needed is needed for and who is specifying that it is needed. From this one might enquire as to whether there are other means than the one asserted to be needed – especially ones that may be more effective, or more cost-effective – and whether the person specifying the need is appropriately qualified (for example, by training, accountability or responsibility). One may also enquire as to the social value, moral worth and so on of the *outcome* for which the thing said to be needed is necessary (if it is necessary). In this way, some analytical content might be injected into what otherwise is in danger of being mere slogan mongering.

It is invariably a good procedure to distinguish between a need for health and a need for health care (the latter may be seen as a kind of *derived demand* from the former). Important and difficult issues remain concerning, for example, whether any particular need ought to be met, whose need it is, and how much of it ought to be met. In prioritizing needs, economists naturally reach for the tools of *cost–effectiveness* and *cost–utility* analysis, which can indeed be helpful, not least in exposing the necessity for making *social value judgments* and interpersonal comparisons of health and illness.

The most frequently met practical measures of need at the community level are *morbidity* and *mortality* data. They plainly imply a need for health, though not necessarily a need for health care (which may not be effective in altering either for the better). Other concepts include *capacity to benefit* from health care (which is an outcome measure if the underlying thing needed is health care) and the resources that are necessary to reduce capacity to benefit to zero (that is, to the point at which the *marginal benefit* falls to zero). There are manifest formidable problems of measurement with both of these.

Need is often used as a criterion for adjusting the *distribution* of health care resources in the interests of *fairness* or *equity*. Again, its usefulness in this role would be much enhanced (in proportion to the reduction in its capacity to do harm) if the questions suggested above were probed.

Negative Predictive Value

Negative predictive value (PV–) is the proportion of individuals with negative test results who really do not have the disease being investigated. In the figure, $PV- = d/(c + d)$. Cf. *Positive Predictive Value, Sensitivity, Specificity.*

| | | Diagnosis | | |
		Present	Absent	Total
Test result	Present	a (true positive)	b (false positive)	$a + b$
	Absent	c (false negative)	d (true negative)	$c + d$
	Total	$a + c$	$b + d$	

Negative Rights Good

Opposite of *positive rights good.*

Negbin Model

An extension of the *Poisson regression model*. Short for 'negative binomial'. In this sort of model the *dependent variable* is in non-negative integers and its expectation is an exponential linear function of the *independent variables*.

The *variance* of the dependent variable is larger than the *mean*, in contrast to the Poisson model, where the variance equals the mean.

Neonatal

Concerning the first four weeks of life after birth.

Nephrology

The medical specialty concerned with diseases and abnormalities of the kidneys. Same as renal medicine.

Nested Case-control Study

Same as *cohort case-control study*.

Net Exports

A national income accounting term: the difference between the value of exports and imports in a time period (usually a year).

Net Investment

A national income accounting term: it is *gross investment* less *depreciation*. See *Investment*.

Net National Product

A national income accounting term: it is Gross National Product less *depreciation* (or *capital* consumption). This is the entity commonly referred to as 'national income' even though it is computed from the output side of the economy. But NNP can also be computed by adding up the incomes accruing to residents of a jurisdiction in a period and allowing for depreciation: incomes from employment, self-employment, profits (including interest and dividends) and rents. Adding net property income from abroad yields Net National Product at *factor cost*.

Net Present Value

The *discounted* value of the differences over time between monetary costs and benefits in each period.

Network Externality

See *External Effects*.

Neumann–Morgenstern Independence

This is an assumption of *expected utility theory* that means, roughly speaking, that adding the same third lottery to two lotteries, whose ranking has already been determined, will not affect that ranking.

Neurology

The science of nerve systems.

New Active Substance

A pharmaceutical or similar product that was not on the market in the European Union before a specified date.

New Chemical Entity

A new chemical entity is a drug containing no active molecule or ion that has previously been approved by a regulatory authority.

New Drug Approval

The term applied to approval by the US Food and Drug Administration of a new drug for inter-state sale.

NHP

Acronym for *Nottingham health profile*.

NICE

Acronym for *National Institute for Health and Clinical Excellence*.

NND

Acronym for *number needed to diagnose*.

NNT

Acronym for *number needed to treat*.

Nominal Income

Income that has not been adjusted for changes in the (usually intertemporal) general price level (inflation). Cf. *Real Income*.

Nominal Price

A monetary price that is not adjusted for changes in the (usually intertemporal) general price level (inflation). Cf. *Real Price*.

Nominal Variable

A *categorical variable* for which there is no natural ordering.

Nomogram

A two-dimensional diagram (sometimes a table) designed to allow the approximate graphical computation of one value given values for another. Its accuracy is limited by the precision with which physical markings can be drawn, reproduced, viewed and aligned. See *Altman's Nomogram*.

Non-cooperative Game

A type of game in *game theory* in which the players may not cooperate in deciding what each will do. Cf. *Cooperative Game*.

Non-diversifiable Intertemporal Risk

A risk in providing private long-term *insurance* is that future costs may be far off in time and may be substantially higher than now. This may be held to account for the fact that most insurance policies offer *indemnity* benefits rather than benefits in kind.

Non-ignorable Non-response

A problem with some survey instruments when non-responders may differ from responders in relevant ways. See *Incomplete Data*.

Non-marketed Good

This is a good that is not traded in any market. In health economics the principal good of this type is *health* itself. The absence of observed prices (even imperfect ones) and even the absence of straightforward quantities requires the imputation of *shadow prices* and indirect ways of measuring the entity (health) of interest.

Non-parametric Methods

Non-parametric statistical methods do not assume any particular family of *distribution* (for example, that the distribution is *normal* or that it is defined by mean and standard deviation, and so do not estimate any *parameters* for such a distribution).

Non-profit

Organizations whose objective is assumed to be other than profit. Any trading surplus is not available for distribution to owners (or 'trustees'). In economics, it is nonetheless usually assumed that hospitals maximize something (like the utility of managers, or that of the senior doctors who work in them). It is a characteristic of health care that is sometimes (as in Canada) required by statute. See *Hospital Economics*.

Non-satiation

One of the axioms of choice theory. It means that if, for any amount of a good or service, more is preferred to less, then more will be preferred to less also at all larger amounts of that good or service. See *Utility*.

Normal Distribution

A probability *distribution* with one *mode*, having the symmetrical shape of a bell. Also known as a *Gaussian distribution*. It is characterized by two *parameters*: the *mean* and the *standard deviation*, with 67 per cent of values lying within one standard deviation on either side of the mean. See *Distribution*.

Normal Good

A good for which a change in income causes a change in demand in the same direction. The income-*elasticity* of demand is positive. This is probably the only sense in which health care can be regarded as a 'normal' good. Cf. *Inferior Good*.

Normative

The adjective is usually taken to mean 'containing one or more social value judgments' and hence implying a 'norm' or standard that ought to be aimed at. *Welfare economics* is entirely concerned with normative matters. It is to be compared with *positive economics*. Positive economics is, however, sometimes used as a kind of Trojan horse for the introduction of implicit social value judgments, as when all varieties of implicitly good or bad things are linked with the operation of 'the market'. See *Interpersonal Comparisons of Utility, Logical Positivism, Welfare*.

Norwegian Centre for Health Technology Assessment

The Norwegian Centre for Health Technology Assessment critically reviews the scientific basis for methods used in health care and evaluates their costs, risks and benefits. Their web site is at www.sintef.no/smm/News/FramesetNews.htm.

Nosocomial

Occurring in a hospital, as in 'nosocomial infection'. Hospital-acquired disease. Cf. *Iatrogenesis*.

Nosology

The art of producing taxonomies of diseases, for example, by *aetiology*, *pathogenesis* or *symptoms*.

Notifiable Disease

A disease, usually infectious or contagious, whose occurrence is required by law to be made known to a health officer or government authority.

Nottingham Health Profile

A profile approach to *health status* measurement covering physical mobility, pain, social isolation, emotional reactions, energy and sleep.

NPV

Acronym for *net present value*.

NSAID

An acronym for non-steroidal anti-inflammatory drug.

Nuclear Medicine

Same as *radiology*.

Null Hypothesis

The prediction that there is no 'effect' or that the theory being tested is not 'true'.

Number Needed to Diagnose

Number needed to diagnose = $1/[Sensitivity - (1 - Specificity)]$.

Number Needed to Treat

The number of patients needed to be treated with a particular therapy in order to prevent one additional bad outcome. Often referred to as NNT. The reciprocal of the *absolute risk reduction* ($NNT = 1/ARR$). Suppose an existing procedure entails a risk of an adverse effect of 0.005, while an alternative has a risk of 0.004; then $ARR = 0.001$ and $NNT = 100$. Switching from the former to the latter procedure yields an expected reduction of one adverse event in every 100 cases.

O

Objective Function

A function that is to be maximized (or minimized) with respect to choice variables of interest (like 'health') and subject to whatever constraints (like 'resources') may apply.

Objectives

The aims or end-states that are sought in health systems or parts of systems. They may be cast in rather general forms such as 'to maximize *utility*' or more specifically in terms of directly measurable achievement (for example, number of patients successfully discharged). Useful statements of objectives are normally cast in terms of *outputs* to be achieved or net *benefits* to be maximized. A characteristic of most planning systems is that objectives are stated, with dates set for their accomplishment, and methods of monitoring progress identified.

Observational Bias

Same as *information bias*.

Observational Cohort Study

Same as *prospective cohort study*. See also *Observational Study*.

Observational Study

Studies that depend merely on observing 'what is' without observer intervention, say, in the form of creating *controls* or *blinding* or *randomizing*. Causal relationships may be hypothesized and tested empirically using data from such studies. The great majority of empirical economics is of this kind.

Observer Bias

A form of *bias* arising from lack of objectivity in those who are recording or measuring subjects' responses in *clinical trials* or social surveys. The cure for this disease is *blinding* (single or, preferably, double).

Obstetrics and Gynaecology

The medical and surgical specialties concerned with midwifery, childbirth (obstetrics) and the reproductive health of girls and women (gynaecology – also spelled gynecology).

Odds Ratio

The ratio of two probabilities. In *case-control* studies it is an estimate of the *relative risk*. The ratio of the probability, for example, of having a disease in a population exposed to certain *risk factors* and the probability of having that disease in another population not so exposed, or the probability that one treatment is more *effective* than another. It is calculated thus: the number of individuals with disease who were exposed to a risk factor (D_e) over those with disease who were not exposed (D_n) divided by those without disease who were exposed (H_e) over those without who were not exposed (H_n). Thus $OR = (D_e/D_n)/(H_e/H_n) = D_eH_n/D_nH_e$.

OECD

Acronym for *Organisation for Economic Cooperation and Development*.

Office of Health Economics

A group of health economists based in London, England, which provides independent research, advisory and consultancy services on policy implications and economic issues within the pharmaceutical, health care and biotechnology sectors. It is funded primarily by the British pharmaceutical industry but has independent policy and editorial boards. Its web address is www.ohe.org.

Official Financing

A component of the *balance of payments*.

OHE

Acronym for *Office of Health Economics*.

Oligopoly

A market with few sellers, whose interaction may involve mutually dependent strategies and tactics. See *Competition*.

OLS

Acronym for *ordinary least squares*.

Omitted Variable Bias

The difference between the expected value of an estimator and the true value of the underlying parameter due to failure to control for a relevant explanatory variable or variables. It is sometimes possible to assess the direction of the bias by using common sense. For example, if a regression of hospital costs finds that the cost per patient episode is higher in teaching hospitals than in non-teaching hospitals, the inference that teaching hospitals are less *cost-effective* than non-teaching hospitals is likely to be false because their costs are in reality increased by the presence of teaching, a variable for which was omitted. So the bias is clear. It is probably better on the whole to err on the side of including the wrong variables than to omit the right ones.

Oncology

The specialty of medicine concerning the diagnosis and treatment of cancer.

One-tailed Test

A statistical significance test based on the assumption that there is *a priori* information that specifies the direction of any departure from the null hypothesis if it is untrue. Cf. *Two-tailed Test*.

Open Cohort Study

This is a *cohort study* in which the subjects are recruited and enrolled via a procedure that allows for in and out migration of people. Cf. *Fixed Cohort Study*.

Open-ended Questionnaire

An interview schedule or questionnaire that does not restrict the respondent to a specific set of predetermined answers but allows answers to be freely determined. Cf. *Closed-ended Questionnaire*.

Ophthalmology

The medical specialty concerned with diseases and abnormalities of the eyes. The word is usually pronounced as though the first 'h' were not there.

Opportunity Cost

Economists use the word 'cost' in a particular way that differs from everyday usage and also from accounting concepts of cost. Cost, in economics, is opportunity cost. Opportunity cost is the value of a resource in its most highly valued alternative use. In a world of competitive markets, in which all goods are traded and where there are no market imperfections, opportunity cost is revealed by the market prices of resources. Where these stringent conditions are not met, opportunity cost and market prices can diverge and *shadow prices* may be estimated to measure the former.

Identification of opportunity cost is a skilled art that can be applied only in the context of a particular decision which enables one to identify the consequences of alternative courses of action. In general, opportunity cost cannot be defined independently of the context in which the term is being used. There are, perhaps, two main reasons for this. First, if the context is, as it frequently is, one of decision making, then the cost of a decision will depend upon such factors as the period of time over which the decision is believed to have consequences, which may either go well beyond a conventional accounting period (for example, when one decides to add a particular drug to a reimbursement tariff for the indefinite future) or fall short of it (for example, as when one wishes to know the cost of acquiring – as distinct from owning and operating – an item of equipment). Secondly, one must ask 'cost to whom?', for example whether the resource-using consequences of a decision are to be seen as limited to the decision maker alone, or to affect a wider set of parties.

At best, market prices can reveal the opportunity cost of resources in their most highly valued uses to people other than the decision taker in question. They do this by showing what the decision maker must pay to bid resources away from others. The opportunity cost of using resources one already owns is not usually revealed in market prices since the best alternative may be an alternative use in one's own organization (unless there is an *internal market*). In such cases, opportunity costs need to be elicited by discussion and judgment, and may not be readily put in monetary terms. Opportunity costs should not be confused with *transfer payments*. Cf. *Opportunity Loss*.

Opportunity Loss

The most highly valued use of resources. It is used especially in the context of decision making under *uncertainty*, when the value attributed to obtaining additional information depends on the opportunities thereby created. Note that *opportunity cost* relates to the most highly valued alternative use of resources. See *Expected-value-of-information*.

Optimism Bias

This is the tendency to be too optimistic in appraising the outcomes of projects or options. Enthusiasm can, in general, be a dangerous attribute in a scientist, especially enthusiasm concerning particular results (for example, results that may support a position to which one has previously committed oneself). See *Bias*.

Optimum

Usually defined in economics as a *Pareto optimum*.

Option Appraisal

This is the use of *cost–benefit analysis* or *cost–effectiveness analysis* and related techniques to assess the desirability of one option relative to another and to help decision makers understand the critical differences between options and to select their preferred one.

Option Value

Option value is the value of the availability of an option at some future date, even if it is not used directly. Its availability for use is the thing valued. For example, the mere availability of a local hospital might be valued even if one had no plan to use it and no expectation of ever having to.

Ordered Probit Model

A statistical model of ordered *multinomial outcomes*.

Ordinal Scale

This is a numerical measure of a *variable* in which the function of the numbers is no more than to indicate the order of the observations (for example, in order of size). See *Utility*.

Ordinal Utility

A numerical indicator/predictor of choice whose particular characteristic is that the entities amongst which one may choose are simply put in order, those that are 'more preferred' receiving a higher number. A 'strong' order is one that does not allow ties; otherwise the order is 'weak'. See *Utility*.

Ordinary Least Squares Regression

This is the standard statistical method of estimating the *linear regression model*. Its essence is finding *parameter* values that minimize the sum of squared *residuals*.

Ordinate

The vertical axis in a two-dimensional diagram commonly referred to as the *y*-axis, or a point on that axis. Cf. *Abscissa*.

Oregon Experiment

In 1989, the US state of Oregon initiated a controversial reform of its *Medicaid* programme by simultaneously increasing the number of people it covered but reducing the number of services that were insured. The services included were to be based on an explicitly prioritized list. The scheme was introduced in 1994, having gained federal approval from the *Health Care Financing Administration*.

Prioritized list

Line 1	Diagnosis: severe/moderate head injury, haematoma or oedema with loss of consciousness Treatment: medical and surgical
Line 2	Diagnosis: insulin-dependent diabetes mellitus Treatment: medical
Line 3	Diagnosis: peritonitis Treatment: medical and surgical
Line 4	Diagnosis: acute glomerulonephritis, with lesion of rapidly progressive glomerulonephritis Treatment: medical therapy including dialysis
Line 5	Diagnosis: pneumothorax and haemothorax Treatment: tube thoracostomy or thoracotomy, medical therapy
Line 576	Diagnosis: internal derangement of the knee and ligamentous disruptions of the knee Treatment: repair, medical therapy
Line 577	Diagnosis: keratoconjunctivitis sicca, not specified as Sjögren's syndrome Treatment: punctal occlusion, tarsorrhaphy
Line 578	Diagnosis: noncervical warts Treatment: medical therapy
Line 579	Diagnosis: anal fistula Treatment: fistulectomy
Line 580	Diagnosis: relaxed anal sphincter Treatment; medical and surgical

A Health Services Commission developed a prioritized list of paired *diagnoses* and treatments. The process entailed much public consultation and many focus groups. Criteria such as the probability of death or disability with and without treatment were used in ranking procedures. The list of approved diagnoses/procedures was subjected to sensitivity analysis and eventually had 745 items (in 1995) of which the top five and borderline five at the cut-off point of 578 are in the table.

The creation of this list represents one of the world's most significant excursions into explicit '*rationing*' of health care. Despite its many imperfections, and although *cost-effectiveness* was not an explicit criterion, there would probably be widespread agreement that treatments above the line are more *cost-effective* than ones below it and that the ones ranked highest are properly so ranked.

Original Position

A vantage point from which to evaluate the justice of various states of the world in *Rawlsian* theory. See *Fairness*.

Orphan Drug

A drug developed for rare diseases and conditions which, in the USA, affect fewer than 200 000 people or, in the European Union, affect five or fewer per 10 000 people.

Orthopaedics

The surgical specialty concerned with the correction of deformities of and damage to bones. Also spelled 'orthopedics'.

Orthotics

The specialty of making and fitting devices (orthoses) to correct or stabilize malformed or weak body parts.

Osteopathy

The treatment of disease through the manipulation of bones.

OTC

Acronym for *over-the-counter drugs*.

Otolaryngology

The surgical specialty concerning diseases of the ears and throat.

Otorhinolaryngology

The surgical specialty concerning diseases of the ears, nose and throat. Same as 'ENT'.

Outcome

This is another term for *output*. It tends to be used in preference to output when the effects in question are not quantitative or when they are characteristics of people, such as their ability to perform activities of daily living, or changes in such characteristics.

Outcomes Programme

This is a *managed health care* plan that includes the collection and analysis of information about the results of prescribed treatments and procedures. An outcome is usually defined as the patient's change in health status at a particular time following treatment. Surveys of patient satisfaction are sometimes included in the data. The information is used by the plan to determine the most *cost-effective* treatments of specific health conditions and to reduce unnecessary medical interventions.

Outlier

An observation that lies outside the range of most of the observations in a *distribution*.

Out-of-network Services

These are services by US health care providers who are not employed by or under contract with a *managed care* plan. Some plans require care to be provided only by doctors approved by the plan and some allow a member to see physicians outside the plan subject to *deductibles* or *coinsurance payments*. Emergency medical care outside the geographic area of a benefit plan is not considered out-of-network, but is usually specifically covered. See *In-area Emergency Services*.

Output

The effects produced by production. Changes in *health status* are the ultimate output of the health service *production function*. However sometimes more proximate throughput measures are used, such as 'patients discharged'. In general, the use of inputs as measures of output is not recommended since the practice begs the question as to the nature and amount of output (if any) that the inputs may generate, particularly at the margin, by assuming essentially that there is a one-to-one correspondence between input and output. Cf. *Outcome*.

Output Budgeting

A method of presenting allocated sums of money in an organization according to the *outputs* or *objectives* that the resources are directed towards. It is in distinction from traditional budgets that focus on *input* classifications like 'wages and salaries', '*capital* expenditure' or 'equipment'. Ideally output budgeting transcends the boundaries of particular agencies, so that a complete picture of the resources devoted to a particular end is obtained. In health care, outputs might relate to intermediate process outcomes like patient discharges from hospital or the number of *finished consultant episodes*. Cf. *Programme Budgeting*.

Overhead Costs

These are *opportunity costs* resulting from resource use that serves a variety of programmes, departments or activities. They pose a 'problem' in any organization if one is interested in discovering the *total cost* of a particular programme, department and so on for the evident reason that they have not been incurred only for the sake of that particular programme or department. Any *marginal* impact on overhead costs arising from a change in the rate of any of the specific activities they support poses less of an intellectual challenge of attribution, though the practical challenges may be considerable.

Over-the-counter Drugs

Drugs that may be purchased without a doctor's *prescription* and from a wider range of suppliers than registered pharmacists. Also known as 'proprietary drugs'.

Overutilization

Too much (somehow defined) use of something. It is not a technical term in economics. See *Utilization*.

P

Paasche Price Index

The Paasche index compares the cost of purchasing the current basket of goods and services with the cost of purchasing the same basket in an earlier period. It is an index number in which prices are weighted by current quantities:

$$P_P = \sum P_n Q_n / \sum P_0 Q_n$$

where P_P is the Paasche price index, P_n is the price per unit in period n and Q_n is the quantity produced in period n. Named after the German economist Hermann Paasche (1851–1925). Cf. *Laspeyres Price Index*.

Paediatrics

The medical specialty concerned with diseases of children. (Also spelled pediatrics.)

Paired Comparison

An experimental method in which raters compare two states of health at the same time and record one as 'better' than the other. An *interval scale* can be derived using this method and *Thurstone's Law of Comparative Judgment*.

Pairwise Comparison

A method of eliciting people's preferences for various characteristics of health services. It proceeds through survey instruments that ask subjects to make such (pairwise) comparisons as whether they prefer a *general practitioner's* surgery to have longer opening times combined with a night time deputizing service or shorter daytime opening combined with the general practitioners taking their own out-of-hours calls. See *Conjoint Analysis*.

Palliative Care

Palliative care is mainly directed at providing relief to terminally-ill people through symptom and pain management. The goal is not to cure, but to provide comfort and emotional ease and to maintain the highest possible quality of life for as long as life remains. Also known as 'comfort care'.

Pandemic

An *epidemic* that is geographically widely dispersed.

Panel

A group of respondents in a survey. As a member of such a panel, each may take part in several surveys or events over the course of a year or sequence of years.

Panel Data

Survey data in which each respondent has been observed several times.

Parallel Export

An outward flow of goods in *parallel trade*.

Parallel Group

A design feature of some *clinical trials* in which the treatment being investigated and the *control* are applied simultaneously to two separate groups of subjects. This is different from a crossover design where each subject gets the treatment and then the control (or the control and then the treatment) in sequence. Cf. *Crossover Design*.

Parallel Import

An inward flow of goods in *parallel trade*.

Parallel Trade

A kind of *arbitrage* in which drugs are imported without the manufacturer's consent into a jurisdiction from a market having lower prices. Since drug prices are regulated in most countries, parallel trading is unlikely, however, to produce the usual implication of arbitrage – the emergence of a single (or close to single) price for each product overcoming inefficiencies arising from uncompetitive practices – because the price differentials reflect efforts to earn a return on research and development (R&D) investment rather than differences in production costs. Parallel trade, though legal in some jurisdictions (for example within the EU), is bitterly opposed by the pharmaceutical industry because it undermines the value of a patented product and because it effectively imports the results of other countries' regulatory schemes. It is not clear that parallel trade redounds particularly to the benefit of consumers or third party payers, as distinct from that of the parallel traders.

Parameter

Parameters do not relate to the actual measurements or *attributes* of a *variable* but are quantities that define a theoretical model. For example, the coefficients on the input variables in a *production function* are parameters, as are the *mean* and *standard deviation* of a theoretical *distribution* which might be used to characterize an empirical distribution having the same estimated mean and standard deviation. The intercept and slope of a simple *regression* line (the regression coefficients) are likewise (like error variance) parameters of the regression model.

Parameters can also be values that are altered to see what happens in a model or a system. For example, the construction of a *partial equilibrium demand curve* normally assumes constant real income but it is often interesting to ask what happens if real income changes. In doing this one is effectively treating real income as a parameter rather than a value in an observed data set. The *cost-effectiveness* of a screening programme will depend on, amongst other things, the *sensitivity* and *specificity* of the screening test. In assuming different values for them in order to discover the consequences for cost-effectiveness, one is treating them parametrically. The term 'parameter' is often misused by, for example, being confused with *variable* or, even more vulgarly, with 'perimeter', as in the awful phrase 'within these parameters'.

Parameter Estimation by Sequential Testing

PEST is a method for eliciting responses from subjects in experimental situations, for example, when measuring *quality-adjusted life-years*.

Parametric Test

A test that makes particular assumptions about *distributions*.

Pareto Efficiency

A state of the world in which no one can have their welfare (as they see it) improved without someone else having their welfare (as they see it) reduced. See *Efficiency*, *Pareto Optimality*.

Pareto Improvement

A change such that at least one person is better off (as judged by them) and no one is worse off (as judged by them). See *Pareto Optimality*.

Pareto Optimality

An allocation of resources such that no one can be made better off without at least one other person being made worse off. In both cases, being better off or worse off is judged from the viewpoints of the individuals in question. Its attraction to economists is threefold: (a) it does not require the direct comparison of individuals' *utilities*; (b) it is readily applicable to market transactions, where compensation takes place as a matter of course, usually in monetary form; (c) it seems to be relatively uncontroversial; after all, if anyone who could conceivably object to a proposed change is adequately compensated (as they see things), then who could – or ought to – possibly object? This gives away the implicit liberal political underpinning of the Paretian approach, which is an attraction to some and unappealing to others.

The Paretian approach is not able to categorize changes as desirable or undesirable when some have uncompensated losses. It is a vulgar error to infer from this that the Pareto criterion rules such changes out. It does not; it is simply silent about them. It is also silent about changes whose purpose is to affect the *distribution* of income, or health (or utilities). It is, in fact, silent on quite a lot of important issues.

Economists have amused themselves (probably not anyone else) by considering awkward cases, like the negotiations that might be successfully concluded between a masochist and a sadist and how they can be regarded in terms of welfare enhancement. They have also examined the situation when transfers of income, otherwise not evaluatable in Paretian terms, are themselves sources of utility (for example to charitably inclined people). The approach is named after Vilfredo Pareto (1848–1923), the Italian economist who was a leader of the Lausanne School of Economics. See *Efficiency, Extra-welfarism, Interpersonal Comparisons of Utility, Pareto Improvement, Welfare Economics*.

Pareto Optimum

A state of the world in which no one can have their welfare (as they see it) improved without someone else having their welfare (as they see it) reduced. Same as *Pareto efficiency*. See *Pareto Improvement, Efficiency*.

Pareto-preferred Move

Same as a *Pareto improvement*.

Partial Correlation

The correlation between two variables controlling for any interaction they may have with other specified variables. Cf. *Multiple Correlation*.

Partial Equilibrium

The 'partial' element in this term refers to a theoretical ploy used in economics to simplify analysis by focusing on the principal relationships and setting aside feedback effects and other effects deemed to be non-central, even at the price of some compromise in logical coherence. '*Equilibrium*' refers to the solution of a set of simultaneous equations, some of which describe behavioural reactions to *parameter* changes. Thus a simple demand and supply analysis might posit a linear demand function, supply function and equilibrium condition:

$$D = a - bP$$

$$S = c + dP$$

$$D = S.$$

The equilibrium price is thus $(a - c)/(d + b)$. All else is held constant (*ceteris paribus*) notwithstanding the fact that a change in price will affect the purchasing power of money income (so *real income* is NOT constant and the good may have a positive or *negative income-elasticity*) and that a change in S might affect the demand for labour and hence a person's income (so money income is not constant either). Absence of side-effects such as these can be regarded as stipulations for the circumstances under which the theory in question is applicable (that is, when the impact of a price change on income is likely to be minute because, say, the good whose demand is being investigated occupies a minute fraction of an individual's expenditure). When this is not sustainable a *general equilibrium* approach must be taken, or at least one that explicitly takes account of the consequential effects of any initial disturbance to equilibrium. See *Nash Equilibrium*.

Partial Equilibrium Theory

Classic demand-and-supply analysis in which each market is treated in isolation from all others. Cf. *General Equilibrium Theory*. See *Partial Equilibrium*.

Partworth Utility

The partworth is the element of the *utility* of a service that attaches to a particular *attribute*. See *Conjoint Analysis*.

Patent

A patent for an invention is a territorial *intellectual property right* granted by an official agency of the government to the inventor, giving the inventor the right for a limited period to stop others from making, using or selling the invention without the permission of the inventor. It is a temporary monopoly. When a patent is granted, the invention becomes the property of the inventor, which – like any other form of property or business asset – can be bought, sold, rented or hired. Patent laws exist in order to reward, and hence encourage, innovation and invention. They have been particularly important for the pharmaceutical industry.

Patent protection is usually for 20 years from the date the patent application was filed. The practical life of most pharmaceutical patents is much shorter than this because it takes many years to bring a product to market, satisfy safety and *efficacy* regulatory agencies and to negotiate prices. Seven to ten years may be a realistic effective patent life over which a product must recoup its development costs (and those of other 'failed' products). Some countries permit extensions to a patent's term for a further term, usually to compensate patentees for delays in securing approval to market a drug.

Some countries allow the production, sale or use of a patented product, without the patent owner's permission, for the purposes of obtaining permission to market the product. Such an exception to patent rights (sometimes known as 'springboarding') is intended to allow generic drugs to enter the market as soon as possible after the patent on the drug expires.

Pathogenesis

The postulated pathway through which an organism (pathogen) such as a bacterium or virus produces disease.

Pathology

The science of diseases of the body. It is also used to characterize the symptoms of a disease.

Payment by Results

This has a special connotation in the National Health Service of England, where it refers to the system, introduced in 2002, of financial controls and rewards through which the central ministry influences providers throughout the care delivery service. Providers are paid for the activity they actually deliver. *Commissioners* will have sufficient funding to look for alternative providers if agreed activity levels are not met. Primary Care Trusts will commission the volume of activity required to deliver service priorities, adjusted for case-mix from a range of providers using standard *national tariffs* for *Healthcare Resource Groups*. The tariff is adjusted for regional variation in wages and other costs of service delivery using a nationally determined formula.

PBAC

Acronym for *Pharmaceutical Benefits Advisory Committee.*

PBI

Acronym for *Pharmaceutical Benefits Scheme.*

Percentile

Same as *centile.* See *Quantile.*

Performance Bias

A form of *bias* in *clinical trials* arising from the use of interventions that are not a formal part of the trial.

Perinatal

The period between the 28th week of pregnancy and the end of the first week of life.

Permanent Income

The regular *annuity* for an individual or organization whose present value equals the *wealth* of the individual or organization. It is used in economics as an alternative to current income on the grounds that people are more likely to consume, save and so on in relation to permanent income than to transitory income which may have substantial ups and downs.

Person Trade-off Method

Originally called the 'Equivalence of Numbers' method of creating a 'Quality of Well-Being' scale, this is a method of assigning utilities to health states that works as follows: subjects are asked a question of the following kind: 'If x people have health state A (described) and y have health B, and if you can only help (cure) one group, which group would you choose?' One of the numbers x or y is then varied until the subject finds the two groups equally deserving of their vote. The undesirability (disutility) of situation B is x/y times as great as that of situation A and this ratio provides the index of the utility of one state relative to the other. See also *Standard Gamble, Time Trade-off Method*.

Perspective

The 'viewpoint' adopted for the purposes of an *economic appraisal (cost–effectiveness, cost–utility* studies and so on) which defines the scope and character of the *costs* and *benefits* to be examined, as well as other critical features, which may be *social value-judgmental* in nature, such as *the rate of discount*. The perspective may be set by a client or determined by the analyst. Most textbooks advocate the use of the social (or 'societal') perspective, according to which all potential costs and benefits are to be included regardless of who bears or receives them. However this is merely a value judgment of the authors that the conscientious investigator need feel no scruple in ignoring. It has the virtue of inclusivity but the vice of demanding much work that may be irrelevant in particular circumstances. It also has the more dangerous vice of encouraging a belief that a single perspective, whether inclusive or exclusive, is the appropriate way to perform such analyses. In some cases, particularly where the potential clients for a study are heterogeneous in their interests and values, it may be desirable to adopt more than one perspective (for example, the perspective of workers and employers is likely to differ concerning the cost-effectiveness of health and safety practices in the workplace). Distributional issues, such as the weights to be attached to health gains accruing or denied to different sorts of people (old/young, fit/ill, geographical location and so on) ought in principle to be settled within any discussion of perspective, but they rarely are. For two contrasting views on perspective, see Marthe R. Gold, Joanna E. Siegel, Louise B. Russell and Milton C. Weinstein (eds) (1996), 'Appendix A: Summary Recommendations', in *Cost-Effectiveness in Health and Medicine*, New York and Oxford: Oxford University Press; chapter 5 in National Institute for Clinical Excellence (2004), *Guide to the Methods of Technology Appraisal*, London: NICE.

PEST

Acronym for *parameter estimation by sequential testing*.

PHARMAC

See *Pharmaceutical Management Agency.*

Pharmaceutical Benefits Advisory Committee

An Australian statutory body that makes recommendations and gives advice to the Minister of Health about which drugs and medicinal preparations should be made available as pharmaceutical benefits. No new drug may be made available as a pharmaceutical benefit unless the Committee has so recommended. The Committee is required by the Act to consider the *effectiveness* and cost of a proposed benefit compared to alternative therapies (not just *placebo*).

Pharmaceutical Benefits Scheme

The Australian public support system for subsidizing approved prescription drugs. Its web site is http://www.health.gov.au/pbs/. See *Pharmaceutical Benefits Advisory Committee.*

Pharmaceutical Management Agency

An agency of the New Zealand government that conducts *economic appraisals* of drugs, maintains a list of approved subsidized drugs and manages the purchasing of hospital pharmaceuticals. Its web address is http://www.govt.nz/urn.php?id=2%7C140.

Pharmaceutical Price Regulation Scheme ·

The Pharmaceutical Price Regulation Scheme (PPRS) regulates the overall profitability of pharmaceutical companies with sales of branded prescribed medicines to the *National Health Service* in the UK. Its objects are to secure the provision of safe and effective medicines for the NHS at 'reasonable' prices; promote a strong and profitable pharmaceutical industry capable of sustained research and development; and encourage the efficient supply of medicines to pharmaceutical markets in the UK and elswhere. It operates through negotiation based on companies' financial records and regulates both the return on *capital* (usually restricted to a range pre-tax of 17–21 per cent on assets) and prices. It allows freedom of pricing for all new chemical entities, requires companies to seek permission for any price increases (which have to meet particular criteria), requires companies with NHS sales in excess of £25 million per annum to submit data on sales, costs, assets and profitability and to repay any excess profits over an agreed return on capital. Its web site is at: http://www.dh.gov.uk/PolicyAndGuidance/MedicinesPharmacyAndIndustry/ PharmaceuticalPriceRegulationScheme/fs/en.

Pharmacoeconomics

The economics of drugs (*cost–effectiveness* and *cost–utility analysis* of their effects) and of the pharmaceutical industry.

Pharmacology

The science of the action and/or mechanism of action of drugs on living tissue.

Phases in Clinical Trials

Clinical trials on humans are conducted in phases, prior to which tests on animals for toxicity will have been completed. Each phase has a different purpose. In Phase I trials, researchers test a new drug or treatment in a small group of healthy people (usually less than 100) for the first time to evaluate its safety, determine a safe dosage range and identify side-effects. In Phase II trials, the treatment is given to a larger group of people (100+) with the disease to see if it is effective and to further evaluate its safety. In Phase III trials, the treatment is given to large groups of people (1000–3000) preferably in *double-blind* trials (sometimes multi-centre) to confirm *effectiveness*, monitor side-effects, compare it to commonly used treatments and collect information that will allow the drug or treatment to be used safely. There are also Phase IV trials: postmarketing studies yielding additional information about the drug's risks, benefits and optimal use. Cf. *Postmarketing Surveillance*.

Physiatry

Same as *rehabilitation medicine*, comprising such specialties as occupational therapy, physical therapy, speech therapy, audiology, prosthetics and orthotics.

Physician Behaviour

Doctors' behaviour is usually assumed by economists to be *utility-maximizing* behaviour in which the main arguments of the *utility function* are personal wealth, personal status (professional and social) and patient welfare/health. The weights attaching to these seem to be highly variable. More in the tradition of *satisficing* theory, some theories posit a target income. Some models have boldly assumed that the medical profession seeks to operate as a wealth-maximizing *price-discriminating monopoly*, and some professional behaviour in some jurisdictions seems consistent with this idea.

Physician Extender

While there is no precise or universally agreed definition of the scope of a physician extender's work, the term always refers to an advanced registered nurse practitioner or a physician assistant whose skills have been enhanced by an appropriate course of training. The idea is to substitute some of the extender for some of the physician.

Physician-induced Demand

Same as supplier-induced demand.

Physiology

The science of the functions of living organisms and their various parts.

Physiotherapy

The use of physical exercise, massage and manipulation for the prevention and treatment of stress or trauma.

Piechart

A figure showing the *distribution* of a non-continuous *variable* (such as social class) in which the size of the slice for each indicated value is proportional to the relative frequency of observations in that category of the variable.

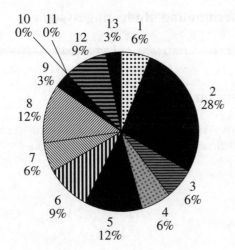

In the figure, the slices are proportional to the frequency of words of various lengths in the first sentence of the entry for *Bar Chart*. The numbers above the percentages are the lengths of words in letters beginning with the smallest (1) and moving clockwise.

Ping-pong Method

A method of ascribing values to entities like *health* states or the equilibrating probability in a *standard gamble* experiment by successive approximations from above and below.

Placebo

A non-active apparent treatment used in a *clinical trial* that is in appearance indistinguishable from an active treatment being investigated. The idea is to identify the effect of the specific treatment under investigation as distinct from 'treatment' in a general sense. From the Latin, meaning 'I will please'. See *Placebo Effect*.

Placebo Effect

The impact on health that a *placebo* may have even though it is not known to contain any active therapeutic ingredient. See also *Hawthorne Effect*.

Planning–Programming–Budgeting System

Broadly including *output budgeting* and *programme budgeting*.

Plumbing Diagram

May refer to Alan Williams' taxonomizing account of the scope of health economics. See *Williams' Schematic of Health Economics*.

Podiatry

Same as *chiropody*.

Point Estimate

A single sample statistic used to estimate a population *parameter*. Cf. a range of plausible values.

Point of Service Plan

Point of Service is a type of plan in the USA whose members can choose their services when they need them, either in a *Health Maintenance Organization* or from a provider outside the HMO at some cost to the member in the form of a reduced benefit level. The term is also used to describe a plan in which the primary provider directs services and referrals.

Point Prevalence

The *prevalence* of a particular condition at a particular date.

Poisson Distribution

A *distribution* having the characteristic that the *mean* is equal to the *variance*. Named after the French mathematician Siméon Denis Poisson (1781–1840).

Poisson Regression

A statistical model for *count data* based on the *Poisson distribution*. See also *Negbin Model*.

Polynomial Regression

A regression procedure for estimating non-linear relationships between *dependent* and *independent variables* (it may be quadratic, cubic and so on). See *Multinomial*.

Population

The total collection of individuals, events, technologies or other entities of interest (of which the human population of a jurisdiction is the most common example) from which *samples* are often taken.

Portability

Refers to the ability of an individual to retain their rights to medical care when they leave one jurisdiction for another or one insurance scheme for another. With full portability one's rights move with one. A characteristic of a health care system that is commonly desired or sometimes (as in Canada) required by statute.

POS Plan

Acronym for *Point of Service plan.*

Positive Controls

The patients in a trial who receive a therapeutically active treatment (that is, not *placebo*) as controls in a trial of another active therapy.

Positive Economics

That branch of economics that is social science in the sense that it offers hypotheses and tests them empirically. It contrasts with *welfare* (or *normative*) *economics* in not making judgments about what is good for society. There is, however, good and bad positive economics, so even positive economics does not free one from the necessity of making *value judgments*, for example about what is 'good science'. Judgments about what is good for society are not a part of positive economics. Not all economists are as scrupulous as they ought to be in making these distinctions (this is a value-judgment) and some claim to be value-free in terms of social values when they are actually not being value-free at all (this is not a value-judgment). See *Interpersonal Comparisons of Utility, Welfare Economics*.

Positive Predictive Value

Positive predictive value (PV+) is the proportion of individuals with positive test results who really do have the disease being investigated. In the figure, $PV+ = a/(a + b)$. Cf. *Negative Predictive Value, Sensitivity, Specificity*.

		Diagnosis		Total
		Present	Absent	
Test result	Present	*a* (true positive)	*b* (false positive)	$a + b$
	Absent	*c* (false negative)	*d* (true negative)	$c + d$
Total		$a + c$	$b + d$	

Positive Rights Good

Although it is not a term in economics, the notion of positive rights is closely linked with the notion of a *merit good*. Positive rights are rights or guarantees to have certain things, in contrast to negative rights which are the rights to be free from certain things, like abuse or coercion. If a right exists at all, it is positive when its realization entails some action on the part of others and it is negative when its realization entails inaction on the part of another. Health care is often used as an example of a positive rights good.

Posterior Distribution

A probability *distribution* that takes account not only of the data but also of the *prior distribution*. See *Bayesian Method.*

Posterior Probability

A belief about the likelihood of an event that is a modified *prior probability* as the result of additional information. See *Bayesian Method.*

Postmarketing Surveillance

Routine follow-up studies of the use of drugs after their licensing for public use. A means of discovering effects of long-term use and any undiscovered adverse effects not revealed during earlier trials. See *Phases in Clinical Trials.*

Postnatal

After, but within one year of, giving birth.

Post-test Odds

The odds that the patient has the target condition after a diagnostic test has been carried out (calculated as the *pre-test odds* times the *likelihood ratio*).

Potential Pareto-efficiency

The idea that, if gainers from a change could compensate losers and still gain, there is an increase in social welfare (even if the compensation is not actually paid). Another version is the idea that, if potential losers can offer gainers an equivalent gain sufficient for them to forgo the proposed change and still be better off than with the change, the change will not enhance welfare (even if the equivalent is not actually paid). These contortions are gone through in order to avoid having to face up to the reality that a dollar of gain may not be of the same value to each person. See *Efficiency*.

Power

See *Statistical Power.*

PPO

Acronym for *Preferred Provider Organization.*

PPP

Acronym for *purchasing power parity.*

PPRS

Acronym for *Pharmaceutical Price Regulation Scheme.*

Pragmatic Trial

A species of controlled *clinical trial*. Pragmatic trials measure *effectiveness* as distinct from *efficacy* and are not so much concerned with scientific questions of explanation (why something works or does not work) as with the degree of beneficial effect to be expected in real clinical practice. The pragmatic trial thus seeks to maximize *external validity*. A pragmatic trial is much less likely to use *placebo* as a comparator procedure than an explanatory trial, since placebo is unlikely in most cases to be a real-world alternative to the technology under review. Cf. *Explanatory Trial.*

Preadmission Review

A review of a patient's needs to determine whether admission to hospital is necessary.

Preclinical Trials

These are trials in the test tube or on animals designed to test such basic characteristics of drugs as toxicity and the strength and frequency of dosages that will be both safe and effective. They are a necessary preliminary stage before trials in humans may be carried out.

Predictive Validity

An instrument or measure that permits accurate predictions of future states of the *construct* in question.

Preference

Choices are usually assumed in economics to be the result of an interaction between preferences and constraints, where preferences are embodied in a *utility function*. 'Preferred' often means 'chosen rather than'. Most economists take preferences as primitive concepts, about which one need not enquire much (for example, as to their origin, causes or merit). Difficulties start to arise when people have preferences about (other people's) preferences or when they have preferences that everyone agrees are appalling (for example, a preference – taste? – for cannibalism). Preferences are usually also taken as constant over time. This poses particular difficulties when studying processes (like much education and some health care) whose aim (or consequence, regardless of aim) is to change people's values and/or preferences.

Preference Function

Same as *utility function*.

Preference Reversal

Preference reversal is a phenomenon widely observed in experiments designed to test the validity of the assumptions usually taken as underlying economic theories of behaviour (see *Utility*). In choices between pairs of simple monetary gambles, it has been found that individuals choose bets involving high probabilities of small gains (so-called P-bets) rather than bets offering a smaller chance of a larger prize (so-called $-bets) but attach a higher monetary value to the $-bets. This evidence has generated a controversy as to whether the preferences that are assumed to underlie people's choices are better seen as context-free (the usual economic point of view, in which the means through which a preference is elicited is supposed to be irrelevant) or context-sensitive (the usual psychological point of view, in which the experimental means can affect the outcome). Preference reversal has not been much researched in health economics and so it is not known whether attempts to measure, say, willingness to pay through experimental means are biased or inconsistent as a result. See *Framing Effect*.

Preferred Provider Organization

A PPO differs from a *Health Maintenance Organization* (HMO) in that (a) the providers are paid not by the prepaying subscriber as with an HMO but by an insurance company or employer on a *fee-for-service* basis and (b) patients are usually able to avail themselves of non-PPO providers, albeit with substantial *copayments*. PPOs can range from a single hospital and its practising physicians contracting with a large employer to a national network of physicians, hospitals and laboratories which contract with insurers or employer groups. PPO contracts typically provide discounts from standard fees, incentives for plan members to use the contracting providers, and other *managed care* cost containment methods.

Prenatal

Same as *antenatal*.

Prepayment

Payment by the individual to the provider in advance of receiving (or needing) treatment.

Pre-post Study

Same as *before and after study*.

Prescription Drug

A drug that is available to a member of the public only when prescribed by a physician and obtained by a formally registered pharmacist. Cf. *Over-the-counter Drugs*.

Present Value

The value at a particular point in time of a future *flow* of income, health and so on. See *Discounting*.

Pre-test Probability

The proportion of people with the target condition in the population at risk at a specific time (point prevalence) or time interval (period prevalence). Same as *prevalence*.

Prevalence

The proportion of a population in which a particular medical condition prevails at a particular date (point prevalence) or over a period (period prevalence). Same as *pre-test probability*. Cf. *Incidence*.

Prevention

Any procedure taken to stop a disease from either occurring (*primary prevention*) or worsening (*secondary prevention*). Some classifications also have *tertiary prevention*.

Price Discrimination

A process through which profit-seeking sellers in *price-searchers' markets* charge different prices for different increments of a good or service provided or charge different prices to different groups of buyers in *segmented markets*. In market-oriented systems of health care provision, the fact that rich patients may be charged more than poor ones for the same service has been held to be price discrimination (though the reasons given by its practitioners are

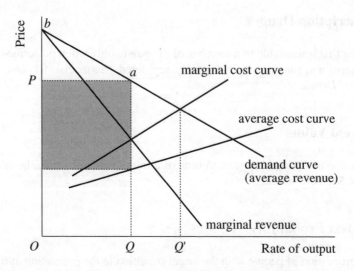

different).The figure shows the profit-maximizing price and output rate for a price-searcher who charges a single price (*P*). It is where *marginal cost* equals *marginal revenue*. Profit is shown by the shaded area. The *demand curve* shows not only the maximum amount that will be purchased at each price but also the maximum amount that will be paid for each additional unit of the good or service in question. For example, the maximum payable for the very first unit is *Ob* and the maximum payable for an additional unit when consumption is already at *Q* is *Qa*. The segment of the demand curve *ba* indicates the maximum amounts that would be paid by a person with this demand curve for increments of output in the range *OQ*. So the maximum the seller could obtain, if it were possible to charge the consumer the maximum willingness to pay, is the succession of prices in the segment, yielding additional profit *Pba*. In fact, in this case, one may readily see that the profit could be further increased by selling each unit at the maximum the buyer will pay up to output rate *Q′*, where marginal cost equals price, which generates the same output rate as under *price-taking* conditions (though there is a transfer of *consumer's surplus* from consumer to seller which does not happen under price-taking).

This form of price discrimination is rarely seen in explicit form. Market segmentation is, however, widely practised. In this situation, the output is produced, we assume, under identical conditions for two (or more) segmented markets as in the second figure. The conventional profit-maximizing price is charged so that in each market the marginal cost is set equal to marginal revenue (whether by careful design or by chance) and the prices P_A and P_B are set in market segments *A* and *B*, respectively. The higher price is charged in the segment with the lower price-*elasticity*.

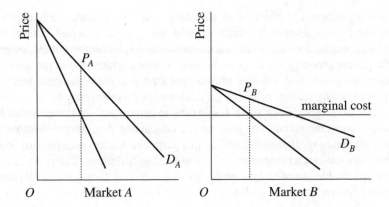

Price Index

A price index measures the average change in prices over time in a basket of goods and services and is used to adjust prices in periods other than the base period so as to make 'real' comparisons at *constant prices*. The *Consumer Price Index* (CPI) is a familiar example of such an index. See *Laspeyres Price Index*, *Paasche Price Index*.

Price-making

A somewhat less satisfactory term for *price-searching*. It is less satisfactory because prices cannot be 'made' by firms independently of the demand for their product. Any firm that is not a *price-taker* has to discover (guessing, searching for, copying similar others, doing market research on, running econometric models of, consulting entrails concerning) the price that is most advantageous to it.

Price Mechanism

The market mechanism that sends price signals to producers about what to produce, to labour about whether to work and at what, and that allocates goods and services amongst consumers. Markets and the rules by which they operate are human creations and, in practice, are rarely perfect (not only in design but also in execution, since their operation is itself costly). It is usually assumed (by economists) that prices settle in an *equilibrium* from which they are disturbed by *exogenous* shocks. Provided the system as a whole is stable, a new equilibrium is expected to be established. The remarkable feature of this mechanism is that it works without any general external control or planning mechanism other than the existence (and enforcement) of exchangeable private property rights in goods and services, which define the uses to which the goods and services may be put (the so-called 'invisible hand'). There are many reasons why any particular market system may be very slow to adapt to change, which are as fascinating to contemplate as is the 'invisible hand' itself. One should not jump to the conclusion that, simply because a particular price mechanism operating in a particular market with its particular set of (human-made) rules succeeds in allocating resources, it does so in the best imaginable (or even best possible) way. See also *General Equilibrium, Market Failure, Partial Equilibrium.*

Price-searching

The market phenomenon that exists when a seller's decision to increase or reduce the rate of supply of a good or service will change its market price. The problem for the seller is to find the output rate and price that maximize their *objective function* (usually assumed to be *profit*). Since the *demand curve* that confronts the seller will have negative slope (cf. the demand curve under *price-taking*) the point on this curve that is best from the seller's perspective may need to be searched for: it is not given (as under price-taking); hence the name. Whatever the method used by the seller to locate the 'best' price, in logic, the profit-maximizing price and rate of output are determined by equality between *marginal cost* and *marginal revenue*. This is

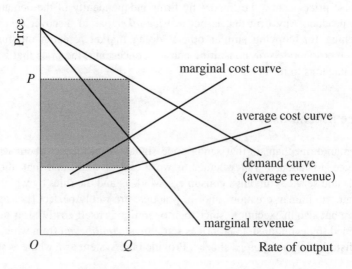

shown in the figure. The boxed area shows profit (maximized) at the price *P* and output rate *Q*, where marginal cost equals marginal revenue.

Price-taking

A market phenomenon under which the seller of a good or service cannot affect the market price by varying their own rate of output. The *demand curve* as it appears to the firm is perfectly *elastic* (a horizontal line) and price is not a choice variable; it is given by the market. Hence the name.

Primary Care

Primary care is that care provided by doctors and other generalists, including nurses, who are usually based in the community (as distinct from hospitals), who practise as generalists (see *General Practitioner*). A primary care professional (not always a physician) will frequently coordinate the care of *ambulatory* patients across various clinical professionals (for example dental, ophthalmic or nursing care) and other local non-clinical professionals (such as social services). They also serve as the first point of contact (*gatekeepers*) to the health care system as a whole. They refer patients judged to be more appropriately diagnosed and treated in other parts of the system. Primary care services commonly include health promotion, disease prevention, vaccination, family planning, health maintenance, counselling, patient education, and the initial diagnosis and first-line treatment of acute and chronic illnesses that are deemed not to require referral to a hospital-based specialist. Cf. *Secondary Care*, *Tertiary Care*.

Primary Care Trust

PCTs are trusts (since 2002) within the UK National Health Service with responsibility both for providing primary care services in their areas and for commissioning health care from hospitals and other specialist centres. They are required to develop health plans for their areas which are integrated with the plans of other agencies such as social services. PCTs have chief executives, chairs and boards comprising executive and non-executive directors. Cf. *Secondary Care Trust*.

Primary Prevention

Primary prevention entails actions intended to deter, delay or prevent the occurrence or development of disease or injury by reducing *risk factors*. The actions include behaviour modifying actions such as health education, safety advice and legislation, as well as clinical interventions such as vaccination. Cf. *Secondary Prevention*. See *Prevention*.

Principal

In health economics, this refers to one of the parties in the *agency relationship*. The principal is the party on whose behalf an *agent* acts. See *Agency Relationship*.

Principal Component

A constructed variable using *factor analysis*, through which many (possibly) correlated *variables* are collapsed into a smaller number of uncorrelated variables.

Prior Distribution

The *probability distribution* of a *variable* in the minds of analysts before they have collected any data. See *Bayesian Method*.

Prior Probability

A view about the probability of an event (which may be objectively or subjectively based) prior to the receipt of other information pertinent to the *likelihood* of that event. See *Bayesian Method*.

Probabilistic Sensitivity Analysis

A technique in *decision analysis* in which *probability distributions* are created for each element about which there is uncertainty. By simulating the consequences of random drawings from these distributions, it enables judgments to be formed about the *robustness* of decisions in relation to each element.

Probability

The proportion of times (as a decimal fraction) an event would occur if an experiment were repeated a large number of times. More generally, the chances (however assessed) of an event occurring. It lies between 0 and +1. See *Bayesian Method, Likelihood*.

Probability Distribution

A mathematical representation of the probability that a variable falls in the specified interval.

Probit Model

A statistical model of binary *dependent variables* based on the *normal distribution*.

Process Utility

The idea that *utility* might be gained from a process, like being reassured that one is well, rather than a health outcome. See *extra-welfarism*.

Producer Sovereignty

Not a standard term of art in economics though, on grounds of fairness, it ought to have the same status as *consumer sovereignty*. If the term existed, it would presumably describe a situation in which producers of goods (and services) determined the character and quantity of *outputs*, who consumed them and on what terms. The medical care market would seem an obviously approximate case, driven by the *information asymmetry* that denies non-doctors the ability to know their own *needs*.

Producer's Surplus

The difference between what a producer receives and the minimum required to compensate the producer for producing/selling. In the figure, the marginal cost curve (supply curve) in a *price-takers' market* defines the

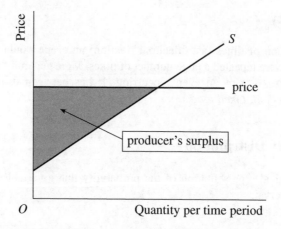

lower boundary of the producer's surplus (the triangle). Cf. *Consumer's Surplus*.

Production Frontier

Same as *production possibilities curve*.

Production Function

A technical relationship between *inputs* and the maximum *outputs* or *outcomes* of any procedure or process, also sometimes referred to as the 'technology matrix'. Thus a production function may relate the maximum number of patients that can be treated in a hospital over a period of time to a variety of inputs like doctor- and nurse-hours, and beds. For econometric purposes the relationship is usually postulated to be in a particular mathematical form, of which one is the so-called Cobb–Douglas production function, $X = kA^{\alpha}B^{\beta}$, where X is the rate of output (or throughput of clients), k, α and β are positive constants, and A and B are rates of use of two inputs. The production function specifies efficient combinations of inputs required at each rate of output, *viz.*, the fewest of each needed to produce that output (see *Efficiency*). Depending on the values of *parameters* like a and b an equal proportional increase in all inputs may entail either a larger, smaller or equal increase in output. This corresponds to *increasing*, *decreasing* or *constant returns to scale*.

Production Possibilities Curve

A locus indicating the boundary between all the combinations of goods and services that an economy can produce with given resources and technologies, and those it cannot. Its slope is the *marginal rate of transformation*, showing in two dimensions the minimum amount of one good or service that must be sacrificed in order to produce an additional unit of the other (or the maximum that can be produced of one for a given sacrifice of the other). Also known as a production frontier or *transformation curve*.

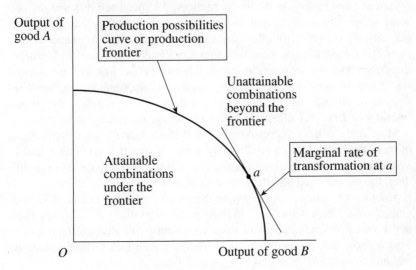

Productivity

This refers to the output of goods and services produced by one or more *factors of production*. Total factor productivity is the rate of output divided by the amount of all inputs used in production where each input is usually weighted by its share in total cost. The rate of growth of total factor productivity is sometimes also referred to as the residual after the contributions of *capital* and labour to the growth of *gross domestic product* have been accounted for. See also *Average Product, Marginal Product*.

Productivity Cost

A substitute term for *indirect cost* (or for a part of indirect costs) often chosen so as to avoid confusion with the accountants' usage of 'indirect cost'. A productivity cost is the *opportunity cost* of an individual's time not spent in productive work activity. The status of this category of cost has been a matter of controversy, with some arguing that, if the (*extra-welfarist*) *perspective* from which a study is being conducted considers health as the only relevant outcome, then costs that do not fall on the health sector ought to be disregarded. It seems more consistent, however, with the extra-welfarist perspective to allow the *objective function* to include whatever those with appropriate responsibility for deciding such matters want it to include. So the minister of health (say) may require that analyses are to take account both of health consequences and of resources costs falling on the health services, the social services and the personal sector. The conventional *welfarist* approach would include any effects that directly or indirectly affect individuals' utilities. If a consequence of a particular intervention to improve health actually does increase work productivity, then, as a strictly practical matter, this might affect incomes, the *demand for health services* (and health care *insurance*) and generate additional resources to produce health care. It would then seem curmudgeonly for any 'minister' to treat such effects as irrelevant and ask analysts to ignore them.

Most analysts have expressed concern at the potential *equity* implications of including work-related productivity costs, fearing that this might lead to systematic *bias* in technologies that favour the working population over children, the unemployed and the retired, or the very productive over the not so productive. Of course, any procedure that ruled these costs out of all consideration would then deny decision makers the opportunity of assessing them and forming a judgment about their significance for distributional equity. This is, however, to encourage an ostrich-like approach to public decision making. See also *Friction Costs, Human Capital*.

Professional Standards Review Organizations

Professional Standards Review Organizations (PSROs) were mandated under United States Public Law 92-603 in order to promote *cost-containment* in hospitals by reducing '*overutilization*' while maintaining 'proper quality of care'. PSROs are locally based vetting agencies responsible for conducting reviews of the quality and appropriateness of hospital services. See *Utilization*.

Profit

The economic concept of profit differs from the accounting concept by deducting from revenue not only the obvious costs of production but also the *opportunity costs* of owner's time (especially important in small businesses like nursing homes) and the opportunity cost of *capital* (effectively the rate of return that could be earned on the assets if they were invested in a risk-free asset like a government bond adjusted for the kind of risk of default common to firms of this size and type). Economic profit is always less than accounting profit. In a perfectly competitive economy, profits are zero when it is in *equilibrium*. See *Competition*.

Prognosis

A forecast of the future progress and pattern of a disease and its symptoms.

Programme Budgeting

Similar to *output budgeting* except that the basis for classification is the target client group (the 'programme') rather than the output or outcome in question. Examples include maternity care, child care and care of the elderly.

Progressivity

Usually relates to the proportion of household or personal income that is taken in taxes; a progressive tax is one for which the proportion of income taken in tax rises as income rises, a *regressive* tax is one for which that proportion falls, and a *proportional* tax is one for which it remains constant. Cf. *Regressivity*. See *Ability to Pay*.

Proportional Hazards Regression Model

Same as *Cox proportional hazards model*.

Proportionality

Usually relates to the proportion of household or personal income that is taken in taxes; a proportional tax is one for which the proportion of income taken in tax is constant as income is the larger, a *regressive* tax is one for which that proportion falls, and a *progressive* tax is one for which it rises.

Proprietary Drug

Same as *over-the-counter drug*.

Prospect Theory

An approach to decisions under uncertainty that provides an alternative account for the phenomenon of *risk aversion* to that of *expected utility theory* and which helps to explain why *framing effects* exist. Prospect theory differs from expected utility theory in assigning 'decision weights' rather than probabilities to outcomes and in assuming that decision weights tend to overweight small probabilities and underweight moderate and high probabilities. It also differs from expected utility theory in that it replaces the notion of *utility* with 'value', defined in terms of deviations from a reference point. The value function has a different shape for gains and losses. For losses it is convex and steep, for gains it is concave and flatter. Although hardly in current use in health economics, it is likely to make an appearance in the future, initially, perhaps, in topics like health status measurement that use experimental methods. Cf. *Expected Utility Theory*, *Regret Theory*. See *Reflection Effect*, *Utility*.

Prospective Cohort Study

An observational study of a *cohort* of initially disease-free individuals whose exposure to *risk factors* and whose health are followed over a period of time. It is usually regarded as the design of choice for an observational study. Same as *observational cohort study*.

Prospective Payment Assessment Commission

A US agency that advises the Congress and the Secretary of Health and Human Services on maintaining and updating *Medicare* payment policies for hospitals and other facility services. It is also responsible for the analysis of *Medicaid* hospital payments and issues related to health care reform.

Prospective Payment System

A mechanism through which US *Medicare* reimburses hospitals on the basis of a given sum per case in a *Diagnosis Related Group*.

Prospective Reimbursement

Used by insurers: a method of reimbursing health service providers (especially hospitals) by establishing rates of payment in advance which are paid regardless of the costs in actual individual cases.

Prospective Study

A trial in which individuals are followed forward from a particular date and the effect of future events on them is investigated.

Prosthetics

The specialty dealing with prostheses or prosthetic devices, like artificial limbs.

PSRO

Acronym for *Professional Standards Review Organizations.*

Psychiatry

The medical specialty concerned with mental illness.

PTO

Acronym for *person trade-off method.*

Public Choice Theory

Based on the idea that individuals in public positions make decisions according to their own interest rather than voluntarily follow any rules for maximizing *social welfare.* See *Median Voter Model.*

Public Good

A good or service that it is not possible to exclude people from consuming once any is produced (clean air is a classic example and clean water another, though one can be avoided by migration to an urban environment and the other by swimming off one of the 47 British beaches named by the European Commission in 1990 where the water was – at that time – too polluted for safe swimming). Public goods are non-rival in the sense that providing more for one person does not entail the other having any less (the marginal *opportunity cost* of provision to another consumer is zero). Most public goods are not wholly public in this sense and whether health care itself has significant public good characteristics is a point of debate. Some programmes (especially those called 'public health') have considerable public good characteristics and even the care consumed by an individual may have a public aspect by virtue of any 'sympathy' that others may feel, so the consumption of one may in this way affect the *utility* of many others. Thus, if the alleviation of someone's ill-health is valued by any other than that individual, and there is more than one such externally affected person, then the *externality* will have the *attribute* of publicness.

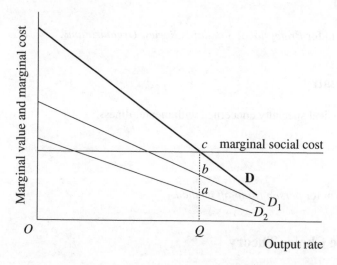

The first-order rule for optimizing the output of a public good entails adding the *marginal value* each consumer attaches to the good at a variety of outputs and selecting that output at which the sum of the marginal values (*marginal social value*) is equal to *marginal social cost*. In the figure, the two *demand* curves D_1 and D_2 are to be interpreted as *marginal value curves* for two individuals, 1 and 2. The boldly drawn curve D is the vertical summation of these two curves. At output rate Q, which is the optimal rate, the individuals value additions to the output rate at amounts Qa and Qb, whose sum, Qc, the marginal social value, is equal to the marginal social cost. Note that, in economics, a public good is not defined by whether it is produced in the public sector – which also produces private goods (that is, ones that do not have the characteristics described above) – or the private (where the charitable sector often produces public goods). See *External Effects, Median Voter Model*.

Public Health Medicine

The study of disease prevention and promoting health through the use of collective agencies and actions (for example, population vaccination, health education, water purification). Virtually the same as social medicine.

Publication Bias

A *bias* in the published literature arising from the criteria (which may in part be arbitrary) used by editors to select articles for journals. The bias includes a preference for 'new' results (rather than confirmation of 'old' ones), 'positive' results (rather than 'we don't know') and familiar languages (rather those that are unfamiliar to the review team). See *Systematic Review*.

Pulmonary Medicine

The medical specialty concerned with diseases and abnormalities of the lungs. See also *Respiratory Medicine*.

Purchaser

A term that has acquired a special meaning in the UK *National Health Service*, where it denotes various collective agencies such as *Strategic Health Authorities* or *Primary Care Trusts* that have statutory powers and centrally determined budgets to commission health care and related services on behalf of local communities. See *Block Contract, Payment by Results, Purchaser–provider Split*.

Purchaser–provider Split

An aspect of *internal markets* for health care in which the purchasing or commissioning of services on behalf of groups of the population (often geographically defined) is not done by providers of services. See *Commissioning*.

Purchasing Power Parity

Rates of currency conversion that eliminate the differences in price levels between countries are termed purchasing power parity rates of exchange. Each is the ratio of price levels in two jurisdictions having different currencies, where the prices used are those of a common bundle of goods and services. This is sometimes called 'absolute purchasing power parity' to differentiate it from relative PPP, which states that the rate of appreciation of a currency is equal to the difference in inflation rates between it and that in another jurisdiction. The purpose of PPPs is to obtain more reliable ways of making international economic comparisons (for example, of health care expenditures) than can be done by using exchange rates (which are subject to many other determinants). The Organization of Economic Cooperation and Development (OECD) publishes PPP rates for OECD countries that are regularly updated and compared with exchange rates. The table on page 283 shows recent PPPs for the countries of the OECD in national currency units per US dollar, together with comparative price levels, which are ratios of PPPs to average exchange rates.

Purposive Sample

A *sample* of a set of subjects chosen not randomly but with particular criteria in mind (for example, they are the children of parents with some genetic characteristic of interest).

P-value

The probability, when the *null hypothesis* is true, of obtaining a sample result that is at least as unlikely as what is observed. It is often called *statistical significance*.

Purchasing power parities for OECD countries, 2004

	Purchasing power parities	Comparative price levels
Australia	1.37	90
Austria	0.908	110
Belgium	0.883	107
Canada	1.27	95
Czech Republic	14.6	55
Denmark	8.47	138
Finland	0.983	113
France	0.897	108
Germany	0.942	114
Greece	0.697	84
Hungary	127.0	61
Iceland	90.0	124
Ireland	1.01	122
Italy	0.839	101
Japan	132.0	119
Korea	771.0	65
Luxembourg	0.984	119
Mexico	7.16	62
Netherlands	0.919	111
New Zealand	1.49	96
Norway	9.47	137
Poland	1.83	48
Portugal	0.660	80
Slovak Republic	17.2	52
Spain	0.768	93
Sweden	9.32	123
Switzerland	1.77	138
Turkey	0.780	54
United Kingdom	0.618	110
United States	1.00	100

Source: OECD. Adapted from table on www.oecd.org/dataoecd/61/54/18598754.pdf.

Q

QALY

Acronym for *quality-adjusted life-year.*

QoL

Acronym for *quality of life.*

Qualitative Analysis

This term is used in two distinct senses. The first refers straightforwardly to any kind of analysis that focuses on the direction of causation or change (for example, positive/negative, better/worse) or their relative size, not their absolute magnitude. The second kind refers to a kind of empirical investigation in which hypotheses may not be clearly formed or intended to be tested but which is designed to generate data from which hypotheses might be invented in inferential ways. Open-ended questionnaires used in surveys of individuals having particular characteristics of *a priori* interest are an example of a qualitative method of this second kind. Cf. *Quantitative Analysis.* See *Qualitative Study.*

Qualitative Effect

The sign (positive or negative) of the effect of one *variable* on another. The magnitude of the effect is quantitative rather than qualitative.

Qualitative Study

A methodological approach to the understanding of social phenomena that is largely exploratory and interpretive and intended to be a means through which general (usually social scientific) presumptions or high-level general theorizing may be crafted into more specific hypotheses and theories. It produces findings not usually arrived at by means of statistical procedures or other quantitative techniques, and includes in-depth (often deliberately unstructured) interviews, observations and participant observation.

Quality-adjusted Life-expectancy

Life-expectancy using *quality-adjusted life-years* rather than years of life.

Quality-adjusted Life-year

The quality-adjusted life-year (QALY) is a generic measure of health-related *quality of life* that takes into account both the quantity and the quality of life generated by interventions. The invention and further development of the QALY was a response to the treatment of health outcomes solely in terms of *survival* without any weight being given to the quality of the additional years of life. A year of perfect health is scaled to be 'worth' 1 and a year of less than perfect health 'worth' less than 1. Death is commonly indicated by 0, though in some situations there may be states regarded as worse than death and which would have negative numbers attached to them. Thus an intervention which results in a patient living for an additional five years rather than dying within one year, but where quality of life fell from 1 to 0.6 generates 5 years' extra life with a quality of 0.6 (= 3.0) less 1 year of reduced quality (1 − 0.6) (=0.4), so the (net) QALYs generated by the intervention are 3.0 − 0.4 (=2.6).

The status of the QALY has been the subject of some debate and not a little confusion. Is it a measure of preference for health states? Is it a measure of health outcome that is independent of health states? Is it a *utility* measure of someone's preferences (the fact that its construction may entail the use of utility theory does not imply that it is)? Is it *cardinal* or *ordinal*? Is it consistent with the conventions of *welfare economics* or is it inescapably a part of *extra-welfarism*? What *value-judgments* does it embody and what is their acceptability? What empirical forms of it exist and how do they differ?

Seen as a measure of preference, the QALY is generated using *expected utility theory* and, in particular, the technique known as the *standard gamble*. This interpretation therefore rests on the applicability of the axioms of expected utility theory with the *independence axiom* being extended to entail that, when constructing QALYs from characteristics (like 'painfulness' or 'physical mobility'), the (dis)utility from any one is independent of the others. That is, the preferences are assumed to be *additively separable*. Further assumptions of this approach are that subjects' preferences have a *constant proportional time trade-off* (that is, they must be willing to sacrifice a constant proportion of future years of life for a given QALY gain) and that a person values health outcomes independently of knowing them ahead of time, including even the extreme outcomes of death and full health. It may seem odd that people are required to be unconcerned about not knowing whether they will live or die but expected utility theory requires people to value each outcome as though it were certain. These assumptions generate a form of cardinal utility measure that is on an *interval scale*. The scale alone does not permit interpersonal comparisons of the sort 'Individual A is twice as ill as individual B'.

The extra-welfarist interpretation of QALYs is that they are socially chosen cardinal indicators of health or health gain that are interval or ratio scales, depending on their method of construction. This is tantamount to saying that the social welfare function is separable into different types of measure, some of which may be utility measures but one of which is, in any event, health or health gain. On this interpretation, interpersonal comparisons can be explicitly made, as can (at least in principle) whole *distributions* of health (or health gain), thus enabling the question of *equity* to be addressed directly. This has given rise to various proposals for weighting QALYs according to who gets them (for example, old v. young, male v. female, married v. single), how many you already have (relatively well v. relatively sick), and how many you have already had (a lifetime of chronic disability v. a recently acquired disability). See *Assessment Quality of Life, Disability-adjusted Life-year, EQ-5D, EuroQol, Health Gain, Health Status, Health Utilities Index, Healthy Year Equivalents, SF-6D, SF-8, SF-12, SF-36.*

Quality of Life

An index of the quality of a year of life, usually measured by a utility number that has been constructed in a fashion described under *utility* and embodying the value judgments of selected judges. See *Assessment Quality of Life, Disability-adjusted Life-year, EQ-5D, EuroQol, Health Gain, Health Status, Health Utilities Index, Healthy Year Equivalents, Quality-adjusted Life-year.*

Quality of Well-being Scale

The QWB is a generic preference-weighted measure combining three scales of functioning with a measure of symptoms and problems on a scale of 0 (death) to 1.0 (full health). This measure is then weighted according to population-based preference weights and combined with expected life-years to generate *quality-adjusted life-year*. Cf. *Assessment Quality of Life, Dis-*

ability-adjusted Life-year, EQ-5D, EuroQol, Health Gain, Health Status, Health Utilities Index, Healthy Year Equivalents.

Quantile

When a continuous *variable* is split for convenience into equal-sized chunks of data the cut-off points between them are called quantiles. Thus, if there are four such groups (*quartiles*), each containing 25 per cent of the data, there are three such cut-off points, the central one being the median. Common divisions are *tertiles* (three groups), *quartiles* (four), *quintiles* (five), *deciles* (ten), *centiles (*or *percentiles)* (one hundred).

Quantitative Analysis

An analysis dealing in measured quantities of entities. Cf. *Qualitative Analysis*.

Quartile

When a continuous *variable* is split for convenience into four equal-sized chunks of data the cut-off points between them are called quartiles. See *Quantile*.

Quasi-experimental Research

Comparative research in which the assignment of subjects to comparator groups is not random or a *control* group is not used.

Quasi-market

Same as *internal market*.

Queue

Queues seem endemic in health care. Most of them are not the standing-in-line type, a major *opportunity cost* of which for the person waiting is the time not available for alternative uses. Queues mostly represent the postponement of care (including diagnostic care), whose consequences can vary from the non-existent (as when restoration to health occurs through natural processes) to the catastrophic (as when a fatal condition goes undiagnosed). In most Western countries with waiting lists, people are mainly waiting for elective surgery. In welfare terms, what probably matters more than the numbers waiting is the time spent waiting and the hazards to which that might expose the waiter: for example, someone waiting for a hip replacement steadily loses muscle strength and becomes more vulnerable to falls, while a large number of waiting people may wait for trivial periods of time.

QuickDASH

The QuickDASH is a shortened version of the *DASH* Outcome Measure. Instead of 30 items, the QuickDASH uses 11 items to measure physical function and symptoms in persons with any or multiple musculoskeletal disorders of the arms, shoulders and hands. Its website is http://www.dash.iwh. on.ca/quickdash.htm. Cf. *Disabilities of the Arm, Shoulder and Hand.*

Quintile

When a continuous *variable* is split for convenience into five equal-sized chunks of data the cut-off points between them are called quintiles. See *Quantile.*

Quota Sample

A *sample* chosen in such a way that the proportion of subjects possessing a certain characteristic is the same as in the population from which the sample comes.

QWB

Acronym for *quality of well-being.*

R

R^2

The proportion of the total variation in the *dependent variable* of a multiple regression that is 'explained'. It is the squared correlation between actual and predicted values of the dependent variable. A measure of the goodness-of-fit of the equation. Also known as the 'coefficient of determination'.

Radiography

The diagnostic use of radiation such as X-rays to make images.

Radiology

The science of X-rays and high-energy radiation in imaging and treatment processes. Same as nuclear medicine.

Radiotherapy

The treatment of cancer by X-rays or gamma rays to destroy cancer cells.

Random Effect Model

A model in which treatments are a random sample from a large population (Cf. *Fixed Effect Model*). A random effect model does not provide any knowledge of the treatment effect at a particular level but it does enable study of the variability due to the effect of treatment.

Random Sample

A simple random sample is a *sample* of individuals or observations drawn from a population where each has an equal chance of being selected.

Randomized Clinical Trial

Same as *Randomized Controlled Trial.*

Randomized Controlled Trial

A *clinical trial* in which patients are allocated to treatments (including *placebo*) in a random fashion. The essential idea is that randomization removes *confounding* effects and reduces *bias* in the result. Also known as a randomized clinical trial.

Randomizing

Allocating patients to alternative treatments in a *clinical trial* in a random fashion (that is, by chance).

Range

The difference between the smallest and the largest in a set of numbers.

Rank Correlation Coefficient

See *Spearman Rank Correlation Coefficient.*

Rank Dependence

A type of model that is often used in the analysis of decisions under uncertainty. In health economics it refers to a system for equity weighting *quality-adjusted life-years* (QALYs) in a *social welfare function.* The weight depends on each individual's relative ranking in terms of expected lifetime QALYs.

Ratchet Effect

An effect in negotiations between purchasers and providers by which the purchaser utilizes knowledge from previous negotiations to ratchet up the expected level of performance at the same price or *global budget*. See *Purchaser–provider Split*.

Rate of Interest

Interest is the amount of money payable to a lender for lending a given amount for a period. The interest rate is that amount divided by the sum that is lent, usually on the assumption that the period is one year, and expressed as a percentage. See *Discounting*.

Rate of Return

The rate of discount (see *Discounting*) that makes the *present value* of a stream of money costs and benefits over time equal to zero.

Ratio Scale

A property of some measures of health and also of some measures of utility. See *Utility*.

Rational Addiction

The idea that addiction may be explained in terms of the usual economic axioms of *utility* or *expected utility theory*. See *Addiction*.

Rational Drug Design

A focused strategy for organizing commercial pharmaceuticals research based on knowledge of the workings of proteins in human biology.

Rationality

Generally intended in economics to refer to behaviour that is consistent with the axioms of *utility* or *expected utility* theory. This idea of rationality has been pretty well attacked. An early assault was from Keynes on the ground that its axioms were not obeyed by at least some financially successful people who ought not to be dubbed 'irrational' in light of the evidence. It has been attacked also because it is too narrow in excluding emotional effects of not knowing things ahead of time, effects such as anxiety, disappointment and regret, and because it is too demanding and its literal pursuit might actually reduce welfare (see *Bounded Rationality*). Moreover identifying rationality as behaviour consistent with the axioms of a theory invites the unhelpful conclusion that every time any of these is actually violated (for example in a controlled experiment) the subject in question is an irrational being and, when this happens frequently – as it does – people are frequently irrational.

It is useful to keep in mind the distinction between *positive* and *normative* economics. In the former, rationality plays no ethical role at all, since theory seeks to account for or predict what actually happens, not what ought to happen if people were different from the analyst's postulates. Any empirical refutation of an axiom is a refutation of the theory (whether one calls it 'rationality' or anything else). In the case of normative economics, the issues are more comprehensive and complex than those that entail the usual notions of 'rationality' and certainly so if the concept requires people to be selfish and to act selfishly. In health policy, for example, 'rationality', like other fundamental value-laden underpinnings, needs to be defined and used in such a fashion as to include what the clients on behalf of whom the analysis is being done find ethically acceptable.

Rationing

Allocating resources according to a rule or administrative arrangement. One rule might, for example, be 'resources shall go to whoever is willing to pay the highest price'. Such a rule does not much commend itself in health care however. The most common general usage of 'rationing' is in connection with (usually wartime) arrangements under which, in exchange for a voucher, individuals (or families) are entitled to purchase fixed quotas of goods at *administered prices*. A lot of tendentious hot air is generated in public de- bates about whether health care in any jurisdiction is 'rationed'. Those with political responsibility are understandably unwilling to concede that health care is rationed in either of the two ways just described, but sometimes less understandably unwilling to concede that some form of rationing mechanism has to be used, the critical question relating not to 'whether?' but to 'which?' There is also debate about the desirability of being explicit about the criteria to be used in determining the 'rules', with most economists apparently strongly in favour of explicitness. See *Need, Pareto Optimality, Price Mechanism*.

Rawlsian

An approach to questions of social justice named after the late American philosopher John Rawls (1921–2002). See *Fairness*.

RBRVS

Acronym for *resource-based relative value scale*.

RCT

Acronym for *randomized controlled trial*.

RD

Acronym for *risk difference*.

Real Income

Nominal (that is money) income adjusted to remove the effect of changes in the price level on purchasing power.

Real Price

Nominal price divided by a general *price index*.

Recall Bias

A distortion in data that arises from people's imperfect memories of events they are being asked to remember. See *Bias*.

Receiver Operating Characteristic Curve

A plot of the *sensitivity* of a test against 1 minus the *specificity* of the test which is used to compare tests or to select an ideal cut-off value in a test.

Recurrent Cost

Expenditures or *opportunity costs* that occur on a regular (usually annual) basis rather than being incurred once and for all.

Redistributive Impact

The effect on the *income distribution* of the arrangements adopted in a jurisdiction for health care financing. It is generally measured as the difference between the *Gini coefficients* for prepayment and postpayment income distributions and, quantitatively speaking, seems to be determined by the average proportion of household income spent on health care, the *progressivity* of the health care financing system, the extent of *horizontal inequity*, and the extent to which households are reranked in the distributions when postpayment and prepayment distributions are compared.

Reference Case

A standard set of methods and assumptions that analysts should follow in performing *cost–effectiveness* or *cost–utility* analyses. For two examples, see Marthe R. Gold, Joanna E. Siegel, Louise B. Russell and Milton C. Weinstein (eds) (1996), 'Appendix A: Summary Recommendations', in *Cost-Effectiveness in Health and Medicine*, New York and Oxford: Oxford University Press; chapter 5 in National Institute for Clinical Excellence (2004), *Guide to the Methods of Technology Appraisal*, London: NICE.

Reference Cost

This pools data returned from (English) *National Health Service* (NHS) providers to compute average costs for all *Healthcare Resource Groups* and a *Reference Cost Index* for each NHS provider. It underpins the *national tariff*.

Reference Cost Index

This is an index used in the English National Health Service (NHS) of the actual cost for each NHS provider organization divided by national average cost for the same activity multiplied by 100. An 'adjusted index' allows for local price variations. .

Reference Pricing

A reimbursement mechanism (usually for pharmaceuticals) whereby a third party payer or insurer determines the maximum price at which it will reimburse the supplier (the reference price). The consumer pays the difference between the reference price and the market price. The reference price is often set at the price of the lowest priced product in the therapeutic group or is the weighted average of the lowest prices in the market. The market prices are set at the discretion of the supplier.

Referral Bias

This occurs when particular physicians and centres of *secondary care* attract individuals with specific disorders or exposures but which are atypical of the general class of referrals or of patients of this type. Also known as centripetal bias. See *Bias*.

Referral Cue

Guidance to help *General Practitioners* and their patients decide when a consultation with a specialist, usually at a hospital, is appropriate.

Reflection Effect

Reflection effects involve gambles whose outcomes are opposite in sign, though of the same size. Compare two choices, one between a certain gain of $20 or a one-third chance of $60 and the other between a certain loss of $20 or a one-third chance of losing $60. Most people choose the certain gain in the first choice but the one-third chance of loss in the second. The effect is predicted by *prospect theory* as a consequence of the S shape of the value function. Cf. *Expected Utility Theory*, *Framing Effect*.

Region of Acceptability

That part of a *cost–effectiveness plane* which indicates that the technology under investigation is cost-effective.

Regression Analysis

Same as *multiple (linear) regression.*

Regression Coefficients

These coefficients give a quantitative account of the relationship between a *dependent variable* and one or more *independent variables* in a regression equation. In the regression equation

$$Y_i = a + bX_i + \varepsilon_i,$$

b is a regression coefficient. See *Multiple (Linear) Regression.*

Regression to the Mean

An empirical phenomenon in which extreme values tend to be followed by more normal ones; for example, parents of exceptional longevity tend to have less long-lived children.

Regressivity

Usually relates to the proportion of household or personal income that is taken in taxes; a regressive tax is one for which the proportion of income taken in tax falls as income rises, a *progressive* tax is one for which that proportion rises, and a *proportional* tax is one for which it remains constant. Cf. *Progressivity.* See *Ability to Pay.*

Regressor

An independent variable in a regression equation.

Regret Theory

An approach to decisions under uncertainty that takes account of the possibility that people anticipate the possibility that they will come to regret making a particular decision even at the time of making it. Cf. *Expected Utility Theory, Prospect Theory.*

Rehabilitation Medicine

Same as *physiatry*, comprising such specialties as occupational therapy, physical therapy, speech therapy, *audiology*, *prosthetics* and *orthotics*.

Reimbursement

A retrospective payment made to someone for out-of-pocket expenses that they have incurred.

Relative Hazard

Same as *relative risk*.

Relative Price

A pure number: the price of one good or service divided by the price of another.

Relative Price Effect

The movement over time of a specific *price index* (for example, one for health care, or expenditure on physician services) relative to a general price index such as the *GDP deflator*. Alternatively, one price relative to another or to the price of a bundle of other goods and services.

Relative Risk

A ratio of two risks, usually the chance of catching a disease if exposed to particular *risk factors* divided by the chance of catching it if one is not so exposed, or the ratio of risk in an experimental group (E) to the risk in the control group (C). It is used in randomized trials and cohort studies and is calculated as E/C. Relative risk is often abbreviated to RR. Cf. *Odds Ratio*, *Relative Risk Reduction*.

Relative Risk Reduction

A measure of treatment effect in trials, calculated as $(C-E)/C$, where C is the risk in the control group and E is the risk in the experimental group. Cf. *Absolute Risk Reduction, Relative Risk.*

Relative Value Unit

A (US) hospital accounting procedure in which each item of service is allotted a weight showing its relative 'value' which, when multiplied by a tariff, yields a cost per item which can then be summed with other such items to calculate a patient's treatment costs.

Reliability

Consistency of repeated measures. There are many kinds. See *Interrater Reliability, Intrarater Reliability, Test–retest Reliability.*

Rent

In economics, this is used in two senses: (1) the income accruing to an owner of a *capital* good, like land or machinery, from contracting for another person to use it; (2) receipts in excess of the minimum amount necessary to keep a *factor of production* in its present use. Receipts in excess of its *transfer earnings.*

Rent Seeking

This is a term used by some economists to describe the processes through which individuals and corporations seek to use government to further their own interests and, in particular, to acquire streams of money (*rents*). An example would be members of a regulated industry manipulating the regulatory agency.

Repeatability

The extent to which the measurements of an observer at one date agree with those the same observer makes in the same circumstances at another date. See *Reliability.*

Replacement Investment

Same as *capital consumption*.

Representative Sample

Same as *stratified sample*.

Reproducibility

The extent to which the same results are obtainable under different circumstances, at another time, in another country, by another researcher and so on.

Reputational Good

Health care is sometimes regarded as a reputational good or service, though the term does not have wide currency or a widely accepted meaning. By this seems to be meant that the market for health care is characterized by *price-searching* and by substantial *information costs*, especially as regards the quality of service offered by different providers in the market. One common means of acquiring information about the *attributes* of various local providers is to ask the opinions of friends, neighbours and the current clients of various providers; that is, to seek information about the reputation of the providers.

Reputational Rent

Income to health care professionals that derives from one's reputation and status (unless income determines reputation and status).

Required Rate of Return

A target average *rate of return* for a public sector trading body in the UK.

Reservation Wage

The minimum wage that an employee will accept to take a job.

RESET

A general statistical test for misspecification of the functional form of a *regression model* and for omitted *variables*.

Residual

The difference between the observed and the fitted values of the *dependent variable* in a regression analysis.

Resource-based Relative Value Scale

A method of determining appropriate reimbursement under US *Medicare* based on the value of the estimated resources used per service.

Resources

Variously used to refer to *factors of production, inputs* or *goods* that have already been produced. It includes human resources.

Respiratory Medicine

The medical specialty concerned with diseases of the lungs and respiratory tract. See also *Pulmonary Medicine.*

Respirology

Same as *respiratory medicine.*

Response Bias

Same as *sample selection bias*.

Retrospective Cohort Study

An *observational study* of a cohort of initially disease-free individuals at some past date whose exposure to *risk factors* and whose *health* is followed over a period of time.

Retrospective Payment

Reimbursement of, say, an insured person by an insurance company, after they have incurred the health care expense. It is also used to describe the compensation paid to a provider of service after the service has been provided. A disadvantage of both forms of payment is that the reimburser has little control over the factors that have caused the expense to be what it is. Another, from the claimant's point of view, is the delay that occurs between incurring the expense and receiving the reimbursement. Cf. *Prospective Payment System*.

Retrospective Review

A review of a patient's past care management.

Retrospective Study

A study in which individuals are selected and past events investigated for their effects on health.

Returns to Scale

Describes what happens to the rate of output as all inputs are increased. See *Production Function*.

Revealed Preference

A person's (usually marginal) *willingness to pay* for an entity as revealed by (for example) market transactions or a controlled experiment. The emphasis is on the preference being revealed through behaviour in the form of a real act of choice or a hypothetical one rather than mere introspection. The theory of revealed preference is a branch of *utility theory* in which either one entity is preferred to another or the other is preferred to the one or, in some versions, neither is preferred to the other: '*indifference*'. It is concerned less with questions about whether choices actually do reveal preferences (sometimes this is taken axiomatically to be the case) than with building a logical structure of consistent axioms for choice theory and one that yields the implication that an individual's *demand curve* will have a negative slope. Cf. *Indifference Curve*. See *Conjoint Analysis* for an experimental version of revealed preference that has become used in health economics to evaluate the quality of health services.

Rheumatology

The medical specialty concerned with the treatment of diseases of the musculoskeletal system of joints and muscles.

Right-censored Data

Data about patients who did not reach the planned *end-point*. Also known as 'suspended data'. More generally, a data set in which some entities in a sample had not experienced the event of interest (for example, some machines had not broken down over the experimental time period of the test).

Risk Adjustment

In health economics, this is generally taken to mean the adjustments made to actuarially calculated health *insurance* premiums in order to promote *efficiency* and/or *equity*.

Risk Aversion

There are various definitions of this in economics. That most frequently met is the definition from expected utility theory: the extent to which a sure and certain outcome is preferred to a risky alternative with the same expected value. It is an implication of diminishing *marginal utility* of income. If people had a constant marginal utility of income they would be risk-neutral and, if an increasing marginal utility, risk-loving. In the finance literature on capital pricing, a quite different concept of risk aversion is used, in which people are classified as risk-averse if, for a given expected return, they prefer a portfolio with a smaller variance. See *Insurance* for an account of the way the diminishing marginal utility of income produces risk aversion.

Risk–benefit Analysis

A limited form of *cost–benefit analysis* that examines the benefits and risks of a particular procedure or alternative procedures.

Risk Difference

In a *clinical trial*, the *risk difference* is the absolute risk in the treated group minus the absolute risk in the control group. Sometimes called the 'absolute risk difference'. Cf. *Relative Risk*.

Risk Factor

A probabilistic determinant of ill-health. An element of behaviour, one's history, genetic inheritance, early parenting, exposure to harmful micro-organisms, environment and so on, that increases the probability of becoming diseased.

Risk-loving

Opposite of *risk aversion*. See *Expected Utility Theory*.

Risk-neutral

Being neither risk-averse nor risk-loving. See *Expected Utility Theory*.

Risk Pooling

Insurance pools risks. Since the costs of health care can be extremely high, uninsured individuals face possible large losses. By agreeing to contribute a small premium to a common pool held by an insurer for use to compensate whoever actually suffers the loss, individuals may be able to reduce the net costs of risk bearing in a way that increases their welfare. Premiums will normally include elements beyond the expected cost of insured events and their probabilities of occurring in order to cover the operating costs of the insurer and a return on *capital* (so-called *loading*). See *Adverse Selection*.

Risk Premium

In general, the reward to one who holds a risky asset as compared to a safe one. See *Moral Hazard*.

Risk Ratio

Same as *relative risk*.

Risk Selection

Forms of distortion in the health care insurance market. Risk selection is usually of two kinds: *adverse selection* and *cream skimming*. Both effects are generated by *competition* and both are harmful to *welfare*. Health *insurance* thus provides an exception (or ought to) to economists' predilection for competition.

Robustness

A test is said to be robust if violations of the assumptions on which it is based do not much affect its distribution when the null hypothesis is true. It is one desideratum by which options may be ranked. Cf. *Sensitivity Analysis*.

ROC

Acronym for *receiver operating characteristic curve*.

Roemer's Law

What has been dubbed 'Roemer's Law' is, according to the late US researcher and public health advocate Milton Roemer, 'the notion that under conditions of insurance or other prepaid support, the supply of beds tends to set a minimum utilization rate as well'. This has been popularly shortened to the adage that 'a bed built is a bed filled'. See Milton I. Roemer (1961), 'Bed supply and hospital utilization: a natural experiment', *Hospitals*, **35**, 36–41.

Rosser Index

An early ratio scale method of measuring *health*. See Rachel Rosser and Paul Kind (1978), 'A scale of valuations of states of illness: is there a social consensus?', *International Journal of Epidemiology*, **7**, 347–58.

RR

Acronym for *relative risk*.

Rule of Rescue

The so-called 'rule of rescue' is often proposed as an alternative (or supplement) to a *cost-effectiveness* criterion for selecting which treatments ought to be made available and to whom. The rule of rescue, in a general sense, reflects the general concern that many people have for those facing the immediate prospect of death (or something else regarded as pretty awful) and, in economic terms, it might be seen as a way of describing a caring *externality*. In situations where cost-effectiveness is being used as the basic criterion for determining the treatments that are to be made available within a health care benefits package, the rule of rescue is suggested as an element to be brought into consideration when the *incremental cost–effectiveness ratio* is highly unfavourable, there is only one treatment option, death is imminent, the situation occurs rarely and the total cost to the third party payer is 'small' (these are criteria used by the Australian Pharmaceutical Benefits Scheme). It is not altogether clear whether such a flagrant breach of cost-effectiveness principles might be avoided, but the intentions of those advocating the 'rule' still realized, by weighting health gains to those with relatively short life expectation or who have chronic past and/or prospective disabilities higher than health gains accruing to others within the cost–effectiveness *algorithm*.

It seems plain however, whatever one may think of its merits, that it is not really a 'rule' at all.

Rule Utilitarianism

Under rule-utilitarianism the rightness of an act is settled first by establishing the best rule of conduct in terms of its utilitarian consequences and then by following it. See *Utilitarianism*.

RVU

Acronym for *relative value unit*.

Rx

Shorthand for prescription drug or recommended course of medical treatment.

S

Sample

A set of data about individuals or other entities of interest that is smaller than the *population* from which it is drawn. There are many ways in which this may be appropriately done, some involving replacement of subjects already drawn from the population (like drawing a number from a hat and then putting it back before drawing again), others not. See, for some common types of sample, *Cluster Sample, Convenience Sample, Purposive Sample, Quota Sample, Random Sample, Sequential Sample, Stratified Sample.*

Sample Selection Bias

The *bias* created from analysing survey data when non-responders in a survey are systematically different from responders. This is also termed *response bias.* Cf. *Selection Bias.*

Sample Size

The number of entities (subjects and so on) in a subset of a population selected for analysis. The size of the *sample* and the way in which it has been drawn from the population are critical issues on any research study. For some, such as *clinical trials*, particularly where one wants the sample to be representative of the population, size is a major indicator of the statistical *power* of the analysis. *Randomization* in the sample selection is usually necessary for statistical tests to be valid. In other cases, however, as is sometimes the practice in *qualitative studies*, samples will be taken in order to reveal other *attributes* of the population that need not be representative.

Sampling Distribution of the Mean

A *distribution* of the sample *means* after taking repeated samples of a given size from a population.

Sampling Error

That element of the difference between what is observed in a *sample* and what is in the *population* sampled that can be attributed to the use of a sample.

Satisficing

A version of *bounded rationality*. Satisficing is behaviour that attempts to achieve a minimum level of a particular objective, but not to maximize it. It has been commonly used in analysing the behaviour of firms (including hospitals), where profit, instead of being the maximand, is a constraint which has to be achieved but, once achieved, enables managers also to choose other goals.

Saved Young Life Equivalent

SAVE is an alternative health outcome measure to the *healthy years equiva-lent* or the *quality-adjusted life-year*. It works via the *person trade-off* method, by asking experimental subjects to determine how many individuals it would take to move from health state X to health state Y (better) for such a change to be judged equivalent to saving one young person's life. For example, if the answer to that question proved to be 15 individuals, then 0.7 (1/15) would be the value ascribed to moving one person from health state X to health state Y.

Scarcity

Economics is founded on the proposition that there is scarcity: that more is wanted of goods and services than is available (either to individuals or to populations). A scarce good is a good having these characteristics, in contrast to a *free good*.

Scatter Diagram

Same as *scatter plot*.

Scatter Plot

A plot of the values of one variable against the corresponding values of another, with the coordinates of each pair marked by a dot. By visually inspecting the plot one can often detect whether the two variables are related and, if so, whether linearly or non-linearly.

Scenario Analysis

A form of *sensitivity analysis* that allows for the possibility that factors affecting *incremental cost–effectiveness ratios* are not independent of one another.

Scitovsky Criterion

A method of judging whether there is an increase in *social welfare*. Named after Tibor Scitovsky (1910–2002). See *Kaldor–Hicks Criterion*.

Scottish Intercollegiate Guidelines Network

A body within the Scottish *National Health Service* which develops guidelines for good medical practice that embody research on cost-effectiveness. SIGN works in conjunction with the *National Institute for Health and Clinical Excellence*. Its web site is http://www.sign.ac.uk/.

Screening

Screening is a means of detecting a disease in its pre-symptomatic stage (that is, when no symptoms are apparent). The number of people screened is typically large and those showing evidence of disease will then normally receive further (typically more costly and/or more risky) confirmatory tests and treatment. The theory is that early detection enables early treatment, though whether this is more *effective* (than, say, watchful waiting) or more *cost-effective*, is an empirical matter rather than one of principle and ought to be so treated. Screening programmes are subject to problems with *false positives* and *false negatives*. See also *Sensitivity* and *Specificity*. Screening programmes are also subject to *bias* (a common one is *lead-time bias*). A screening programme is a *health technology* that is often a suitable subject for a *clinical trial* and for *cost–effectiveness* or *cost–utility analysis*.

SD

Acronym for *standard deviation*.

SE

Acronym for *standard error*.

Search Cost

The costs in money and time of finding and exploiting opportunities to trade, including advertising and purchasing information about possible buyers/sellers.

Seasonal Variation

A variation in a *variable* that is attributable to the times of the year at which it was measured.

Second Best

A theorem in welfare economics to the effect that correcting one or more, but not all, *market imperfections* will not necessarily increase *social welfare*. For example, well-conducted *health technology appraisals* may indicate that the use of a particular set of technologies should be encouraged in a publicly funded health care system because the *incremental cost–effectiveness ratio* (ICER) exceeds a policy threshold, so local health care *commissioners* are instructed by a central authority to commission these services. In doing this, however, unless the budget is adjusted appropriately, the local commissioner will be forced, at least in the *short run*, to reduce expenditures on some other technologies which may have higher ICERs. Thus removing the one imperfection (underuse as revealed by the appraisals) may not enhance outcomes if another (the budget) is left unaddressed.

Second Fundamental Theorem of Welfare Economics

The proposition that any *Pareto optimum* can be achieved, given particular assumptions, through competitive markets and the ability to select the starting distribution of resource *endowments*. Cf. *First Fundamental Theorem of Welfare Economics*.

Second Order Uncertainty

You will not be in any doubt that a head is a head and a tail a tail but you will be in doubt as to which a throw of a fair coin will result in (first order uncertainty). If you doubt the fairness of the coin, then that is second order uncertainty. See *Uncertainty*.

Secondary Analysis

Using data collected for one purpose to explore other hypotheses.

Secondary Care

Health care provided in a hospital or institution to which a patient has been referred by a health care professional. Cf. *Primary Care, Tertiary Care*.

Secondary Care Trust

In the *National Health Service* of the UK, a hospital or other health care provider to which patients are referred which is also a *trust*.

Secondary Prevention

This term has two slightly different meanings, both of which are widely used. In the public health literature it is used to describe actions taken to prevent disease or injury when other *risk factors* are known to be present but before symptoms or other adverse consequences have become evident. In clinical epidemiology it means preventive actions intended to slow or stop the progress of a disease during its early clinical stages or to moderate the adverse consequences of disease or injury, especially through the prevention of recurrence. Screening tests are examples of the 'public health' approach, as these are done on populations at risk of diseases with significant latency periods like hyperlipidemia, hypertension, and breast and prostate cancer, but without clinical presentation. The amelioration of adverse consequences or slowing of deteriorations becomes classed as 'tertiary prevention' on this view. Cf. *Primary Prevention*. See *Prevention*.

Segmented Market

A *price-searcher's* market that is divided by a producer or seller in such a fashion as to enhance profitability. See *Price Discrimination*.

Selection Bias

A *bias* created when using data from a sample that differs systematically in its characteristics from the general population owing to a feature of the selection process. Such a bias will enter, for example, if the selection rule is 'take those whose names start with A', or 'those who live on the corner', or 'those who respond to a mailed questionnaire'. It also refers to the selection by patients or physicians of treatments that they believe will confer the greater benefits. It may also arise as a direct form of scientific fraud. *Blinding* is no safeguard against this form of bias. Measures taken to prevent it include taking the appropriate steps to minimize specific forms of it (such as *volunteer bias*), to require full disclosure of scientific procedures and possible conflict of interest, or to correct for it by multiplying an observed *odds ratio* by the inverse of the 'selection odds ratio'. Cf. *Randomizing, Sample Selection Bias, Sample Size*.

Selective Contracting

One of the means used by health care insurers to control costs, selective contracting entails the insuring agency contracting with local providers (doctors and hospitals) to provide specific services at pre-agreed prices and often with agreed quality assurance mechanisms. See *Managed Care, Preferred Provider, Organization*.

Self-referral

This has two common meanings. One is the ability of a patient to refer themselves directly to a specialist without going through a *gatekeeper*. The other is when physicians make referrals to institutions in which they have a direct or indirect financial relationship.

Semantic Differential Technique

A scaling device used in health measurement. A common form, in which the respondent is invited to rate an entity (like 'health' or 'satisfaction') on a scale, is to circle a number:

Good 3 2 1 0 1 2 3 Bad,

where 0 is neutral and one moves outwards from it towards the extremes of goodness and badness (of 'health' and so on).

Semi-Markov Model

A type of *Markov model* in which the *transition probabilities* are not constant but are related to the passage of time.

Semiparametric Model

A statistical method that combines parametric assumptions (such as that the relation between *dependent* and *independent variables* is linear) and non-parametric assumptions (such as that the *distribution* of the error term is unknown).

Sensitivity

The proportion of individuals with a condition who are correctly identified as such by a test. It is calculated thus: Sensitivity = $TP/(TP+FN)$, where TP is the number of true positives and FN is the number of false negatives. The

| | | Diagnosis | | |
		Present	Absent	Total
Test result	Present	a (true positive)	b (false positive)	$a + b$
	Absent	c (false negative)	d (true negative)	$c + d$
	Total	$a + c$	$b + d$	

terms 'positive' and 'negative' are used to refer to the presence or absence of the condition of interest. In the figure, sensitivity $= a/(a + c)$. Cf. *Negative Predictive Value*, *Positive Predictive Value*, *Specificity*.

Sensitivity Analysis

Sensitivity analysis is a procedure which adds further information to that derived in *clinical trials* and *cost–effectiveness analyses*. There are broadly two kinds: variable-by-variable analysis (sometimes called univariate sensitivity analysis) and scenario analysis (or multivariate sensitivity analysis). In variable-by-variable analysis one lists the important factors that affect the size of the costs and outcomes and for each of them a range of plausible values around the mean (for example, 'optimistic', 'most likely', or 'pessimistic') is specified. *Incremental cost–effectiveness ratios* (ICERs) are then calculated for each value of each factor, holding all other factors at their expected or most likely values. Thus, if there are three important factors and three estimates for each factor, seven different ICERs will be calculated. In this way one hopes to identify the source(s) of the biggest variations about which decision makers will have to make a judgment (and which may identify priority areas for future research). Scenario analysis allows for the possibility that factors affecting ICERs are not independent of one another, as is assumed in variable-by-variable analysis. In this case, one selects a variety of generalized states of the world (for example, worst case, middling case, best case) and takes all the worst case outcomes, middling, best (as the case may be) to calculate the ICERs that would result under the circumstances specified. Typically this method produces much more extreme variations than the variable-by-variable method. See *Modelling*.

Sentinel Event

A serious adverse health event that might have been avoided through appropriate care or alternative interventions or one that might indicate an important change in a population's characteristics. In the USA the Joint Commission on Accreditation of Healthcare Organizations (JCAHO) uses the term to describe serious medical errors.

Separation

Hospital separation is a discharge from hospital (alive or dead).

Sequential Sample

A procedure for creating a *sample* by adding subjects drawn from a population up to the point at which some predefined requirement for accuracy is satisfied.

Serial Correlation

Serial correlation occurs when a *variable* is *correlated* with itself in successive time periods.

SF-6D

The SF-6D is a simplification of the *SF-36®* index. It is a method by which *quality-adjusted life-years* may be derived empirically. It has six dimensions. Any patient who completes the *SF-36®* or the *SF-12®* can be uniquely classified according to the SF-6D. The SF-6D includes preference weights obtained from a sample of the UK general population using the *standard gamble* technique. Potential users may contact the owners on www.shef.ac.uk/sf-6d/info.htm.

SF-8™

The SF-8™ is an eight-item version of the *SF-36®* that yields a comparable eight-dimension health profile and comparable estimates of summary scores for the physical and mental components of health. The instrument, in both this and its other versions (SF-36 and SF-8), is copyrighted. Permissions can be sought at www.qualitymetric.com/products/descriptions/sflicenses.shtml.

SF-12®

A 12-item shorter form of *SF-36®*. The instrument, in both this and its other versions (SF-36 and SF-8), is copyrighted. Permission to use it can be sought at www.qualitymetric.com/products/descriptions/sflicenses.shtml.

SF-20

A 20-item short-form health survey covering physical functioning, role functioning, social functioning, mental health, current health perceptions and pain. It was developed for the RAND Health Insurance Experiment which was probably the most ambitious health insurance study ever conducted. Its web site is at www.rand.org/health/hiedescription.html.

SF-36®

The SF-36® is a multi-purpose, short-form health survey of 36 questions which yields an eight-scale generic profile of health status and psychometrically based physical and mental health summary measures and a *preference*-based health *utility* index (*quality-adjusted life-years*). The instrument, in both this and its smaller versions, is copyrighted and permission to use it can be sought at www.qualitymetric.com/products/descriptions/sflicenses.shtml.

SG

Acronym for *standard gamble*.

Shadow Price

The marginal *opportunity cost* of using a resource as estimated in a situation where there is no market price or the market price is believed to reveal opportunity cost sufficiently imperfectly to warrant the exercise. It may also be the *marginal valuation* of a service as revealed by methods such as *conjoint analysis*. Often used in *cost–effectiveness* and *cost–utility analyses*. See *Willingness to Pay*.

Short Run

A notional period in which some but not all *inputs* or *factors of production* are treated as *variable*. The ones treated as *fixed* may not necessarily be literally fixed in any technological sense (for example, the organization may be bound by a contract not to vary them). A dramatic example (not from health care) of a factor of production that might appear to be quite decidedly technologically 'fixed' – but was not – comes from railway history. When the English Great Western Railway's old broad gauge track was changed to the modern standard narrow gauge in 1892, the entire stretch of 213 miles from Exeter to Penzance was changed in one weekend. Moreover 177 miles of this had to be altered from the old longitudinal timbers to the modern cross-sleepers (ties). Of course, it took an army of platelayers to do it – 4200 of them. The point is that almost anything is possible given sufficient resources. The key issue is what is chosen or assumed to be fixed for the purposes of the particular question being addressed. See *Time*.

In general, the faster one seeks to make any change in input use, the more costly such changes will be. Some inputs are costlier, for many reasons, than others to alter and those that are costliest will tend to number amongst those most frequently treated as fixed. The real point, however, is that what to treat as fixed and what variable is itself a choice problem and any decision about this will restrict the scope of inputs to be considered variable. See *Long Run*.

Shortage

All too frequently 'shortage' is used in an assertive way by people having a vested interest of some sort in the entity asserted to be in short supply. The way economists would address any question of the adequacy of the supply of an entity relates to the value to be attached to the increase (and by whom it is attached) compared to the cost of creating the increase. If the value exceeds the cost, there is a shortage in the sense that (*ceteris paribus*, and given a few other assumptions) more ought to be consumed. More crudely, if demand exceeds supply at the going price there is said to be a shortage. However it does not follow that this shortage ought to be eliminated (for example, by allowing price to rise, supply to increase or demand to fall, or any combination of these three) unless there are grounds for believing that the *efficient* (or *equitable*) allocation of resources would be enhanced thereby. Likewise, in comparing the *marginal value* with the *marginal cost*, the interpretation given above applies only if illegitimate omissions from marginal cost and marginal value do not cause the ratio to fall below 1.0. Cf. *Excess Demand*.

Sick Role

A concept in medical sociology. In contrast to the 'medical model', in which illness is seen as a physical malfunctioning of the body or its microbiological invasion, the sick role is a temporary, medically sanctioned form of deviant behaviour by patients. The role entails being excused one's usual duties and not being held responsible for one's condition. In return, one is expected to seek professional advice and to adhere to treatments in order to 'get well'. Medical practitioners are empowered to sanction temporary absences from work and family duties.

Sickness Impact Profile

A behaviourally based measure of *health status* covering sleep and rest, eating, work, home management, recreation and pastimes, ambulation, mobility, body care and movement, social interaction, alertness behaviour, emotional behaviour and communication.

SID

Acronym for *supplier-induced demand*.

Sign

Indications of disease that can be seen or measured by a person other than the one experiencing them (for example, high blood pressure, fever or skin rash). Cf. *Symptom*.

SIGN

Acronym for *Scottish Intercollegiate Guidelines Network*.

Significance Level

A threshold probability which will require the rejection of the *null hypothesis* if the *p-value* is below it. It is generally 0.05, though this is a *convention*.

Simulation

Simulation is an analytical method or model for imitating a real-life system. See *Monte-Carlo Simulation*.

Single Blind Trial

A trial where the patient (or clinician) is aware of which arm a patient is in but the clinician (or patient) is not. See *Blinding*.

Single Factor Design

An experimental design having only one *independent variable*.

SIP

Acronym for *sickness impact profile*.

Skew

A *distribution* is said to be skewed if it is asymmetrical, having either a long tail to the left (negatively skewed) or a long tail to the right (positively skewed). In a positively skewed distribution, the *mean* is larger than the *median* and vice versa for a negatively skewed distribution. In *cost-effectiveness* studies, the cost data often display right-skewedness partly because costs cannot be negative and partly because a small fraction of patients often consume a disproportionately large amount of health care resources. In the distribution of income most people make under $50 000 a year, but some make lots more and a small number make many millions a year. The right-hand tail therefore stretches out while the left-hand tail stops at zero. See *Kurtosis*.

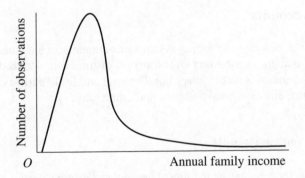

Skimping

Providing less intensive or lower-quality care than that specified in some standard or protocol in order to reduce costs in relation to the reimbursement due to the provider. This is believed to be particularly a problem in payment systems that are prospective and when doctors are paid by *capitation* or salary. When skimping is actually detrimental to patient health or welfare is harder to ascertain than to assert.

Small Area Variations

A term usually applied to the observed wide variations in clinical practices within jurisdictions having otherwise similar health care organizational structures and payments systems, and having populations with similar demographic, economic, social and epidemiological characteristics. These variations appear to be entirely arbitrary and most likely reflect uncertainty about or ignorance of best professional practice. See *Surgical Signature*.

SMM

See *Norwegian Centre for Health Technology Assessment.*

SMR

Acronym for *standardized mortality rate.*

Social Accounts

Used both to describe the formal systems of national accounts that measure economic activity in a country over a period of time and also to describe a wider set of statistics that embrace non-financial entities like life expectation, health status, environmental pollution and crime rates.

Social Cost or Benefit

Social costs (or benefits) are the sum of *internal* and *external costs* (or *benefits*). Social costs (or benefits) include internal costs (or benefits) together with any other effects that may create costs (or benefits) for other members of the community. Social costs are all *opportunity costs*. Thus the social cost of a medical procedure will include its effects on the household and other sectors and not just the costs that are private to a hospital or clinic. Social costs do not include *transfers* (transfer payments) since what one gains another loses.

Social Decisions Approach

A method of deriving values for entities not readily measured in other ways for the purposes of public decision making. It works by assuming that past decisions in the public sector have been consistent and that one may infer from the sums expended that the benefits thereby gained must have been valued at least as highly as this expenditure (or, if not expended, then the benefits cannot have been worth this much). For example, if a programme to introduce child-proof bottle caps for drugs at a cost of $50 per expected life saved was not adopted, then it is inferred that the average value of an expected life for children at risk was not greater than $50. Plainly the method also involves the absence of *confounders* that may have affected the past decisions but which may be irrelevant to the one under current consideration. The method's advantage seems to be mainly in exposing apparent inconsistencies in public decision-making. See *Value of Life*.

Social Discount Rate

This is the *discount rate* that is stipulated for use in public decision making. In evaluating health-related projects, there is controversy as to whether *benefits* (as distinct from *costs*) ought to be discounted at all. Most economists take the view that future health benefits ought to be discounted but there is disagreement as to the principles that ought to govern the choice of discount rate(s). One view is that the *opportunity cost* of *capital* for the economy as a whole ought to be used so that health-related investments are costed in similar ways to other investments (some argue that this rate might be modified in the case of public sector health investments to reflect a presumed lower risk, others that risk adjustments ought to be made separately and not confounded with time discounting). There is no agreement on whether a marginal or an average opportunity cost of capital ought to be used. A second view is that the rate ought to correspond to the average (or possibly marginal) rate of *time preference* in the community as a whole. A third view is that, because of the high degree of *publicness* of health investments, the social rate ought to be a rate deliberatively chosen by society's representatives (effectively politicians or people appointed by accountable politicians) bearing in mind whatever ethical and other considerations they choose. See *Cost–benefit Analysis, Cost–effectiveness Analysis, Cost–utility Analysis.*

Social Medicine

Same as *public health medicine.*

Social Opportunity Cost

Opportunity cost viewed from the standpoint of all members of a society and not just that of a particular private decision maker.

Social Rate of Time Preference

The rate at which it is appropriate to trade off present and future consumption for purposes of public investment. See *Time Preference.*

Social Welfare

The overall well-being of a society. It is generally assumed by economists to depend upon the welfares of the individuals who make up that society but how they are linked is a matter for much controversy. See *Arrow Impossibility Theorem, Arrow Social Welfare Function, Bergson–Samuelson Social Welfare Function, Extra-welfarism, Pareto Optimality.*

Social Welfare Function

A function that relates overall *social welfare* to its determinants, especially the preferences of those individuals taken as members of a society. See *Arrow Impossibility Theorem, Arrow Social Welfare Function, Bergson–Samuelson Social Welfare Function, Extra-welfarism, Pareto Optimality.*

Socialized Health Care

Although it is not a technical term in economics, 'socialized' health care seems generally to be a term used to describe a system in which a third party payer like an insurance agency (which may be private or public) covers its members (membership will usually be compulsory for people with defined characteristics like area of residence) for a specified list of procedures (usually ones deemed to be *cost*-effective) for a fee that is unrelated to need and which may be part of the tax structure. It is similar to *managed care* both in terms of its potential for containing *health care expenditures* and in its promotion of *evidence-based medicine*, though managed care organizations (in the USA) are on a smaller scale than most systems described as 'socialized' (for example, restricted to particular employee groups or people with specific eligibilities as under Medicare or Medicaid).

Societal Perspective

A view often adopted in *cost–effectiveness* and *cost–utility* analyses to the effect that all the costs and outcomes of the use of a technology ought to be taken into account regardless of any characteristics of the person or individual on whom they fall.

Spacing out Bias

A *bias* that is sometimes met when using instruments for measuring *health status*. It occurs when subjects space out their scores to fill the available range offered and there are grounds for believing that their scores ought to be more concentrated.

Spearman Rank Correlation Coefficient

The Spearman rank correlation coefficient (r_S) is a means of measuring the strength of the association between two *ordinally* ranked entities. It has limits of +1 and −1.

$$r_s = 1 - 6\sum \frac{d^2}{n(n^3 - 1)}$$

where d is the difference in the rank order and n is the number of ranks. Cf. Pearson's *correlation coefficient r*. Named after the British psychologist and statistician Charles Edward Spearman (1863–1945).

Specificity

The proportion of individuals without a condition who are correctly identified as such by a test. It is calculated thus: Specificity = $TN/(TN+FP)$, where TN is the number of true negatives and FP is the number of false positives. The terms 'positive' and 'negative' are used to refer to the presence or absence of the condition of interest. In the figure, specificity = $d/(b + d)$. Cf. *Negative Predictive Value, Positive Predictive Value, Sensitivity*.

| | | Diagnosis | | |
		Present	Absent	Total
Test result	Present	a (true positive)	b (false positive)	$a + b$
	Absent	c (false negative)	d (true negative)	$c + d$
	Total	$a + c$	$b + d$	

Spectrum Bias

This exists when the *sensitivity* and/or *specificity* of a test varies in different populations that have different characteristics such as sex ratios, age or severity of disease.

Spillovers

Same as *external effects*.

Springboarding

The production, sale or use of a patented product, without the *patent* owner's permission, for the purposes of obtaining marketing approval.

Standard Deviation

A measure of the dispersion of a set of numbers around the *mean* value of a *variable*. It is the square root of the *variance*. A large value of *SD* implies a large dispersion about the mean and vice versa.

Standard Error

SE is the estimated *standard deviation* of the sampling *distribution* of the sample *mean* or of some other estimator. It is a measure of precision rather than of statistical significance. In *multiple regression* analysis, the estimated *SE* is usually placed beneath the estimated value for each coefficient: the smaller it is, the more accurate the estimate is likely to be. Sometimes, however, the *Student's t* or the *z-statistic* is placed beneath the estimated value for each coefficient. In these cases, the larger the number the smaller the *p-value*.

Standard Gamble

A method of measuring *health status* (or some aspects of quality of life) using *expected utility theory*. It proceeds by asking an appropriate panel of judges to rank the entities to be measured. Any two of these are then assigned numbers that preserve their relative ordering (any numbers will do). A less preferred third entity is then offered each judge in uncertain combination with the more preferred entity and each is asked to say whether they prefer the uncertain prospect to the certainty of the less preferred of the initial two entities. The probability in the uncertain prospect is adjusted until the judge is indifferent between it and the certain prospect, at which point the judge will have implicitly assigned a numerical value to the third entity. In this way many entities can be measured on an interval scale (see *Utility* for an explanation of this). Thus, if $H(.)$ denotes the index of health status, and three styles of living are ranked $H(A) > H(B) > H(C)$, then letting $H(A) = 4$ and $H(B) = 2$, the value for $H(C)$ can be found by adjusting p (the probability) until the following equation holds:

$$pH(A) + (1-p)H(C) = H(B).$$

If, in an experiment, $p = 0.4$, then the values are $H(A) = 4$, $H(B) = 2$ and $H(C) = 2/3$. Of course, the set of values ($H(C)$ and so on) obtained in this manner yields valuations of health states only if the subjects of the experiments are people who choose as though they are expected utility maximizers. See *Person Trade-off Method*, *Time Trade-off Method*.

Standardized Mortality Rate

Same as *standardized mortality ratio*.

Standardized Mortality Ratio

The standardized mortality ratio (SMR) is the number of observed deaths in a study population divided by the expected deaths in the study population and multiplied by 100. The expected deaths are the number of deaths that would occur if the study population experienced the same age-specific, sex-specific (and sometimes ethnicity-specific) mortality as the reference population. Thus, if the SMR is less than 100, the mortality experience of the study population is less than that of the reference population. The statistic enables easy calculation of the 'excess mortality' which is due to variables other than age, sex or race. Cf. *Crude Death Rate*.

Starting Point Bias

A bias sometimes found in responses to *contingent valuation* questionnaires and similar instruments. The final amount settled upon is determined in part by the initial amount bid, or prompted. See *Bias*.

State-dependent Utility

The idea that expected utility from consumption in general is not the same if one is (say) well as when one is ill or that the value of health care is not the same if one is well as when one is ill. In other words, the utility of consumption (or investment) is dependent on one's own state (of health, amongst other things) and external characteristics (an ice cream in the rain is not the same thing as an ice cream in the sunshine). The idea also introduces another role for uncertainty, *viz.* uncertainty about one's health state (how high is my 'bad' cholesterol? Am I a carrier of that gene?) or about the weather (and so on). Oddly the idea is much less used and discussed in health economics than one might expect.

State-preference

Same as *state-dependent utility*.

Stated Preference

Willingness to pay for a non-marketed entity as derived from questionnaires or experiments. It is 'stated' verbally (orally or in writing) rather than revealed by actual behaviour in experiments or in real life. Another term for it is *contingent valuation*. See *Conjoint Analysis, Revealed Preference*.

Statistical Inference

Statistical inference is the inference of properties of an unknown *distribution* from data that have been generated by that distribution. There are many forms, such as graphical analysis and *Bayesian* analysis, as well as more formal methods of hypothesis testing.

Statistical Power

'Power' is the probability that a test will reject an untrue *null hypothesis*. In health economics, 'power' most frequently refers to the statistical power of a *clinical trial*. In general, a trial ought to be big enough to have a high chance of detecting a *statistically significant* effect and one that is also clinically or biologically significant – if one exists. *Sample* size is therefore critically important. The researcher needs to decide the degree of difference between two groups being compared that would constitute a minimally clinically significant effect. How large the sample needs to be to deliver statistically significant results can be determined by using a statistical *nomogram*. The power of the study (moderate, high or very high) is the chance of detecting a prespecified true clinically relevant difference between the groups at a prespecified *p-value* (usually $p < 0.05$).

Statistical Significance

In general, a measure of how confidently an observed event or difference between two or more groups can be attributed to a hypothesized cause. The *p-value* is the most commonly encountered way of reporting statistical significance. The (*frequentist*) interpretation of a p-value of 0.05 is that, if you repeated the experiment a very large number of times, you would expect that result, or a more extreme one, 5 per cent of the time by chance alone. More formally, one forms a null hypothesis about what the underlying data or relationships are. The null hypothesis is typically that something is not present, that there is no effect or that there is no difference between the populations comprising the experimental group and the controls in an experiment. One then calculates the probability of observing those data if the null hypothesis is correct, using an appropriate statistical test (which will depend on the shape of the *distribution* of the sampled variables). If the p-value is small (0.05 is conventionally used) the result is said to be 'statistically significant' (that is, it is highly unlikely that the null hypothesis is true). The precision of an estimated value is not the same thing as its statistical significance.

Clinical significance and policy significance are entirely different from statistical significance. One can have highly statistically significant estimates of things that are wholly irrelevant clinically, biologically or in terms of public policy. One reason why it may be irrelevant is that an effect may be highly statistically significant but so small in its absolute effect as to be completely uninteresting. Similarly, an important clinical difference may not be reflected by a statistically significant outcome. Cf. *Statistical Power*.

Steering

A term used in the US health care insurance industry. It describes a process by which people who are enrolled in insurance plans are directed by the insurers towards particular providers. See *Managed Care, Preferred Provider Organization*.

Stepwise Regression

This involves entering *independent variables* one at a time in order to assess the additional impact each has.

Stochastic

A synonym for 'random'.

Stochastic Frontier

Econometric attempts to estimate *production possibility curves* (frontiers) tended to assume that deviations from the frontier implied inefficiency rather than random shocks or other *exogenous* effects. Stochastic frontier analysis is a method for overcoming this problem.

Stochastic Model

A model that allows randomness in one or more of its *parameters* or *variables*. Cf. *Deterministic Model*.

Stochastic Regression Imputation

A method of dealing with *incomplete data*.

Stock

The quantity of an entity (like housing, health or money) that exists at a point in time. Cf. *Flow*.

Stop-loss

The maximum annual out-of-pocket payment by an insured person. See *Insurance*.

Stopping Rule

In randomized controlled trials and similar systematic research designs, stopping rules define circumstances in which the experiment will cease, bearing in mind the statistical reliability of the evidence. The evidence might take the form of clear *dominance* of one of the procedures being compared over the other before the trial has been completed.

Strategic Health Authorities

Statutory bodies of the *National Health Service* (NHS) in England, of which there are 28, with responsibility for planning the health care arrangements in their localities and for overseeing the effective functioning of local NHS organizations.

Stratified Sample

A *sample* drawn from a population that is divided into strata from each of which a random sample is taken. The strata selected may relate to features of the population that are expected to alter the impact of the treatment being investigated. For instance, a vitamin may be anticipated to have smaller effects on families that grow many of their own vegetables compared to ones who do not. If the sample is not stratified to include an adequate proportion from those who do and do not grow their own vegetables, it may turn out, by chance, that all selected by random come almost exclusively from only one of these two groups. This may result in the effect of vitamin supplements being overestimated or underestimated for the population as a whole, underestimated if there were an unrepresentatively large group of vegetable growers in the sample, overestimated in the reverse case. The problem is reduced if the total sample size is large enough to allow for stratified sampling with respect to factors expected to alter the effectiveness of a treatment. In addition, if the stratified sample is large enough, the differential impact of the treatment on the different subgroups can be estimated.

Structural Unemployment

Structural unemployment exists when an individual's marginal value to any employer is lower than the minimum wage conventionally or legally payable (in the limit, a person's value could be zero, in which case their value is lower than any wage payable). This is the main constituent of most countries' unemployment statistics. Since being active in searching for work is usually a part of the definition of (involuntary) unemployment, some (perhaps many) who are structurally unemployed are not included in unemployment statistics because after a time these people may have become so convinced that they will not find a job that they stop trying. Structural unemployment frequently accompanies the wholesale decline of industries that are geographically concentrated.

Student's *t*-test

See *t-test*. A test based on the t-*distribution*. An important example uses the result that

$$t \equiv \frac{\bar{x} - \mu}{s/\sqrt{n}}$$

has a *t*-distribution with (*n*–1) degrees of freedom, where a simple random sample is taken from a normal population, where $\bar{x}$ is the sample *mean*, μ is the population mean and *s* the sample *standard deviation*. It was invented by William Gossett (1876–1937) a chemist employed by Guinness in Dublin and, later, London. He used the nom-de-plume 'Student' because Guinness employees were not permitted to publish. The only other students in question seem to have been Gossett's consumers (of his extensive statistical work, of course).

Study Arm

Refers to the experimental group in a *clinical trial* having a *control* or other comparison group.

Subgroup Analysis

In *clinical trials* and *cost–effectiveness analyses*, particular interest might focus on particular subgroups of patients defined by characteristics such as gender, race, age, study centre, country, comorbidity or disease *risk factors*. Subgroup analysis is the epidemiological and economic analysis of such groups. It can degenerate into *data-mining*. Many *confounders* such as sex, age, race, centre, smoking status, stage of disease or coexistent disorders can affect outcome. When these are examined post hoc, the risk of *false positives* and false inferences is high: there may be statistically significant differences in outcome between subgroups even when neither arm of the study receives any intervention. In one study (the Second International Study of Infarct Survival) there was found to be a slight adverse impact of aspirin therapy on patients born under the star signs Gemini and Libra.

Subjective Uncertainty

Same as *second-order uncertainty*. See *Uncertainty*.

Substitutes

Goods or services whose demand rises or falls as the price of another good rises or falls. The cross-*elasticity* of demand is positive. They tend to be goods that serve similar purposes, like the *NSAIDs* Fiorinal and Lanorinal, two drugs each containing aspirin (acetylsalicylic acid) and both in capsule form. In other markets, you can get *generic* aspirin under the name 'aspirin'. But beware! In some markets, 'Aspirin' is a protected name and is owned by the German company Bayer AG. In these markets, Aspirin sells at a higher price than the generic form. So chemically identical goods – perfect substitutes (unless you prefer your medicines to be initially capped) – do not always cost the same and the higher-priced version still finds buyers.

Substitution Effect

The effect on the demand for a good or service of a change in its relative price, holding *real income* constant and *ceteris paribus*. See *Income Effect*.

Substitution in Production

The common property of most health and other *production functions* that one *input* may be replaced by some amount of another without output changing.

Sunk Cost

A cost that has already been incurred. By virtue of their being 'sunk', costs of this kind are not *opportunity costs* at all as they represent no current or prospective sacrifice that is necessarily entailed in a decision. This does not necessarily mean that they are irrelevant to current decision making, however, even though standard (*normative*) theory holds them to be of interest only insofar as the past may be thought to hold useful lessons for the future, not least because the idea of managerial commitment, especially to major investment projects, may be an important element in the future credibility of the people who make major decisions of that sort. It is a common experience that sunk costs often do weigh heavily with firms and households and it seems preferable to explore the possibility that this ought not to be dismissed as 'irrational' without exploration of possible reasons for its actually being rational.

Superior Good

Another name for *normal good*.

Supplier-induced Demand

The effect that doctors (or some other group of professionals), as providers of services, may have in creating more patient demand than there would be if they acted as perfect *agents* for their patients. There appears to be some adjustment of physician behaviour in order to maintain incomes. For example, as female fertility has fallen, obstetricians in the USA appear to have increased the rate of caesarian section deliveries relative to vaginal. The former carry a higher fee and the switch enables a partial compensation for the diminishing business available to obstetricians. Supplier-induced demand (SID) has commonly been alleged to arise when there is an increase in the number of doctors; however the fact that the supply of services increases as doctors increase may be the ordinary result of an increase in supply (demand constant) rather than the result of a shift in both supply and demand. Testing for the presence and extent of SID has been bedevilled by this *identification problem*. *Fee-for-service* is often held to encourage unnecessary supplier-induced demand, though the evidence for this is hotly contested. The debate is clouded by a number of other mysteries: how 'unnecessary' is any demand that might be induced? Might not inducement be a good thing in the presence of certain kinds of *externality*? See *Agency Relationship*, *Asymmetry of Information*, *Small Area Variations*, *Target Income Hypothesis*.

Supply Assurance

A term indicating that a health care *provider* is contracted with a specific purchaser to have sufficient capacity set aside to deal with peaks in demand from that purchaser's patients. See *Purchaser–provider Split*.

Supply Curve

A bivariate geometrical representation of a *supply function* where the *dependent variable* is quantity supplied per period and the *independent variable* is price. In general, a supply curve shows both the maximum rate of supply per unit of time at a variety of prices and also the minimum price that must be paid to induce the supplier to provide that amount, *ceteris paribus*. (A so-called 'backward bending' supply curve shows only the maximum that will be supplied at a variety of prices.) Conventionally the price variable is measured on the *y* axis and the quantity on the *x* axis, even when quantity is the dependent variable. Under *price-taking* conditions, the *marginal cost* curve is the supply curve.

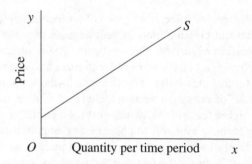

Supply Function

The supply function is a mathematical representation of the rate of supply as the *dependent variable* and its various determinants. The *supply curve* is a two-dimensional representation of a supply function, with supply shown as a function of price (*ceteris paribus*).

Supply-side Cost Sharing

See *Cost Sharing*.

Surgical Signature

Surgical signature describes the striking and persistent differences in the frequency of performance of particular surgical procedures such as prostate operations, back surgery and coronary artery bypass grafting, even among neighbouring regions with very similar demographic, social and economic characteristics and where the health care systems have similar reimbursement mechanisms. The variations seem to be completely arbitrary and are usually conjectured to arise from physician uncertainty, the absence of agreed protocols and other *clinical guidelines*, and/or physicians' ignorance of or unwillingness to adopt best practice as determined by senior professional peers. There are also marked variations across jurisdictions, where to 'surgical signature' get added the variety in reimbursement systems, different demographic characteristics, differences in medical education and so on. See *Small Area Variations, Supplier-induced Demand*.

Surveillance Bias

A *bias* in *clinical trials* arising from some groups in a sample being more closely investigated than others (and the consequential discovery of spurious differences between them).

Survival

See *Survival Analysis, Survival Curve, Time to Event*.

Survival Analysis

The analysis of trial data in terms of time to an outcome (such as death). Mean survival is the time to the outcome in question divided by the number of subjects in a trial who reached the outcome.

Survival Curve

In some *clinical trials*, the outcome is the difference in the *distributions* of survival times of an experimental and a control group. Survival curves (functions) plot the proportion of all individuals in a population or sample surviving at a variety of dates. The term 'survival' sounds like life-and-death, which it sometimes is, but survival curves can be used to study times required to reach any well-defined endpoint (for example, discharge from hospital, return to work).

The analysis of survival data in clinical trials can pose problems because some observations are *censored* as the event of interest has not occurred for

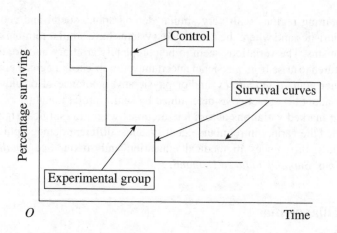

all patients over the study period. For example, when patients are recruited over, say, three years, one recruited at the end of the study may be alive at follow-up after a year, whereas one recruited at the start may have died after two years. The patient who died has a longer observed survival than that for the one who still survives and whose ultimate survival time may be unknown. The *Kaplan–Meier Method* is a method of estimating the proportion of patients surviving to any given date, which is also the estimated probability of survival to that time for a member of the population from which the sample is drawn. A survival curve (Kaplan–Meier curve) plots the estimated probability of survival for a sample of data (not the actual proportion surviving) against time on the horizontal axis in such a fashion that the censoring is allowed for and the maximum use is made of the available data.

Survival Rate

The number of subjects in a trial who have survived at time t, divided by the number of subjects.

Swiss Network for Health Technology Assessment

Switzerland's national association for people engaged in *health technology assessment*. Its website is at www.snhta.ch/about/index.php.

Switching Value

That value of a *variable* that renders the decision maker indifferent between taking an action and not taking it (or taking another).

Symptom

An indication of a disease or health condition that a patient feels (for example, pain, dizziness or nausea). Cf. *Sign*.

Systematic Review

A systematic review differs from other types of review in that it is a comprehensive and relatively unbiased synthesis of the research evidence. Essential features include the explicit identification and scoping of research questions, the use of explicit methods for searching the literature, explicit criteria for including or excluding material, explicit criteria for appraising quality and reliability, and a systematic analysis/synthesis of research findings (for example, by *meta-analysis*).

T

Tangibles

A term that is sometimes used to describe the outcomes of decisions that are either in the form of priced consequences or in some other measurable form. The term is unsatisfactory (as is its antonym '*intangible*') on the ground that consequences that are not measured are unmeasured usually because no one has yet invented a measure for them rather than because they are in principle immeasurable. Even 'psychic' effects yield to various forms of *utility measurement*. The critical judgments that need to be made usually concern the adequacy of particular extant measures (for example, prices) or the characteristics that a measure ought to have if it is to be regarded as a good one for a particular set of purposes.

Target Income Hypothesis

A hypothesis that physicians (and possibly others) have a target income (which need not be fixed over time) which their rate and style of work is adjusted to achieve, given a fee schedule specifying the fee per service provided.

Tarification à l'activité

The French *prospective payment* system for hospital financing based upon a common national tariff for *groupes homogènes de malades*.

Technical Efficiency

Equivalent to being on an *isoquant*, that is, not using more of any one input than is strictly necessary, given the amounts of others in use. See *Cost-effectiveness*, *Efficiency*.

Technological Change

This refers to new knowledge and inventions (see *Patent*) and generally falls into two classes: embodied technological change, when increased productive potential is created by the use of new or upgraded *capital*, and 'disembodied technological change', when the change takes the form of new methods of management, or marketing, or other processes. 'Capital' here includes *human capital* and might also include drugs, which classically embody new technologies. See *Productivity*.

Technology Matrix

A table showing the relationship between *inputs* and the maximum *outputs* or *outcomes* of any procedure or process. See *Production Function*.

Terms of Trade

The ratio of an index of a jurisdiction's export *price index* to its import price index. The terms of trade are said to 'improve' if weighted export prices rise faster or fall more slowly than import prices.

Tertiary Care

Specialized hospital care, usually available only on referral from *primary* or *secondary* medical care personnel, provided by specialists working in regional or national centres having the personnel and facilities for special investigations, treatment and training.

Tertiary Prevention

This term is sometimes used to describe procedures elsewhere known as *secondary prevention*: the amelioration of the consequences of disease, symptomatic relief and palliative care. Secondary prevention, when the tripartite distinction is made, becomes concerned mainly with *screening*. See also *Prevention, Primary Prevention*.

Tertile

When a continuous *variable* is split for convenience into three equal-sized chunks of data, the cut-off points between them are called tertiles. See *Quantile.*

Test Discount Rate

The discount rate required by government to be used in the public service. See *Option Appraisal, Perspective, Social Discount Rate.*

Test–retest Validity

The degree to which scores in an experiment as awarded by a judge are the same when the experiment is repeated using the same judge.

Therapeutic Personality Bias

This *bias* occurs when the observer is not *blinded*. The observer's beliefs about *effectiveness* may influence outcomes and their measurements.

Thermometer

In health economics, reference to a thermometer is likely to be to a device known as a *visual analogue scale* by which subjects in an experiment assign numbers to *states of health.*

Third Party Payer

A payer, typically a private or public insurance agency, who compensates the provider for the expense of providing a service to the patient or the patient after they have paid the provider's bill. Patients and providers are the other two 'parties'.

Thoracic Surgery

The branch of surgery concerned with diseases of the chest (between the neck and the pelvis).

Threshold Analysis

A type of *cost–effectiveness* or *cost–utility* study in which estimates are made of the maximum *costs* or minimum *benefits* that would have to be yielded by a technology if it were to meet a predetermined threshold (minimum for acceptability) *incremental cost–effectiveness ratio*. See *Acceptability Curve, Cost–effectiveness Threshold*.

Thurstone's Law of Comparative Judgment

A procedure used in *pairwise comparisons*, under which the placement of descriptions of states (for example, of health) on a scale is quantified by requiring subjects to compare statements in pairs and to indicate which statement of the pair presents greater 'intensity'. Thurstone's Law is a probabilistic expression for the strength of this intensity. Named after the American psychometrician Louis Leon Thurstone (1887–1955). See Louis L. Thurstone (1928), 'Attitudes can be measured', *American Journal of Sociology*, **33**, 529–54.

Time

Time plays at least four distinct roles in economics. First, time enters most economic functional relationships either because one is considering rates of consumption (for example of drugs) or rates of inputs (for example, so many X-ray machine hours per period of time) or rates of enjoyment of particular states (for example, such and such a state of health) or because one is considering entities at a particular point in time, such as *stocks* of health. Second, time enters explicitly as a factor in intertemporal choice theory, concerning the optimal pattern of consumption, investment or the use of a resource over time. Third, time is used to classify 'runs' in production theory as in *short run* and *long run*. Fourth, time is itself a kind of resource having *opportunity costs* and it can be either efficiently or inefficiently utilized; thus the patient's time is an inherent part of many processes of healing, as it is frequently an inherent part of gaining access to health care (*waiting*). See *Time Preference*.

Time Costs

Reflects the idea that people's time has alternative uses which are valuable and are, hence, *opportunity costs*. Not all time costs in health care are, however, costs in this sense. For example, although waiting in a doctor's waiting room may involve some sacrifice of time (whose value will depend on the alternative use to which it would have been put), waiting for admission as a hospital inpatient does not (though it may have other disadvantages). See *Queue, Time Price*.

Time Horizon

A fixed point of time in the future which is an *end-point* in a *clinical trial* or the point at which consideration of the consequences (*costs* or *benefits*) of an earlier decision is deemed to cease.

Time Preference

An individual's preference for consumption now rather than consumption later. It is measured by the *marginal intertemporal rate of substitution*: the minimum future sum required to compensate an individual for forgoing consumption now. Thus, if the time preference rate is 3 per cent per annum, the individual will be indifferent between $1.03 next year and $1.00 today. It is also the slope of an *indifference curve* where the horizontal axis shows consumption today and the vertical axis shows consumption at a future date. As the name implies, the usual presumption is that the rate of time preference will be positive. The distinction between marginal and average time preference rates ought to be borne in mind. The average rate relates to a total bundle of goods and services consumed now or in the future. The marginal rate relates to a small incremental bundle. Quite why future consumption (setting aside all considerations of uncertainty) should be considered less valuable to individuals than the same level of current consumption has never been satisfactorily explained (at least, not by economists), though it seems plausible to accept that people with large current consumption and small and uncertain future consumption may have a negative rate of time preference. See *Discounting*.

Time Price

Reflects the idea that money prices are not the only access barrier to health services. Just as money price and the rate of use are negatively associated, so is time price (for example the time spent travelling to a facility) and the rate of use. The *direct cost* of travelling also plays a similar role. These time costs are nowadays generally regarded as direct costs in *cost–effectiveness* and *cost–utility analyses* rather than *indirect* or *productivity costs* which include the value of lost working and leisure time. Note that time spent waiting need not be a cost in the same way as it is when standing in a line or queue: standing in line or sitting in a waiting room represents *opportunity cost* (the time has alternative valuable uses); time on a list waiting for admission to hospital is a postponement of treatment and does not involve current opportunities being forgone. See *Queue*.

Time to Event

In *clinical trials* patients are recruited over a period and followed up to a fixed date or possible event such as death or recurrence of a tumour (negative), conception or discharge from hospital (usually positive) or cessation of breast feeding (neutral). The time between recruitment and the event is 'time to event' or *survival* (even when death is not the event in question). Subjects in the trial who survive to the fixed date but for whom the event has not occurred are said to have a *censored* survival time.

Time Trade-off Method

A preference-based method for assigning utilities to health states, in which the subject is asked how much time they are willing to sacrifice from a given lifespan in one health state to have a given number of years in perfect health. Thus, if $H(.)$ denotes the index of health status, and two styles of living are ranked $H(A) > H(B)$, one seeks experimentally to find how much shorter the time spent with $H(A)$ should be to be of the same utility as a longer period in state $H(B)$. Let t be the time spent in state $H(B)$ and x the time spent in state $H(A)$. One then seeks experimentally to vary x until the subject is *indifferent* between the two states:

$$x.U(H(A)) = t.U(H(B)).$$

The ratio x/t provides the utility of state $H(B)$ relative to state $H(A)$. If the latter is arbitrarily set as 1.0 (= perfect health), then the *(ratio) scale* for all such states of lower utility may be revealed. See *Healthy-years Equivalent, Person Trade-off Method, Standard Gamble*.

Timing of Costs and Benefits

Dating the occurrence of *costs* and *benefits*, usually as a prelude to their *discounting*. See *Discounting*.

Tobit Models

A procedure for doing *multiple regression* when the data are *censored*. It has nothing to do with the book of the Apocrypha but is named after economics Nobel prize-winner James Tobin (1918–2002). See James Tobin (1958), 'Estimation of relationships for limited dependent variables', *Econometrica*, **26**, 24–36.

Top-down Studies

A term used in costing methods for *cost–effectiveness* and similar analyses, according to which data sources for costs are precollected data, often routine and often gathered for purposes other than the purposes of the study in question, or else designed for a variety of uses (for no one of which they may be ideal). Cf. *Bottom-up Studies*.

Total Cost

The sum of *fixed* (or *overhead*) costs and *variable costs* when output is produced in a technically *efficient* way.

Total Factor Productivity

The *productivity* of all factors involved as a whole in a production activity.

Townsend Index

An index of social deprivation developed by Peter Townsend and used mainly in the UK. See Peter Townsend, P. Phillimore and A. Beattie (1988), *Health and Deprivation: Inequality and the North*, London: Croom Helm. Cf. *Jarman Index*.

Toxicology

The science of poisons.

Trade-off

The idea that every individual will voluntarily sacrifice some of one good or service in exchange for a sufficient increase in the amount of some other. In *production functions* the idea that some of one *input* or *factor of production* can be sacrificed without loss of *output* if there is a sufficient increase in some other input.

Trade-off Matrix

An instrument used in *conjoint analysis*. It presents in matrix form how the subject can have more of one *attribute* of a service only by having less of another. In complex cases where the attributes are many, the matrices usually reduce the number of comparisons to pairs (*pairwise comparisons*) or some other manageable number.

Trade-related Aspects of Intellectual Property Rights

The World Trade Organization's TRIPS (not TRAIPS) covers a variety of intellectual property rights such as trademarks, copyright and *patents*. It introduced a greater degree of international uniformity in their treatment, for example by setting standard patent lives at 20 years.

Transaction Cost

The cost of making any kind of transaction in a market. It includes the costs involved in searching for possible providers of service, the range of services offered, assessing their quality, their fees and charges, any *agent*'s or broker's charges, any time spent in waiting rooms, and any other cost that is not a part of the money price actually paid for the service.

Transfer Earnings

The minimum payment required by the owner of a factor of production to prevent it from being transferred to another use. Transfer earnings are usually lower than actual earnings (which is why the owner has not transferred the factor). See *Rent*.

Transfer Payment

A transfer of purchasing power from one group (for example, taxpayers) to another (for example, health care beneficiaries). It is not to be confused with *opportunity cost*, since transfer payments do not measure the most highly valued alternative use of resources, whether human or non-human.

Transfer Price

This is a procedure used in the pharmaceutical and other industries to exploit the differences in tax rates in different countries. For example, when a manufacturer transfers goods to overseas subsidiaries, a high price is charged to those operating under high tax regimes so that the subsidiaries will have relatively low profits and a low price is charged to subsidiaries in low tax regimes, which will have larger profits. The idea is to achieve a net tax saving to the parent company from its global operation.

Transformation Curve

Same as *production possibilities curve*.

Transition Matrix

A matrix of *transition probabilities* in a *Markov chain*. The rows list the probabilities of moving from one state to another (or remaining in the existing state) and sum to 1.0. The columns list the states.

Transition Probability

The probability of transition from one state of health to another in a *Markov model*.

Transitivity

The axioms of all utility theories include this one, to the effect that, if entity *A* is preferred or indifferent to entity *B*, and entity *B* is preferred or indifferent to entity *C*, then *A* will be preferred or indifferent to *C*. See *Utility*.

Transitory Income

Opposite of *permanent income*.

Triage

The word 'triage' comes from the French word 'trier', to sort. It seems to have originated with a Frenchman, Baron Dominique Jean Larrey (1766–1842), a surgeon in Napoleon's army, who devised a method for evaluating and categorizing the wounded in battle quickly so as to evacuate those requiring the most urgent medical attention. Its usage today varies from place to place and circumstance to circumstance but in general it still involves the classification of patients according to judgments of their *capacity to benefit* and the urgency of their case. For example, people injured and at the site of an accident might be sorted into the dead for whom one can do nothing; the injured who need immediate transfer to hospital; the injured whose transport can be delayed; and the walking wounded who may need only *primary* rather than *secondary care*. A 'triage nurse' (in the USA) is one who performs a telephone interview and makes an assessment of the health status and health service needs of the caller.

Triage Nurse

A nurse in the USA who performs a telephone interview and makes an assessment of the health status and health service needs of the caller. See *Triage*.

Trial

See *Clinical Trial*.

Triangular Distribution

A frequency *distribution* with three parameters: minimum, maximum and mode. It may be symmetrical, or positively or negatively *skewed*. Cf. *Normal Distribution.*

Triple-blind Trial

A *clinical trial* in which subjects, observers/clinicians and analysts are unaware of patient assignment to the arms of the trial. See *Blinding.*

TRIPS

Acronym for *trade-related aspects of intellectual property rights.*

True Negative

A test result indicating that a disease-free individual is disease-free.

True Positive

A test result indicating that a diseased individual is diseased.

Trusts

Trusts were established in 1991 in the UK National Health Service (NHS). NHS trusts are established under statute as corporate bodies with legal personalities. Statutes and regulations prescribe the structure, functions and responsibilities of the boards of these bodies and prescribe the way chairs and members of boards are appointed. The function of trusts is to provide hospital and community services on behalf of the Secretary of State for Health. A trust is managed by a board of directors made up of executive directors and non-executive directors. The non-executive directors are part-time and are paid an honorarium. Foundation trusts are a new (2004) type of NHS hospital having a greater degree of autonomy than conventional trusts. NHS foundation trusts have the freedom to decide at a local level how to meet their obligations, and have constitutions that make them accountable to local people, who can become members, directors and governors, and are authorized, monitored and regulated by an Independent Regulator of NHS Foundation Trusts.

t-test

A method of comparing the means of a treatment group and a control group when the true mean is not known in order to differentiate the between-group difference from the within-group differences. In multiple regression analysis, the t-statistic of a *coefficient* estimate is the estimate divided by its *standard error*. See *Student's t-test*.

TTO

Acronym for *time trade-off method*.

2SLS

An acronym for *two-stage least squares*.

Two-stage Least Squares

A method of statistical *regression* used as an alternative to (OLS) *ordinary least squares* when some of its assumptions are violated. The two stages are (a) the creation of new *regressors*, derived from regressions on *exogenous* variables, to replace original ones, and (b) computing the regression OLS fashion, but using the newly created variables rather than the original *endogenous* regressors.

Two-tailed Test

A statistical significance test based on the assumption that there is no *a priori* information about the direction of departure (up or down) from the null hypothesis. Cf. *One-tailed Test*.

Type I Error

Rejection of the *null hypothesis* when it is true; for example, concluding that a relationship exists, when it does not.

Type II Error

Non-rejection of the *null hypothesis* when it is false; for example, concluding that there is no relationship, when there is.

Type III error

With a somewhat different emphasis from Types I and II, this additional form of error has been suggested and consists in producing right answers to wrong questions, especially when the answer is limited because the scientific methods chosen to answer the question are not well-suited. For example, one might ask the question, 'What causes this disease?' but the research actually addresses a (significantly more limited) question, 'Why is the prevalence of this disease higher in group A than in group B?' There are also other usages, such as inappropriate choice of alternative hypotheses when testing a particular one, but health economists are probably most likely to come across this one.

U

Unbalanced Panel

A *panel* in which one or more waves of data are missing for some respondents. In contrast, a balanced panel is one in which only respondents with complete data for all waves are included.

Uncertainty

Usually applied to future events, costs and benefits, even though interpretation of the past is notoriously subject to many uncertainties. Sometimes attempts to 'quantify' uncertainty are made by assigning probabilities based on past experience or derived by judgments of various kinds. Sometimes alternative scenarios of the future are devised. Out of the infinity of possible futures, the art lies in trying to narrow down the range to a manageable set of imaginable possibilities that, between them, encompass what are seen as the main characteristics of these possibilities. The reduction of uncertainty about the financial consequences of ill-health (health care expenditures and loss of earnings due to sickness) is the principal advantage of and rationale for health *insurance*.

Analysts distinguish between stochastic uncertainty (sometimes 'first-order uncertainty') and subjective uncertainty (sometimes 'second-order uncertainty'). The former is uncertainty arising from randomness in the data studied. The second is uncertainty relating to *parameter* values and is due to insufficient knowledge. See *Bayesian Method, Cost–effectiveness Plane, Expected Utility Theory, Frequentist Approach, Insurance, Prospect Theory, Regret Theory, Sensitivity Analysis.*

Unconditional Mean Imputation

A method of imputing missing values when there are *incomplete data*.

Unemployment

The definitions vary from jurisdiction to jurisdiction but most follow the following general character: the number of jobless people who are available for work and are actively seeking work. The fact that unemployment can be both caused by and a cause of ill-health is, of course, a field of study, even for some health economists. See *Friction Cost, Full Employment, Involuntary Unemployment, Natural Rate of Unemployment, Structural Unemployment*.

Uniform Distribution

A probability *distribution* having two *parameters*: the minimum and maximum. The probability of being in an interval between the minimum and the maximum depends only on the width of the interval and not its position between the limits. Cf. *Normal Distribution*.

Unimodal Distribution

A *distribution* of a *variable* that has one peak (*mode*).

Unit Non-response

One of a number of non-sampling sources of potential *bias* in surveys. It occurs when selected subjects fail to respond to a questionnaire. Other errors and possible biases include defective questionnaire wording and format, interviewer errors, and coding and/or inputting errors.

Univariate Analysis

Analysis involving a single *variable*.

Univariate Sensitivity Analysis

A type of *sensitivity analysis* in which there is variable-by-variable adjustment to examine the impact on critical outcomes like *incremental cost–effectiveness ratios*.

Universality

A characteristic of a health care system that is commonly desired or sometimes (as in Canada) required by statute. It refers to the coverage of people with entitlement to use a service; a fully universal system is one in which all members of a jurisdiction have the same entitlements. Cf. *Comprehensiveness*.

Unquantifiable Costs and Benefits

Consequences of decisions that are very costly to quantify, unconvincingly quantified or not worth quantifying. See *Opportunity Cost* and *Benefit*.

Urology

The medical specialty concerned with diseases and abnormalities of the urinary system.

User Charges

Prices payable by a user at the time of use.

Utilitarianism

This is the ethical doctrine, a variant of which underlies nearly all *welfare* (and *extra-welfare*) economics, which specifies *utility* as the principal good characteristic of society: what humankind as a whole ought to maximize. The moral object for a society to pursue under utilitarianism is 'the greatest utility for the greatest number'. Under utilitarianism, that which is right is any action or arrangement whose consequences are good in the sense of increasing total utility measured as the sum of each person's individual utility. Hence utilitarianism is a *consequentialist* moral theory. 'Rule utilitarianism' maintains that a code or rule of behaviour is morally right if the consequences of adopting it are more favourable for total utility than not adopting it. 'Act utilitarianism' maintains that the morality of an action is determined by the balance of the favourable or unfavourable consequences in terms of utility that flow from it.

The view that policy ought to be based on individuals' preferences under a *veil of ignorance* has a long history. Amongst its attractions are the idea that 'everyone counts' in the sense that everyone's utility is treated equally or, in a variant (*maximin*) form, that the social goal ought to be to maximize the utility of the least well off individual.

The classical economists treated utility as a *cardinal* entity accruing to individuals which could be added up (like their weights). Since the 1930s, welfare economics has tended to shy away from the *interpersonal comparison of utilities* (on the somewhat odd ground that it is 'meaningless' to compare them, when everyone ordinarily compares such things on a daily basis) in favour of the *Pareto criterion* under which a change is judged to be a social improvement only when at least one gains and no one loses utility from it (this does not imply that other changes are not social improvements; only that one cannot say whether they are). Pareto himself, however, used cardinal and interpersonal comparisons of utility whenever he felt it necessary to do so.

Utility theory has also tended to treat utility as measured by linear instruments (like temperature), which enable one to distinguish rising or falling increments of it (*marginal utility*). Considerable controversy attaches both to the question of the people whose utility is to be 'counted', the ways in which the utilities accruing to different people are to be 'added up', and the character of the entities that are deemed to yield utility or disutility. Goods and services are always 'in', but the following, to illustrate a few possibilities, are not always allowed: prospects of consuming goods and services, the relative consumption of goods and services by others, the *distribution* of goods and services generally, characteristics of goods and services, others' consumption, others' utility, the means of acquisition of goods and services, the processes of change as ownership bundles change, characteristics of people such as their health and cognitive skill, and capabilities of people like their talent for survival. See *Entitlement Theory*, *Fairness*, *Interpersonal Comparisons of Utility*, *Social Welfare Function*, *Utility*.

Utility

Utilities are numbers assigned to entities (usually benefits or things presumed to be the objects of people's *preferences*) according to a rule. This enables the entities to be quantified and ranked according to preference, desirability or choice (these are not, of course, synonyms). There are four common scales of measurement: *categorical*, in which entities either belong to a category ('able to wash self') or not ('not able to wash self'); *ordinal*, in which rank order is revealed and any numbers will serve that preserve the correct order (for example, the entity 'dead' is worse than the entity 'getting along'); *interval*, in which, like temperature measurement, the ratios of intervals between the points on the scale are the same for each set of possible numbers and the zero point is arbitrary; and *ratio*, in which, like measures of weight or distance, zero means 'none' and 'twice as much' is indeed twice as much, whichever set of numbers is being used. The sort of measurement normally used in *indifference curve* analysis is ordinal. The final two are both forms of *cardinal* measurement.

The table illustrates three kinds of utility measurement for the four entities which here correspond to health states, or diseases, where high numbers denote better states. The first set of three columns shows some possible numbers (out of an indefinitely large set) that rank the four entities ordinally. Each column is equally valid and each ranks them in the same order. The differences between the numbers assigned in each column mean nothing, so it is not possible, for example, to speak of increasing or diminishing *marginal utility* from health. The second set of three columns shows three sets of numbers that have been attributed to the entities according to a different rule. The same order is preserved but this time column 6 = 10 + 2(column 5) and column 7 is –10 + column 5. Each is a linear transformation of the other, having the general form $A = a + bB$. With this second set of numbers one can speak of increasing or diminishing marginal utility of health as each column will show the changes between cells as increasing or decreasing. The final three columns are related as follows: column 9 is column 8 multiplied by 0.035 and column 10 is column 8 multiplied by 35. Here the form of the equation relating them is $A = bB$, where $b = A/B$, a constant. Not only does this measure rank the entities in the same order, and preserve increasing or decreasing marginal utilities, but we can also say that if 'good health' is 1.67 times as good as 'better health' on one scale, so will it be on any other.

Examples of utility scalings

| Entity | Ordinal | | | Cardinal | | | | | |
| | | | | Interval | | | Ratio | | |
1	2	3	4	5	6	7	8	9	10
Poor health	1	23	66	1	12	–9	1	0.035	35
Better health	2	24	67	6	22	–4	6	0.210	210
Good health	3	77	68	10	30	0	10	0.350	350
Excellent health	4	987	69	13	36	3	13	0.455	455

The *welfare* connotations of 'utility' are important in economics although, when used simply as an index or preference, utility theory can be seen as a part of the economist's approach to behaviour: it is predictive, explanatory and conventionally *positive*. The usual axioms underlying utility theory are, where the As, Bs and Cs are 'bundles' of goods or services:

- completeness: either A is preferred to B, or B to A or an individual is indifferent between them;
- transitivity: if A is preferred or indifferent to B and B is preferred or indifferent to C, then A is preferred or indifferent to C;
- continuity: there is an indifference curve such that all points to its north east are preferred to all points to its south west;
- convexity: the marginal rate of substitution is negative;
- non-satiation: more is always preferred.

These are essentially positive and experimentally refutable (and have all been more or less frequently refuted empirically).

The welfare connotations arise in welfare economics, when the preferences of individuals form the basic building blocks used to identify improvements or deteriorations in social welfare via a *social welfare function*. Here 'more utility' is a 'good thing'. 'More utility' would also be a good thing if the basic building block consisted of entities ranked by something other than 'preference' but no less value-laden, for example entities that one was duty-bound to select, or ones which, on some ethical grounding or other, ought to be ranked higher than the rest. The fact that one may feel that what one wants to choose is not what one ought to choose is rarely reflected in discussions of utility, even though there is no reason why the workhorse of utility numbers could not do duty in ranking either. The point is that 'utility' is not inextricably wedded to 'preference'.

In a rather different way that is special to health economics, there are welfare connotations arising from the use of utility theory as the analytical framework for constructing indices of health, as in the use of, say, *expected utility theory* in the *standard gamble* approach to *quality-adjusted life-year* (QALY) construction. Here two common, but different, value assumptions may be met. One is that the values embodied in entities (like QALYs) intended to inform public decision making ought to reflect the preferences of the community on whose behalf the decisions are being made; the other is that the values ought to reflect the preferences (or rankings on other grounds) of decision makers who are accountable to the public via the usual processes of representative democracy. In either approach, difficulties arise when any of the underlying axioms (assumptions) of utility theory are violated. See *Extra-welfarism, Interpersonal Comparisons of Utility, Utility Frontier, Utility Maximizing*.

Utility Frontier

A utility frontier is a locus of points in a figure that connects the *utility* of all allocations of two goods between two people such that the *marginal rate of transformation* is equal to the *marginal rate of substitution*. Each such point is a *Pareto optimum*. Thus each of the points *a*, *b* and *c* on the downward sloping curve in the figure is such an optimum: it is not possible to move from one point to any other without one person losing utility even though the other gains, so such points cannot be ranked using the Pareto crierion. The frontier shows the maximum utility attainable by one individual, given the utility level of another. Point *d* is unattainable, given the resources available and the exant technologies that define the maximum outputs that can be produced from them. These background conditions determine the position of the frontier. Note that *d* cannot be ranked in relation to *a* or *c* using the Pareto criterion, nor can *e* in relation to *a* and *c*. Point *e* is not an *efficient* point since it is possible to move from it to a point on the frontier in such a way that both gain utility (or at any rate neither loses). This is shown by the area enclosed by the two arrows from *e*: any point within this space has more utility for both individuals than point *e* and some point on the frontier in this space is going to be better for at least one of the individuals than some point below it. To choose between points on the frontier requires a *social welfare function* that permits the *interpersonal comparison of utilities*. See *Interpersonal Comparisons of Utility, Utility*.

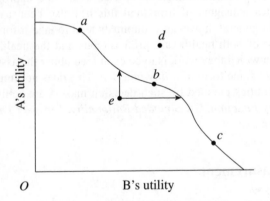

Utility Function

A mathematical function that relates *utility* to the rate of consumption of various goods and services or, in some sophisticated cases, to the characteristics of consumer goods and services. The general form of the function is usually

$$U = U(Q_1, Q_2, Q_3...Q_N),$$

where the Q_i are goods or services, and where $dU/dQ_i > 0$ is *marginal utility*.

It is possible to model *altruism* in *utilitarian* terms by postulating that some of the arguments (the Q_i in the utility function) are entities that accrue to other people and from which they derive utility. That is to say, the choosing individual derives utility from the consumption, experience and so on of another person: put plainly, one is pleased to see another person healthier or with greater access to health care than would otherwise be the case. Conversely, of course, a malevolent person, by analogy, derives utility from arguments in their utility function that are negative arguments of another's behaviour or utility. A non-economist may readily imagine what economists make of trading between a sadist and a masochist. See *Utility Maximizing*.

Utility Maximizing

This (or its variant, expected utility maximizing) is the basic motivating drive for human behaviour most frequently used by economists. In some conditions (for example, where there is intense *competition* for the owner-ship of a firm) profit maximization is used as a good approximation for what motivates managers of firms and this has also been used in health economics. In general, however, economists tend to take it for granted that the behaviour of both health care professionals and the health service or-ganizations in which they work is to be examined under the assumption that they maximize some form of *utility function*. This does not imply necessar-ily that the entities pursued by such decision makers are selfish ones. See *Utility, Utility Function*. Cf. *Bounded Rationality, Prospect Theory, Regret Theory, Satisficing*.

Utility Measurement

Ascribing numbers systematically to entities so as to indicate (usually) pref-erence. See *Utility*.

Utility Scales

See *Utility Measurement*.

Utilization

The intensity of use of medical resources per period. Overutilization is use in excess of some optimal, preferred, stipulated (and so on) rate: the benchmark implied varies from context to context and is too frequently left asserted but undefined. The reader should be alert to its ambiguity: it may be propaganda from someone in pursuit of a larger slice of the cake.

Utilization Review

Monitoring programmes in the USA that seek to determine the appropriateness of the care delivered and its cost. Reviews, which may be retrospective, current or prospective, usually evaluate the need, appropriateness and *efficiency* of health care services, procedures and facilities, including review of the appropriateness of admissions, services ordered and provided, length of stay and discharge practices. Utilization reviews in the USA are performed both by peer review groups and by public agencies.

V

Validity

In a general sense, the extent to which a measurement instrument measures what it is designed to measure. More specifically, see *Construct Validity, Convergent Validity, Criterion Validity, Discriminant Validity, External Validity, Face Validity, Predictive Validity, Test–retest Validity*.

Value

In economics, value is usually taken as the maximum amount that an individual or group is willing to pay for a particular good or service rather than go without it. *Marginal value* is the value of *marginal benefit*: the maximum amount individuals are willing to pay for an increment of benefit. *Value in exchange* is a term sometimes used to describe the market value of traded goods or services. The difference between value in use and value in exchange is *consumer's surplus*. See *Demand Curve, Value in Use*.

Value in Exchange

The market (exchange) value of a good or service. See *Value*.

Value in Use

The maximum amount someone is willing to pay for a particular rate of use of a good or service rather than go without it. See *Value*.

Value Judgment

An ethical opinion made either implicitly or explicitly that a particular course of action, institutional arrangement or method of analysis ought to be implemented, or is itself good. For example, the judgment that consumers' *willingness to pay* ought to determine the allocation of health care services is a value judgment. The judgment that the location and type of services actually provided is determined by willingness to pay is not a value judgment (it is a hypothesis that can be tested empirically). The judgment that economics ought to be value-free is a value judgment. The judgment that economics is value-free is not a value judgment (it is also a false statement). *Option appraisals, cost–effectiveness analyses* and similar evaluative methods typically involve many kinds of judgment, only some of which are judgments of value. A particular class of value judgment is to do with the *welfare* of the members of society: how it ought to be measured, how changes in it or in its *distribution* may be assessed, or whether a particular measure is likely to have an impact on it for better or worse. See *Interpersonal Comparisons of Utility, Welfare Economics*.

Value of Information Analysis

A method for evaluating the value of additional (usually research) information in terms of reduced uncertainty about *parameter* values in *health technology assessments*.

Value of Life

Reduced mortality and increased life expectancy are common benefits of health programmes whose *appraisal* will sometimes require a value to be placed on 'life'. There are broadly three approaches to this valuation. The *human capital* approach assesses the value as the *present value* of expected future earnings. This has been widely discredited partly for its partial nature (effectively treating people as though they were carthorses) and partly because of the discrimination it implies against the very young, the old, females, chronic sick and so on. The second, the *social decisions approach*, infers values from decisions made in the public sector. The third approach enquires experimentally and via surveys about the value placed by individuals on reductions in the size of the risk of death they confront with respect to any particular hazard. This approach is based on people's *preferences* and is thus that which is most consistent with the economic concept of *efficiency*. It also directly approaches the matter in a context of uncertainty which is the characteristic practical context for most decisions.

Variable

Characteristics of individuals, usually quantified, such as blood pressure, age, income or region of residence will vary and, hence, are termed 'variables'. So are other elements in a model that can vary but are not characteristics of people, such as *inputs*, price, *GDP* or *industrial concentration*. Some variables are *binary*. Such variables usually indicate either the presence or the absence of a feature of interest (such as male or female, black or white, alive or dead). Cf. *Parameter.*

Variable-by-Variable Analysis

Same as *univariate sensitivity analysis*.

Variable Costs

Costs that vary as the *output* rate varies.

Variable Factor

A *factor of production* that varies as *output* varies. See *Production Function*.

Variable Proportions

See *Law of Variable Proportions*.

Variance

A measure of the dispersion of a set of numbers. The *standard deviation* squared. The variance of a *population* is the expected value of the squared deviations of the measurements from their mean. The variance of a sample uses the sample mean in the calculation of the squared deviations and the sample size minus one as the denominator in calculating the unbiased estimate of the population variance:

$$s^2 = \sum (x_i - \bar{x})^2 / n - 1.$$

Cf. *Standard Deviation*.

Variance Ratio Distribution

Same as *F distribution*.

VAS

Acronym for *visual analogue scale*.

Vector

In mathematics, a vector comprises numbers (called 'elements') arranged in a row (row vector) or column (column vector). A vector of *n* elements is referred to as *n*-dimensional. There is a special algebra for vectors. In *epidemiology*, a vector is an agent, usually insect or animal, able to carry *pathogens* from one organism to another.

Veil of Ignorance

A device used in moral philosophy, most famously by Immanuel Kant (1724–1804) and, more recently, by John Rawls (1921–2002) in the theory of 'justice as fairness' to eliminate prejudice. See *Fairness*.

Verification Bias

Same as *work-up bias*.

Vertical Equity

Treating appropriately unequally those who are unequal in some morally relevant sense. Commonly met vertical equity principles include 'higher contributions from those with greater *ability to pay*', 'more resource for those with greater need for resource' and 'lower priority for lower deservingness'. Cf. *Horizontal Equity*. See *Equity*.

Vertical Integration

This entails the bringing together in managed units activities or firms that were previously separate. It generally comes in one of three forms: backward vertical integration, forward vertical integration and balanced vertical integration. Under backward vertical integration, an organization has subsidiaries producing inputs used in the production of its 'upstream' products. Under forward vertical integration, an organization has subsidiaries that distribute or market products 'downstream' to customers or use the products themselves. Under balanced vertical integration, an organization has both upstream and downstream subsidiaries. Health care is characterized by a variety of types of integration (or lack of it). Examples of its absence are the existence (in the USA) of doctors contracting with hospitals for use of their beds and provision of professional services to the patients in them, and (in most countries) the complete absence of any kind of coordination between health care services and community-based social care services.

Viatical Settlements

A means by which people with terminal disease may retrieve some of the value of their life insurance. In a viatical settlement, people with terminal illnesses assign their life insurance policies to 'viatical settlement companies' in exchange for a percentage of the policy's face value. The viatical settlement company may in turn sell the policy to a third party. The purchaser continues to pay the premiums, and collects the face value of the policy when the original policyholder dies. The word comes from the Latin word for 'to travel' and relates to the provisions made for subsistence while travelling, with the metaphorical use in the Roman church of preparation for the passage from life to death and the last Eucharistic rite or 'viaticum'.

Visual Analogue Scale

VAS is a graphical method for rating health states directly. A common instrument is a figure akin to a thermometer, on which are marked two anchor states, and on which the rater is asked to mark his or her rating of some other state, usually lying between the two anchors. Used in deriving *quality-adjusted life-years* and related measures of *health status*.

Volunteer Bias

Volunteers in *clinical trials* may exhibit exposures or outcomes which differ systematically from those of non-volunteers. A form of *selection bias*. See *Bias*.

W

Wage-risk Studies

Preference-based studies that value health or reduction in the risk of death through the wage differentials required to induce people to accept jobs having differing degrees of risk to health or death.

Waiting List

A list of people waiting, usually for an outpatient examination by a hospital doctor or for admission to hospital as an inpatient. See *Queue*.

Washout Period

The gap between the end of a treatment period and the start of another in a *crossover trial*. The lapsed time 'washes out' the effects of the first period's treatment.

WB

Acronym for *World Bank*.

Weak Dominance

Same as *extended dominance*.

Wealth

The value of all *assets* owned by an individual or group minus the value of all debts.

Web of Causation

A term used by some epidemiologists to describe a multifactorial and multi-layered set of interlinked determinants of health (or ill-health) outcomes.

Weibull Model

A parametric statistical model for *duration analysis*. Named after Waloddi Weibull (1887–1979) a Swedish engineer. See Waloddi Weibull (1951), 'A statistical distribution function of wide applicability', *Journal of Applied Mechanics*, **18**, 293–7.

Weighted Least Squares

A method used in *least squares* regression of weighting *dependent* and *independent variables* to correct for *heteroskedasticity*.

Welfare

The quality that is taken by economists to indicate the well-being of a society or of the arrangements (or changes in them) that a society adopts. It is usually measured as an index. Higher levels of welfare are inherently better for that individual or society, as judged by the economist constructing or using the index. Economists, philosophers, sociologists and psychologists differ among themselves over what constitutes a higher level of welfare and whether useful empirical measurements of welfare can be made (*construct validity*).

Economists most frequently use per capita GDP (*Gross Domestic Product*) as the index of well-being. Some modify this welfare index with allowance for unpaid activity within households (which GDP excludes) or for environmental and related effects (which GDP treats erroneously from a welfare viewpoint: GDP rises if there is an oil spill and resources need to be used to clean it up). *Extra-welfarists* believe that, even with such modifications, GDP is inadequate since welfare involves much more than the mere satisfaction of wants through the consumption of goods and services.

Other words sometimes used by economists for welfare include *utility* and satisfaction. These alternatives are often used, however, without any implication that an individual or society is better off by having a higher level of either utility or satisfaction. They can merely denote that the chooser (the individual or society) has as a goal a higher level of this index, and not that the economist endorses their goal as a desirable one or that this is the only or the ultimate goal. Sometimes all that is meant by a utility number is a particular level of pain or pleasure for the individual or society in question. This, despite its wide currency, seems a pathetically inadequate measure of either individual or societal welfare.

Some economists try to avoid the concept of welfare entirely and, indeed, deny that the concept of welfare is meaningful. Such economists are broadly in the *logical positivism* school. Since health economics is largely inseparable from policy issues, in which questions deemed 'metaphysical' by analysts in that tradition are central, those who dodge the welfare implications of economic policies are severely limited in their ability to contribute to health economics. See *Positive Economics, Rationality, Welfare Economics.*

Welfare Cost

Same as *deadweight loss.*

Welfare Economics

That branch of economics concerned with identifying the conditions that make for a good society and identifying changes in allocations of goods and services, or arrangements for allocating goods and services, that are better for society. In welfare economics, the noun 'society' is generally taken to encompass all adult rational individuals. How the separate 'welfares' of these individuals are 'added up' to enable an overall judgment of 'good' or 'better' to be reached has been an important part of welfare economics. Cf. *Extra-welfarism, Pareto-optimality, Positive Economics, Welfare.*

Welfare Loss

Same as *deadweight loss.*

Welfarism

The approach to evaluating states of society that assumes that *welfare* is the appropriate maximand, that (economic) welfare in the form of *utility* is to be had only from goods and services and that only utilities matter for social welfare. See *Pareto-optimality*, *Welfare Economics*. Cf. *Extra-welfarism*.

What-if Analysis

Same as *sensitivity analysis*.

WHO

Acronym for *World Health Organization*.

WHO-CHOICE

This is a *World Health Organization* project to facilitate the transfer of information on economic evaluation between countries or regions in such a way as to allow it to be modified and applied in another setting. There are regional databases reporting the costs and *effectiveness* of key interventions for 17 subregions, grouped together on the basis of epidemiology, infrastructure and economic situation. Its web site is at www3.who.int/whosis/cea/guide.

Wilcoxon Rank-sum Test

This is used to test the hypothesis that two independent *samples* have come from the same population. Because it is non-parametric, it makes only limited assumptions about the *distribution* of the data. The method employed is a sum-of-ranks comparison. It is an alternative to the two sample *t-test*, and is based only on the order in which the observations from the two samples fall. It is of evident use when data are *ordinal* in nature and a comparison of means is meaningless. See Frank Wilcoxon (1945), 'Individual comparisons by ranking methods', *Biometrics*, **1**, 80–83.

Williams' Schematic of Health Economics

A comprehensive taxonomizing framework that systematically embraces the various topics studied by health economists. Its form is as in the 'plumbing diagram'. The letter labels for each box in the schematic indicate the (approximate) order in which things flow, with various feedbacks and so on indicated by the arrows.

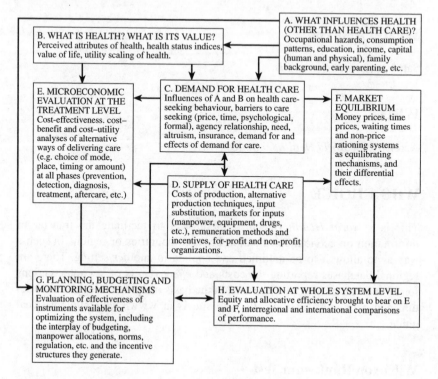

Source: Adapted from Alan Williams (2003), 'Health economics: a bird's eye view of the structure of the discipline', in *Health Care Economics for Health Care Professionals: Module 1, Basic Economic Concepts (Module Workbook)*, York: University of York, p. 132.

Willingness to Accept

The minimum compensation an individual is willing to accept in exchange for giving up some good or service, or the minimum sum that an individual is willing to accept to forgo a prospective gain. It is usually elicited from *stated* or *revealed preference* experiments. Cf. *Willingness to Pay*. See *Kaldor–Hicks Criterion*.

Willingness to Pay

The maximum sum an individual is willing to pay to acquire some good or service, or the maximum sum an individual is willing to pay to avoid a prospective loss. It is usually elicited from *stated* or *revealed preference* experiments. Cf. *Willingness to Accept*. See *Kaldor–Hicks Criterion*.

Withdrawal Bias

A *bias* in trials arising from patients who withdraw from studies being different from those who remain.

Workers' Compensation

A general term to describe the arrangements in many jurisdictions that are designed to ensure that employees who are injured or disabled on the job receive appropriate medical care and monetary awards. It is common for schedules to be used which list the compensation available for both economic and non-economic losses on a no-fault basis, thus eliminating the need for litigation. Provision is also often made for dependants of those workers who are killed in work-related accidents or illnesses. In Australia, Canada and the USA, these are state/provincial programmes. In Italy and New Zealand, the system is national. Other jurisdictions, such as the UK, employ mixed systems via national regulation and social security coupled with compulsory private employer liability insurance. In Germany, the public insurance agencies are organized by industry.

Work-up Bias

Same as *verification bias*. It occurs when patients with negative and positive test results are not evaluated by the same gold standard test. See *Bias*.

World Bank

The World Bank consists of two major international organizations: the International Bank for Reconstruction and Development, and the International Development Association. Together with the International Finance Corporation, the Multilateral Investment Guarantee Agency and the International

Centre for the Settlement of Investment Disputes, they form the World Bank Group. The Group's mission is to fight poverty and improve the living standards of people in the developing world. The group is effectively a development bank which provides loans, policy advice, technical assistance and knowledge-sharing services to low- and middle-income countries to reduce poverty. It is the world's largest external source of funding for education and HIV/AIDS programmes.

Its shareholders are nations, with votes proportionate to their *Gross Domestic Products* and it has a board of governors made up of national directors (usually ministers of member states). It has major interests in investing in health care facilities in the third world and in measuring international inequalities in health, health care and health care financing. Its web address is www.worldbank.org/.

World Health Organization

The World Health Organization (WHO) is the United Nations' specialized agency for health. It was established on 7 April 1948. WHO's objective, as set out in its constitution, is the attainment by all peoples of the highest possible level of *health*. The famous, if unachievable, WHO concept of health in its constitution is 'a state of complete physical, mental and social well-being and not merely the absence of disease or infirmity'.

WHO is governed by 192 member states through the World Health Assembly, which comprises representatives from WHO's member states. The main tasks of the World Health Assembly are to approve the WHO programme and the budget for the following biennial and to decide major policy questions. WHO member states are grouped into six regions, each with a regional office: Africa, the Americas, South-East Asia, Europe, Eastern Mediterranean and Western Pacific.

The WHO is responsible for a host of statistical services; advice, support and training services for member states; international agreements; and broad area strategies for achieving its aims. Its web address is: www.who.int/en/.

WTA

Acronym for *willingness to accept*.

WTP

Acronym for *willingness to pay.*

X

X-inefficiency

X-inefficiency is the difference in costs between *efficient* and inefficient firms engaged in essentially the same activity and on the same scale; that is, it does not arise from differences in product mix and is not a consequence of *economies* (or diseconomies) *of scale* or *scope*. It generally arises in situations when either or both of the product market or the *capital* market (the market for the firm's ownership) are not *competitive*, resulting in *price-searching* behaviour and an increase in the costs to owners of monitoring and enforcing their own interests within the firm (sometimes referred to as a 'separation' of ownership from control). This enables managers to act in ways that may not be in the interest of owners but that are consistent with *utility-maximizing* behaviour by managers. Since most sources of (on-the-job) utility are costly, this necessarily implies that costs will be higher in utility-maximizing firms than in profit-maximizing firms. The difference is X-inefficiency. See *Bounded Rationality, Satisficing*.

Y

Yardstick Competition

An industrial regulatory procedure under which the regulated price is set at the average of the estimated *marginal costs* of the firms in the industry.

Z

Zero Sum Game

A game in which whatever one player wins the other loses. See *Game Theory*.

Z-test

A test of the *null hypothesis* that a population parameter such as the *mean* is equal to a given value. It differs from the t-test in being based on the *normal distribution* rather than the t-distribution.

INDEX

ability to pay 29, 105, 127, 363
absolute advantage 57
absolute purchasing power parity 282
absolute risk aversion 17
absolute risk difference 303
absolute risk reduction 235
accident insurance 371
act utilitarianism 353
actuarially fair premium 4, 19, 53–5,
    130, 177, 198, 220, 221, 302
addiction 291
additive separability 285
administered prices 292
adverse outcomes 2
adverse selection 304
aetiology 234
Africa 196
age, patient's 65, 109, 170
age-specific mortality rate 221
agency relationship 127, 207, 223–4,
    272, 333
aggregate demand 9
aging processes 143
algorithms 86
Allais, Maurice 11
Altman, Douglas G. 12
altruism 358
analysis of variance 131
animal testing 257, 265
annuitized value 117
appreciation 94
arithmetic mean see mean
arm, disabilities of 86, 98, 288
Arrow, Kenneth J. 16, 17
Arrow social welfare function 182
artificial limbs 279
ascertainment bias 95
aspirin 332
asymmetry of information 8, 164, 175,
    207, 273
atorvastatin 142
attention bias 147–8
attributable fraction 7
attributes
    of addictiveness 4–5

of health 153, 222
of services 4, 30, 41, 48, 64–5, 100,
    252, 299, 345
Australia 18
    health care expenditures in 123
    health care system in 36, 150, 214,
        371
    Pharmaceutical Benefits Scheme in
        256, 305
    purchasing power parity for 283
Austria 123, 150, 283
average cost 161
average product 193
average revenue 161

balance of payments 40, 85, 238
balanced panel 351
barriers to access 3
barriers to entry 70, 161
Barthel, Dorothea W. 25
Baumol, William 26
Bayer AG 332
Bayes, Thomas 28
Bayesian approach 122, 137, 327
Beattie, A. 344
before and after studies 110
Belgium 123, 150, 283
benefit–cost ratio 75, 88
bequest value 121
Bergson, Abram 30
beta distribution 140
bias 65, 72, 188, 276
    techniques to reduce 33, 156, 178,
        237, 290, 312
    types of 11, 12, 20, 28, 59, 86, 94, 95,
        113, 120, 139, 147–8, 155, 156,
        162, 163, 171, 175, 184, 193,
        195, 212, 237, 238, 240, 254,
        281, 293, 295, 301, 307, 309,
        312, 323, 324, 326, 335, 340,
        352, 365, 371
binary variables 105, 197, 199, 273, 362
biomedicine 215
biostatics 209
Black, Sir Douglas 32, 33

blinding 104, 236, 237, 257, 312, 319,
        340, 348
block contracts 4
blood
    diseases of 135, 181
    physiology of 147
body, diseases of 253
bones 243, 244
Boole, George 33
bounded rationality 88, 292, 308
Briggs, Andrew H. 41
budget constraint 7, 36, 67, 73, 84, 161,
        179, 185
budget impact 7

caesarian sections 333
call centres 57
Canada 39, 154
    drug reviews in 56
    health care expenditures in 123
    health care system in 3, 23, 60, 150,
        214, 233, 261, 352, 371
    purchasing power parity for 283
    see also Quebec
cancer 226, 238, 289, 311
capacity to benefit 228, 347
capital cost 14, 97
capital goods, value of 94
capital-intensive industries 26
capital markets 161, 374
capital stock, changes in 184, 339
capitation 131, 173, 204, 223–4, 320
card sorts 64
Carides, George W. 41
case control studies 71, 95, 237
case mix 162, 163, 253
case notes 43
ceiling ratios 76
cells and tissues 159, 176
censoring 41, 45, 156, 302, 335–6, 343,
        344
certification 3
charities, hospitals as 162–4
chest, diseases of 340
Chi-squared test 90, 205
childbirth 181, 237
children, diseases of 247
choice modelling 64
choice theory 60, 212, 233, 341
chromosomal disorders 181

chronic conditions 209
circulatory system, diseases of 181
Citizens Council 65
clinical guidelines 226
clinical trials 27, 200, 309, 314
    bias in 11, 33, 94, 95, 120, 155, 178,
        212, 237, 254, 290, 365, 371
    blinding in 33, 104, 237, 257, 312,
        319, 348
    censoring in 41, 45
    control group in 2, 71, 72, 160, 191,
        248, 261, 303
    effect of treatment in 140, 257
    end-point in 342
    inclusion/exclusion criteria for
        entering 170
    outcomes beyond period of 28
    outcomes in 2, 114, 191, 335–6, 343
    phases in 3
    placebos used in 259, 290
    sample size in 12, 307
    statistical power of 12, 327
    stopping rules for 329
    subgroup analysis in 331
    types of 55, 83, 117, 124, 225, 248,
        264, 279, 290, 348
    validity of results of 180
closed panel health maintenance
        organizations 152–3
Cobb, Charles W. 51
Cobb–Douglas production function 274
coefficient of determination 289
cohort modelling 218
cohort studies 133, 200, 229, 239, 278,
        301
coinsurance 220, 245
    see also copayments; deductibles
comparative health systems 151
compensation test 189–90
competition 161–2, 304, 310, 358, 374
completeness axiom 121, 356
concentration curve 60–61, 189
concentration index 189
concentration ratio 59
conditional probability 27, 28
confidence intervals 2, 62, 63, 64, 76,
        216, 217
confidence limits 131, 219
confounding variables 28, 107, 124,
        147, 290, 321, 331

congenital malformations, deformations
and chromosomal disorders 181
conjoint analysis 4, 20, 30, 41, 48, 70,
100, 138, 159, 302, 316, 345
consensus panels 48
constant proportional time trade-off
285–6
construct validity 28, 72, 367
consumer price index (CPI) 269
consumer's surplus 120, 268, 360
consumer sovereignty 273
consumption, utility from 326, 342
contingent valuation 326, 327
continuing professional education 2
continuity axiom 121, 346
control group 2, 71, 160, 191, 248, 261,
303
convexity axiom 192, 356
copayments 53, 80, 152, 220, 266
see also coinsurance; deductibles
copyright 315, 316, 345
corner solutions 179
coronary heart disease 226
corporation tax 162
cost–benefit analysis 29, 79, 80, 88, 127,
151, 241, 303
cost containment 203, 276
cost–effectiveness analysis 36, 151, 241,
314
agencies associated with 147
alternative to 305–6
confidence intervals/limits in 2, 34,
62, 63, 131
cost–effectiveness ratio in 78
costs in 319, 343
decision rule in 88
of effects of drugs 257
incomplete data in 171
methods and assumptions of 103,
294
models/techniques used in 2, 34, 76,
122, 131, 209, 218, 219, 316
outcome measures in 79, 80–81, 155,
165–6
perspective adopted for 255, 323
popularity of 29, 227
rationality of 127
of screening programmes 309
subgroups in 331
terms used in 65, 137, 177, 344

types of 79, 341
uncertainty in 2, 28, 76, 122
value judgments in 361
weighting in 130
cost-effectiveness league tables 193–4
cost–effectiveness plane 295
cost–effectiveness ratio 190
cost functions 41
cost–utility analysis
agencies associated with 96, 147
confidence intervals in 62, 63
cost–effectiveness ratio in 78, 190
direct costs in 343
of effects of drugs 257
methods and assumptions of 294
models/techniques used in 209, 219,
316
outcome measures in 77, 79, 80–81,
155
perspective adopted for 255, 323
popularity of 29, 227
of screening programmes 309
terms used in 137
types of 341
coupon 14
covariate 13
Cox, David F. 82
cream skimming 304
Cretin, Shan 190
criterion function 201
Cronbach, Lee J. 83
cross-elasticity of demand 59, 112, 332
crossover trials 248, 366
Culyer, Anthony J. 84
cumulative scaling 146
Czech Republic 123, 283

DASH Outcome Measure 288
data mining 331
Davidson, Nick 33
deadweight loss 220
death 2, 80, 100, 109, 181, 226, 305,
366
censoring due to 45, 201, 336
as outcome 6, 33, 114, 115, 163, 285,
286, 335, 343
probability of 88, 216, 243
death rates 89, 145, 155, 174, 180, 196,
209, 221, 227–8, 361
standardized 326

Debreu, Gerard 16
decision analysis 18, 88, 272
decision rule 75
decision tree 208, 209
decision weights 278
deductibles 53, 54, 104, 152, 214, 215, 245
demand curves 53, 69–70, 71, 92, 125, 126, 212, 268
  partial equilibrium 249
  relevance of 221
  shifts in 204
  slope of 143, 192, 218, 220, 270, 271, 302
  vertical summation of 280–81
demand function 90, 251–2
demand-side cost sharing 80
Denmark 123, 150, 283
dentistry 60, 210, 271
  see also teeth
depreciation 40, 145, 229
derived demand 91, 92, 227
descriptive statistics 35
Detsky, Alan S. 191
diabetes 226
diagnosis 27, 163, 221, 243, 271, 288
diagnostic related groups 4, 87, 96, 105, 146, 195, 278
difference principle 130
digestive system, diseases of 181
disability 147, 243
disabled persons 213, 214–15
discharges 100, 163, 245, 314, 335, 343
discount factor 99
discount rate 74, 100, 180, 190, 255, 291, 321–2, 340
discounting 218, 230, 344
discrete choice analysis 64
disease costing 151
disease prevention 281
diseconomies of scale 109
doctors
  balance billing by 215
  behaviour of 164, 258, 333
  methods of paying 41, 68, 131, 173, 204, 223–4, 266, 320, 333, 338
  primary care 204, 271
dominance 125, 329, 366
double-blind trials 33, 257

Douglas, Paul H. 51
drugs
  approval of 103, 105, 134, 172, 184, 230, 256
  brand name 35, 142
  ceiling effect 44
  dosage 89
  dose–response curve 104
  economics of 257
  evidence in support of use of 159
  experimental versions of 133
  follow-up studies of use of 263
  generic 142, 253, 332
  new technologies embedded in 339
  orphan 65, 243
  over-the-counter 246, 278
  prescription 80, 104, 267, 306
  prices of 193, 211, 249, 256–7, 295, 332
  promotion of 95
  reviews of 56
  science of action of 257
  substitute 332
  trials *see* animal trials; clinical trials
  used in combination 59
  see also narcotics
dumping 203
duopoly 58
duration analysis 140, 367

ear, diseases of 21, 244
ecological fallacy 9
economic appraisals 28, 67, 132, 168, 255, 256
economic goods 173
economies of scale and scope 25, 374
Edgeworth, F.Y. 109
Edgeworth Box 71
effectiveness 49, 50, 119, 217, 256, 257, 264, 309, 340, 369
efficacy 49, 50, 110, 124, 264
efficiency 84, 359, 361
  see also Pareto-optimality
elasticity of substitution 112
elderly people 143, 214–15, 221, 226
Ellsberg, Daniel 13
Ellsberg Paradox 13
emergency care 105, 169, 245
empirical modelling 218
endocrine glands 113

endocrine, nutritional and metabolic diseases 181
endogenous regressors 176
England and Wales 48
    see also English National Health Service; Welsh National Health Service
English National Health Service 132, 135, 155, 164, 225, 226, 253, 294, 330
environmental effects 368
epidemiology 49, 169, 363
episodes of care 96
equity 2–3, 43, 81, 84, 96, 102, 103, 111, 114, 130, 151, 161, 183, 207, 210, 228, 276, 286, 302, 363
error term 158, 160, 176, 241, 313
ethics 1, 66, 116, 118, 182, 188, 203, 210, 292, 322, 353, 356, 360–61
    see also value judgments
etiological fraction 7
etiology 7
European Union (EU) 109, 243
evidence-based medicine 323
excess burden 220
exchange rates 282
exchangeability 142
expansion path 160
expected utility theory 18, 48, 53, 97, 135, 222, 278, 302–3, 325, 356
    axioms of 34, 46, 121–2, 230, 285–6, 291
    paradoxes of 10–11, 112
expenditure controls 76
experience rating 19
export price index 339
external validity 264
externalities 42, 97, 163, 207, 215, 220, 280, 305, 320–21, 324
extra-welfarism 29, 75, 111, 183, 276, 285, 353, 367, 368
eyes, diseases and abnormalities of 239

F-test 13
factor analysis 272
fair premium *see* actuarially fair premium
fairness *see* equity
Federal Medical Assistance Percentage 213

fee-for-service 68, 173, 204, 223–4, 266, 333, 338
feet, treatment of 47
Feldstein, Martin 162
fertility rates 333
fertility service quality 64–5
Fieller, E.C. 131
finished consultant episodes 245
Finland 123, 132, 150, 283
Fiorinal 332
fiscal policy 84
Fisher, Sir Ronald 131, 133
fixed factors of production 316–17
fluoxetine 142
focus groups 48, 65, 243
follow-up studies 200, 263
foreign-born residents 9, 107
forest plots 216–17
foundation trusts 348–9
framing effects 278
France 8, 55, 123, 146, 150, 283, 338
free goods 308
frequentist approach 28, 122

Gail, Mitchell H. 140
game theory 72, 122, 225, 232, 376
gatekeepers 271, 312
Gauss, Karl Friedrich 141
Gaussian distribution 233
GDP see Gross Domestic Product
general equilibrium theory 16, 252
genitourinary system, diseases of 181
geometric mean 133
Germany 95, 123, 150, 283, 371
Giffen, Sir Robert 175
Giffen goods 175
Gini, Corrado 143
Gini coefficient 171, 189, 294
global budget 33, 74, 197, 291
Gold, Marthe R. 255, 294
Gompertz, Benjamin 145
Gossett, William 331
graphical analysis 327
Great Western Railway 317
Greece 123, 150, 283
gross domestic product (GDP) 26, 208, 367, 372
Guttman, Louis 146

hand, disabilities of 86, 98, 288

Hawthorne effect 20
health
    demand for 91–2, 94, 151
    distribution of 84, 143, 183, 286
    measurement of 232, 305, 313
        see also health status
    need for 227–8
    as policy objective 111, 127, 128, 276
    production of 151
    WHO concept of 372
health care
    demand for 91–2, 94, 124, 151, 276,
        305, 370
    distribution of resource consumption
        143, 228, 292
    expenditures on 122–4, 282, 323
    financing of 132, 144, 149, 151, 294
    market failure in 207
    need for 227–8
    postponement of 287–8, 341, 342, 343
    production of 151
    public good characteristics of 280
    rationing of 243
    standards 187
    utility from 179
Health Care Savings Accounts 214
health frontier 84
health insurance 149, 151
    access to 3
    coinsurance 53–5, 73, 80, 89, 104,
        119, 152, 245
    competition in market for 59
    compulsory 204, 233, 261, 323
    cost control by providers of 312, 323,
        328
    employment-based 112, 146, 178,
        187, 223, 371
    and hospital utilization 305
    information asymmetries in 19, 175
    inter-country comparisons 150
    Medicaid program 213, 221
    Medicare program 214–15
    moral hazard and 53–5, 219–21
    premia 4, 6–7, 19, 53–5, 57, 82, 125,
        130, 177, 198, 220, 221, 302,
        304
    private 82, 105, 150, 232, 371
    rationale for 351
    retrospective reimbursement 152, 172,
        301

    taxation and regulation of 211
health maintenance organizations
    (HMOs) 149, 166, 169, 173, 203–4,
        260, 266
health outcomes
    in clinical trials 2, 114, 191, 335–6,
        343
    definition and/or measurement of 95,
        99, 114, 115, 128, 166, 218, 244,
        285–6, 308
    probability of occurrence of 148
    research on 182
    social value of 227
health promotion 281
health status 29, 43–4, 113, 150–51,
        165, 234, 318, 320
    assigning values to 64, 154, 155–6,
        197, 254–5, 259, 278, 285, 315,
        316, 323, 325–6, 340, 343, 355,
        364
    outcome defined as change in 244,
        245
health technologies 36, 39, 43, 110, 174
    assessment of 52, 55, 96, 181, 207,
        214, 225, 226, 310, 336, 361
    cost-effectiveness of 62, 63, 103,
        193–4, 214, 226, 309, 310
Health Utilities Group (HUG) 154–5
Healthcare Resources Groups (HRGs)
        149, 226, 253, 294
healthy-year equivalent 308
hearing 21
heart, diseases and abnormalities of 41,
        135, 226
Heckman, James 156
heredity 143
heterogeneity 140, 160, 191, 255
heteroskedasticity 160, 367
Hicks, Sir John 189
hierarchical choice 64
HIV/AIDS 196, 372
homoskedasticity 158
hospital-acquired diseases 234
hospital beds 39, 46, 274, 305, 364
hospital closures 25
hospital costs 43, 214–15, 238, 276, 298
hospital discharges 100, 163, 245, 314,
        335, 343
hospital economics 151
households, activity within 367

human capital 1, 18, 40, 137, 339, 361
human races and cultures, study of 118
Hungary 123, 283
hypothesis testing 11

Iceland 123, 150, 283
identification problem 333
immunity disorders 181
imperfect competition 58
imperfectly rational models 5
import price index 339
income distribution 9–10, 60–61, 116,
    130, 143, 171, 200, 251, 294, 319
income-elasticity of demand 10, 90, 92,
    112, 124, 171, 175, 201–2, 233,
    252
income tax 98, 214
incomplete data 59, 192, 201, 329, 351
incomplete markets 207
inconsistency 176
incremental cost-effectiveness ratio 45,
    62, 63, 76, 88, 193, 194, 305, 309,
    310, 314, 341, 352
independence axiom 285
independent practice associations 153
India 57
indifference 46, 60, 302, 337, 342, 343,
    356
indifference curves 36, 71, 97, 173–4,
    179, 206, 302, 342, 355, 356
indirect cost 275
individual preferences 17
individual welfare 68
infant mortality rates 196
infectious disease 56, 70, 181
inferior goods 143, 192
inflation 15, 66, 79, 90, 94, 226, 231,
    282, 293
information, study of 175
information asymmetry 8, 164, 175,
    207, 273
information costs 299
injuries 181
inpatient care 60
insurance *see* accident insurance; health
    insurance; life insurance; sickness
    insurance
intellectual property rights 178, 195,
    252, 345
interest group theory 164

interest rates 79, 81, 84, 99
internal markets 56, 226, 240, 282
internal validity 124
International Bank for Reconstruction
    and Development 371
International Centre for the Settlement
    of Investment Disputes 371–2
International Development Association
    371
International Finance Corporation 371
International Health Economics
    Organization 16
interpersonal comparisons 182–3, 286,
    354, 357
interquartile range 35
interval scales 41, 286, 325
interviews 285
intestine, diseases and abnormalities of
    140
investment 40, 84, 145, 229, 321, 332
invisible hand 270
Ireland 123, 150, 283
isocost lines 121, 185
isoquants 112, 121, 160, 162, 206, 338
iso-utility curves *see* indifference curves
Italian Association for Health Econo-
    mists 18
Italy 22, 123, 150, 283, 371

Japan 123, 150, 196, 283
Jarman, Brian 187
Joint Commission on Accreditation of
    Healthcare Organizations (JCAHO)
    314
joint probability 196, 210
joint products 187, 188
journal articles 215, 281
justice 130, 195, 243, 363

Kakwani, Nanek C. 189
Kaldor, Nicholas 189
Kant, Immanuel 93, 363
Kaplan, E.L. 190
Kaplan–Meier method 336
Keeler, Emmett B. 190
Keynes, J.M. 291
kidneys, diseases and abnormalities of
    214, 229
Kind, Paul 305
Korea 123, 283

L'Abbé, Kristin 191
labour costs 16, 97
    see also wages
Lanorinal 332
Larrey, Baron Dominique Jean 347
Laspeyres, Etienne 192
Laspeyres index 133
Lausanne School of Economics 251
lead-time bias 309
liabilities 24
liberty principle 130
licences 25, 70, 103
life expectancy 89, 98–9, 320, 361
life insurance 364
likelihood function 210
Likert, Renis 197
line of equality 60–61, 200, 201
linear programming 86
linear regression model 223, 241
linear transformations 183
Lipitor 142
literacy rates 9, 107
literature reviews 215–17
living organisms, science of functions of
    258
loading 53, 54, 220, 304
logical positivism 182, 368
logistic distribution 199
logistic regression analysis 100
logit model 199
longitudinal cross-sectional studies
    200
longitudinal studies 83
Lorenz, Max 200
Lorenz curve 144, 189
lung, diseases and abnormalities of 135,
    281, 300
Luxembourg 123, 150, 283

Mahoney, Florence I. 25
male sex, diseases of 14
mammography 27–8
managed care 8, 59, 152, 203, 244, 245,
    266, 323
manpower planning 151
Mantel–Haenszel test 47
marginal benefits 125, 228, 360
marginal costs 76, 91, 125, 157, 185,
    219, 220, 268, 270–71, 273–4, 334,
    375

    see also marginal external cost;
        marginal private cost; marginal
        social cost
marginal external cost 206
marginal intertemporal rate of substitu-
    tion 342
marginal private cost 206
marginal product 193, 206
marginal rate of substitution 97, 112,
    173, 192, 356, 357
marginal rate of transformation 275,
    356–7
marginal revenue 268, 270–71
marginal social cost 125–6, 280–81
marginal social value 125–6, 185,
    280–81
marginal utility of health 355
marginal utility of income 177, 189, 303
marginal valuation curves 53, 69–70, 90,
    93, 125, 126, 212, 220–21, 268,
    280–81
    see also marginal social value
market failure 208, 215
market imperfections 310
market share 61, 157
Markov, Andrei Andreyevich 209
Markov chain 2, 346
Markov model 313, 346
Massachusetts 135
mean 52, 64, 102, 199, 233, 249, 260,
    319, 349, 376
    sample mean 81, 307, 325, 331, 362
    see also geometric mean
means testing 213
median value 35, 102, 199, 287, 319
Medicaid Program 8, 45, 150, 221,
    242–3, 278, 323
Medical Outcomes Study 222
medical supply industries 151
medical technologies *see* health
    technologies
'medically necessary' services 60
Medicare Program 6, 8, 16, 36, 45, 96,
    104, 150, 213, 278, 300, 323
Meier, Paul 190
mental and behavioural disorders 181,
    279
mental health care 203, 226
merit goods 262
meta-analysis 191, 337

Mexico 123, 283
micropopulation simulation modelling 218
midwifery 237
minimum wage 300, 330
mixed systems 150
mode 233
monopoly 42, 58, 207, 258
monopsony 59, 109
moral hazard 53, 54
morbidity 37, 156, 181, 227–8
Morgenstern, Oscar 122
mortality rates 89, 145, 155, 174, 180, 196, 209, 221, 227–8, 361
    standardized 326
multi-disciplinary groups 49
Multilateral Investment Guarantee Agency 371
multiple regression *see* regression analysis
multivariate sensitivity analysis 314
muscles and movement, physiological study of 190
musculoskeletal system and connective tissue, diseases of 181, 302
myopic irrational models 5

NAIRU (non-accelerating inflation rate of unemployment) 138, 226
narcotics 25
Nash, John 225
National Center for Biotechnology Information (NCBI) 153
national health insurance 150
national health services 150
    see also English National Health Service; Northern Ireland National Health Service; Scottish National Health Service; UK National Health Service; Welsh National Health Service
national income 229
National Institute for Health and Clinical Excellence 48, 49
national tariff 208, 253, 294
negligence 203
neoplasms 181
nerve systems 230
nested case-control study 52
Netherlands 87, 96, 123, 150, 211, 283

New Zealand 123, 150, 256, 283, 371
nomogram 327
non-accelerating inflation rate of unemployment (NAIRU) 138, 226
non-profit institutions 162–4, 187
non-satiation axiom 108, 356
normal distribution 102, 141, 190, 199, 273, 376
normal profit 1
normative economics 182, 292
Northern Ireland National Health Service 225
Norway 4, 123, 150, 283
nose, diseases of 244
null hypothesis 11, 13, 47, 239, 282, 304, 318, 327, 328, 349, 350, 376
number needed to treat (NNT) 2
nursing care 271
nursing homes 277

O'Rourke, K. 191
objective function 197, 270, 276
odds ratio 216, 312
OECD 123, 282, 283
Office of Health Economics 150
older people 143, 214–15, 221, 226
oligopoly 58
omitted variables 64, 86, 162, 163, 300
opportunity cost 77, 79, 97, 110–11, 132, 136, 185, 246, 276, 277, 280, 287, 294, 316, 321, 322, 332, 341–2, 343, 346
opportunity loss 122
opthalmic services 60, 271
option appraisals 12, 151, 361
ordered probit model 183
ordinary least squares (OLS) 142, 158, 223, 349, 367
Oregon 242–3
otorhinolaryngology 114
outcomes *see* health outcomes
outpatient care 60
output budgeting 260, 277
overutilization 276, 359

p-value 318, 325, 327–8
Paasche, Hermann 247
Paasche index 133
pain
    measures of 178

relief of 13, 33, 248
pairwise comparisons 64, 341, 345
panel data 20, 118, 351
parallel groups design 83
parallel trade 208
parameters, number of 90
Pareto, Vilfredo 251
Pareto criterion 182, 354, 357
Pareto-improvements 58
Pareto-optimality 71, 73, 87, 109, 111,
    125–6, 133, 189, 207, 310–11, 357
parthenogenesis 234
partial equilibrium theory 142
patents 25, 35, 70, 142, 178, 195, 249,
    324, 339, 345
pathogens 363
patients' records 61
pay-off to research 37
Pearson, Karl 74
Pearson χ^2 test 47
Pearson's correlation coefficient 74
perfect competition 58, 277
permanent income 347
person trade-off method 308
perspective of a study 74–5
pharmaceutical industry 11, 207, 253,
    257, 346
pharmaceuticals *see* drugs
pharmacoeconomics 182
pharmacy 60
Phillimore, P. 344
physicians *see* doctors
placebos 290
Point of Service plans (POSs) 166,
    203–4
poisonings 181
poisons 345
Poisson, Siméon Denis 260
Poisson distribution 261
Poisson regression model 228–9
Poland 123, 283
population, characteristics of 92, 93,
    174, 288, 320, 326, 330
population variance 362
Portugal 123, 150, 283
positive economics 182, 233–4, 292,
    355, 356, 368
posterior probability 27–8
potency, quantitative assessment of 32
potential health gain 19, 39

potential Pareto-efficiency 111
potential Pareto-improvements 58
Pratt, John W. 17
preferred provider organizations (PPOs)
    149, 203–4
pregnancy 181, 254
present value 14, 40, 74, 100, 117, 165,
    180, 254, 291, 361
price discrimination 208, 258
price-elasticity of demand 80, 92, 112,
    208, 219–20, 268, 271
price index 66, 68, 89, 133, 191–2, 247,
    293, 297, 339
price-searching 269, 299, 312, 374
price-taking 58, 268, 269, 270, 273–4,
    334
Primary Care Trusts 56, 180, 253, 281
prior probability 27–8, 263
priorities for treatment 37
prisons 95
private employer liability insurance 371
private sector providers 161
producer's surplus 120
production functions 78, 110, 176, 249,
    345
    Cobb–Douglas 51, 274
    constant elasticity of substitution
        (CES) 66
    diagrammatic representation of 104
    features of 67, 97, 160, 172, 193, 332
    health service 84, 245
production possibilities curve 206, 329
productivity 15, 19, 26, 37, 339, 344
productivity cost 137, 174
professional organizations 42
profit maximization 161, 268, 358
programme budgeting 260
progressive taxation 189, 277, 294, 296
property rights 16, 133, 270
    intellectual 178, 195, 252, 345
proportional taxation 189, 277, 296
prospect theory 135, 295
prospective payment systems 338
Prozac 142
public choice theory 212
public goods 136, 163, 207, 212
public health medicine 56
public ownership 163
publication bias 139

qualitative data 21, 307
quality-adjusted life-years (QALYs) 67,
    77, 79, 80, 91, 100, 115, 119, 128,
    147, 156, 222, 250, 285, 286, 290,
    308, 315, 316, 356, 364
quality of life 37, 43–4, 67, 147, 153,
    154, 285
Quality of Well-Being scales 254
quality standards 3
Quebec 8
questionnaires 50, 352

RAND Health Insurance Experiment
    222, 316
randomized controlled trials (RCTs) 55,
    114, 307, 329
rate of return 91, 277, 299
ratio scales 41, 286, 305, 343
rational addiction 5
rationality assumptions 91, 127, 207
Rawls, John 130, 195, 293, 363
real income 171, 192, 249, 252, 332
real interest rate 79
regression analysis 64, 158, 222, 249,
    289, 300, 325, 349
    forms of 82, 100, 118, 194, 197, 223,
        228–9, 241, 261, 344, 367
regressive taxation 189, 277
regulatory agencies 25, 208, 298
regulatory capture 208, 298
rehabilitation medicine 257
relative frequency 24, 159
relative price 332
relative risk 110, 237
renal disease 214, 229
rent 176
replacement investment 40
research and development 11, 31, 37,
    162, 182, 188, 249, 256, 291
respiratory system, diseases of 181, 300
response bias 307
revealed preference 70, 371
rheumatoid arthritis 59
risk analysis 147
risk aversion 17, 46, 278
risk factors 7, 42, 53, 114, 237, 272,
    278, 297, 301, 311, 331
Robbins, Lionel (*later* Lord Robbins)
    108, 182
Roemer, Milton I. 305

Rosser, Rachel 305
rule utilitarianism 353
rules of thumb 34
Russell, Louise B. 255, 294

sample mean 81, 307, 325, 331, 362
sample selection bias 156, 301
sample size 12, 20, 90, 139, 327, 330,
    362
sample variance 362
sampling 174, 222, 261, 282, 288, 289,
    315, 325, 330
Samuelson, Paul A. 30
satisficing 258
savings 221
scalogram analysis 146
scenario analysis 224, 314
Scitovsky, Tibor 189, 309
Scitovsky Criterion 189
Scottish National Health Service 154,
    225, 309
screening programmes 27–8, 193, 195,
    249, 311, 339
search algorithm 31
second best optimum 55, 220–21
Second International Study of Infarct
    Survival 331
Secondary Care Trusts 132, 135, 162,
    164
secondary prevention 339
segmented markets 267, 268
sensitivity analysis 218, 224, 243, 272,
    309, 352
service industries 26
severity of illness 67
sex-specific mortality rate 221
SF-8™ 315
SF-12® 315
SF-20 222
SF-36® 315
shadow prices 79, 232, 239
shoulder, disabilities of 86, 98, 288
sickness insurance 150
Siegel, Joanna E. 255, 294
Sierra Leone 196
signs and symptoms 50, 96, 98, 181,
    234, 253, 277
Simon, R. 140
simulations 219
single-blind trials 33

skewed data 34
skin, diseases and abnormalities of 94, 181
Slovak Republic 283
social benefit 74
social cost 74
social decisions approach 75, 361
social deprivation 187
social preferences 17–18
social welfare function 17–18, 30, 182, 286, 290, 356, 357
societal perspective 75, 255
Spain 43, 123, 150, 283
Spanish Association for Health Economics 18
Spearman, Charles Edward 323
standard deviation 12, 52, 110, 138, 199, 233, 249, 325, 331, 362
standard error 349
standard gamble 155, 259, 285–6, 315, 356
standardized difference 12
standards, national 226
State Children's Health Insurance Program 45
stated preference analysis 64, 70, 370, 371
statistical significance 12, 217, 282, 327, 349
stochastic uncertainty 351
stomach, diseases and abnormalities of 140
Strategic Health Authorities 281
stratified sampling 15
Student's t 325
subjective uncertainty 351
subsidies 208
substance abuse care 203
supply curves 170, 273–4, 334
supply function 251–2, 334
supply-side cost sharing 80
survival functions 41, 148
survival times 148, 195, 196, 211, 285, 335–6, 343
Sweden 123, 150, 283
Switzerland 123, 150, 283
symptoms 50, 96, 98, 181, 234, 253, 277
systematic reviewing 33, 159, 170

t-distribution 331, 376

t-test 369, 376
taxation 101, 129, 150, 208
   burden of 37–8, 169–70
   corporation tax 162
   direct 38, 98, 149, 214
   earmarking of 107, 149
   fair 1
   indirect 37–8, 149, 170, 174
   of insurance business 211
   inter-country differences in 346
   progressivity/regressivity of 189, 277, 294, 296
taxpayers 8, 37, 80, 120, 212, 346
teaching hospitals 109, 162, 188, 238
technical efficiency 111, 162, 185, 344
technology matrix 274
teeth 103
   see also dentistry
terminal illness 248, 264
territorial resource allocation 151
tertiary prevention 312
theoretical modelling 217–18
threshold values 183
throat, diseases of 244
Thurstone, Louis L. 341
Thurstone's Law of Comparative Judgment 247
time horizon 218
time preference 99, 321
time series data 200
time trade-off 155
tissues 159, 176
Tobin, James 344
Tobit model 156
total factor productivity 275
Townsend, Peter 33, 344
trade-off matrices 64
trademarks 345
trading partners, selection of 19
transaction costs 175
transfer payments 101, 240, 321
transformation curve 275
transition probability 2, 313, 346
transitivity axiom 121, 218, 356
travellers, diseases and treatments of 113
triple-blind trials 33
Trusts, NHS *see* Primary Care Trusts; Secondary Care Trusts
Turkey 123, 150, 283

UK Department of Health and Social
Security 32–3, 225
UK National Health Service 49, 56, 65,
150, 180, 208, 225, 226, 256–7,
271, 281, 311, 348–9
see also English National Health
Service; Northern Ireland
National Health Service;
Scottish National Health
Service; Welsh National Health
Service
uncertainty 2, 12, 28, 46, 75, 76, 88, 91,
121, 122, 240, 290, 296, 320, 326,
361
types of 133, 311, 332, 351
unemployment 137, 138, 185, 226, 330
United Kingdom 123, 187, 283, 299,
371
see also UK National Health Service
United Nations 372
United States 8, 9, 107, 211, 243, 314,
333
health care expenditures in 123
health care system in 6, 16, 46, 96,
98, 104, 105, 112, 150, 152–3,
161, 166, 178, 187, 203, 213,
214–15, 223, 245, 260, 278, 298,
323, 328, 359, 364, 371
purchasing power parity for 283
univariate sensitivity analysis 314
urinary system, diseases and abnormalities of 353
US Department of Health and Human
Services 45, 134
US Food and Drug Administration 103,
105, 184, 230
US National Center for Health Statistics
48
US National Library of Medicine 153,
215
utility functions 1, 5, 12, 17, 51, 97,
161, 258, 265, 358
utility maximization 36, 48, 121, 127,
161, 233, 236, 258, 326, 353, 368,
374
utility measurement 5, 41, 285, 291,
338, 354–5
utility theory 218, 222, 285, 302, 353–6
axioms of 71, 72, 108, 121–2, 192,
218, 291, 347, 355–6

see also expected utility theory; utility
maximization

vaccination 157, 271, 272, 281
value function 278, 295
value judgments 75, 102, 111, 116, 127,
128, 183, 188, 227, 233–4, 255,
262, 285, 286, 356
variable-by-variable analysis 314
variance 64, 107, 158, 160, 229, 260
variance ratio distribution 131
vectors 210
veil of ignorance 130, 353
visual analogue scale 340
volunteer bias 312
von Neumann, John 122
von Neumann–Morgenstern (VNM)
axiom 121–2

wages 208, 300, 366
see also labour costs
Wagstaff, Adam 84
waiting lists 288, 341, 342, 343
wealth 1, 7, 24, 254, 258
Weibull, Waloddi 367
Weinstein, Milton C. 255, 294
welfare economics 182, 188, 233, 278,
285, 310, 353–4, 355, 356
fundamental theorems of 133, 310–11
welfare-enhancing change 58
welfare loss, measure of 87
Welsh National Health Service 225,
226
Western Electric 147
Wilcoxon, Frank 369
Williams, Alan 194, 260, 369–70
willingness to pay 29, 31, 48, 65, 69–70,
127, 266, 302, 327, 360–61
workers' compensation 149, 178
working environment 117
World Health Assembly 372
World Health Organization 148, 196,
369
International Classification of
Diseases 180–81
International Classification of
Functioning, Disability and
Health (ICF) 98, 168, 181
World Trade Organization 345

x-axis 1
x-inefficiency 161, 162
x-rays 289

y-axis 242

z-statistic 325